# A THEORY OF
# URBANITY

# A THEORY OF
# URBANITY

## THE ECONOMIC AND CIVIC CULTURE OF CITIES

## ANTON C. ZIJDERVELD

Transaction Publishers
New Brunswick (U.S.A.) and London (U.K.)

Library of Congress Catalog Number: 97-26786
ISBN: 1-56000-317-0
Printed in the United States of America

Library of Congress Cataloging-in-Publication Data

Zijderveld, Anton C., 1937–
    [Steden zonder stedelijkheid. English]
    A theory of urbanity : the economic and civil culture of cities / Anton C. Zijderveld.
        p.  cm.
    Rev. translation of the author's Steden zonder stedelijkheid.
    Includes bibliographical references and index.
    ISBN 1-56000-317-0 (alk. paper)
    1. City planning—Netherlands. 2. Urban policy—Netherlands. 3. City planning. 4. Urban policy. I. Title.
HT169.N4Z5413   1997
307.76'09492—dc21                                        97-26786
                                                          CIP

For Gabi Zijderveld

*A city is not just a place but a state of mind, a symbol of a distinctive style of life whose major attributes are variety and excitement; a city also presents a sense of scale that dwarfs any single effort to encompass its meaning.*

—Daniel Bell

# Contents

# Preface

In the 1980s organizational culture became a much debated issue in the areas of public and business administration. It is generally viewed as the hardly quantifiable source of social and economic energy which is essential to the organization's performance. In comparison there is still little reflection and discussion about urban culture. What is it that keeps a city going economically, socially, and politically, despite all its diversities and fragmentations? What is it that makes a city, despite its often chaotic appearance, into a meaningful order that some people love and identify with, yet others loath and reject as the source of multiple evils? This book tries to discuss and answer these and related questions. The concept *urbanity* is used throughout as synonym for *urban culture*.

This book is a complete overhaul of an earlier Dutch publication. It was some ten years ago that an enlightened civil servant of the Dutch Ministry for Housing Affairs asked me to write an essay on the culture of cities with the explicit request not to repeat all the well-known theorems and concepts of mainstream urbanologists. "It is strange," he said to me, "that the two well-known and eternally criticized essays on urbanism by Wirth and Simmel are still very readable. You find them in almost every urban sociology reader." "Substantively and methodologically, they may have been wrong," he went on, "but unlike many present-day urban specialists, they managed to put life in the big cities into perspective."

This was, I still believe, a wise observation, because Wirth, Simmel, and others, like Redfield, Mumford, and Jacobs, may indeed lack methodological and empirical sophistication, yet after one reads their publications carefully, one begins to look at cities, and at the people living and working within them, differently. It is as if they, unlike most of today's urbanologists, somehow put the qualitative dimensions of urban life into focus. They caught, so to say, its pulse, its rhythm, its cultural infrastructure, maybe even its meaning.

The above-mentioned civil servant asked me to put things into the proper theoretical perspective and to offer him and his colleagues something to ponder. The study should not be burdened with learned expositions of the urbanological discourse, nor be hindered by the standard methodological and theoretical demands of urban sociology. I was not even allowed to worry in advance about my study's possible applicability to issues of public policy. That, of course, was quite remarkable, since all research contracted by government agencies usually ought to contribute in the end to the solving of social and economic problems. The civil servant in this case believed—and that is why I called him "enlightened" before—in the rather indirect usefulness and applicability of theory: it puts things into a perspective that renders practical policies and the problems to be addressed more rational in a substantive manner. Policy may in this way even end up being more effective and more efficient.

I fully shared these conceptions of theory and policy, complied with his wish, and sat down to read the "classics" on the city once again. But I also plunged head first into the ocean of urbanological publications, some of which were helpful and enlightening. I completed the manuscript rather hastily within six months. (This was the only concession I had to grant to the policy makers who apparently are always in a hurry.) I began the treatise, as I shall do in this essay, with Max Weber's theory of the city as developed in "Economy and Society," and in his seminal series of lectures, published posthumously as "Economic History." But I also dealt with the anti-urban animus which is, in my view then and now, fostered by state centralization and in particular by a centralized and interventionist welfare state. In view of the Dutch welfare state, still thriving in the beginning of the 1980s, I called my little book programmatically (translated) "Cities without Urbanity."

I have always wanted to rewrite and expand this Dutch essay, particularly since I became acquainted with Peter L. Berger's concept of *economic culture*. I realized that this concept which evidently belongs to the tradition of Institutional Economics (Weber, Sombart, Veblen, Schumpeter, Malinowski, Jacobs, etc.), would help to strengthen the notion of urbanity as I developed it in my short Dutch study. However, I soon discovered that the concept of urbanity should also be tied to the concept of *civic culture* as developed in the sixties by Almond and Verba. It ties in, of course, with the present debates on civil society. Urbanity, I shall argue, has been, from its start at the end of the Middle Ages in Europe, an economic as well as civic culture, and as such the source of energy and inspiration for Western urban democracy—the prime example of a truly civil society.

There was still another reason for a complete overhaul of the Dutch essay. During the 1980s the (predominantly post-modernist) argument gained prominence that the idea of the city as a distinct phenomenon is outdated in view of a world which has become increasingly fragmented and borderless, if not limitless, and highly flexible due to the seminal impact of electronic technologies. Consequently, it is argued, the notion of a specifically urban culture has become superfluous. We have allegedly entered the age of cyberspace and virtual reality, the informational society that is no longer characterized by more or less fixed structures and a centered order. Informational society and the informational city of today are rather characterized by incessant flows, by mobilities of sorts, by decentered fragmentations. In this new world, the idea of the city, let alone of urbanity, is, it is believed, meaningless. In view of such urban behemoths like Los Angeles, often professed as the model for urban life in the twenty-first century, but also in view of the recent evolution of suburbia, in particular the rapid emergence of so-called *edge cities*, decentered or polycentered urban satellites, the idea of urbanity as explored in the present book seems to be out-of-date, and certainly not applicable to the American scene. In short, cities-without-urbanity are rapidly becoming the normal condition of urban life, certainly in North America.

Indeed, urbanity is, in origin, a European phenomenon (see ch. 1) and the present discussion is nourished primarily by the European experience. Yet, after the merits and faults of the post-modernist arguments have been discussed, it will be argued that urbanity is analytically, as well as normatively, still a crucial phenomenon that ought to be taken into account, if one deals, either scientifically or in terms of public policy, with cities and city life. The final judgment is, of course, left to the reader. Moreover, I do believe that the European experience of urban culture is relevant to the present urban scene in America which is, as ever, much in development and in many places subjected to multiple symptoms of anomie. However, it should be added immediately that what is usually held to be "typically American" in urban life, is currently observable in most European cities. If there are differences, they are differences in degree, not in kind. In fact, what we are discussing here is not "Americanization" but *modernization*. That point is discussed specifically in chapters 2 and 4, but is actually the leading motif of the entire book.

As always (our co-operation lasts for more than thirty years now), I am grateful to the intellectual stimuli I received from Peter and Brigitte

Berger while preparing this book. During the past years I could at several intervals escape the teaching duties and administrative chores of my university, and stay at the Institute for the Study of Economic Culture (ISEC) of Boston University, of which Berger is the founder and the director. It enabled me to catch up with my reading, particularly in the stacks of the Boston University library, and to discuss various issues related to economic culture with the Bergers, and with several staff members and visiting scholars of the institute. I am grateful to the administrative staff, Laurel Whalen in particular, for the invaluable assistance in scores of bureaucratic and administrative issues.

This book is dedicated to my oldest daughter Gabriele Maria (Gabi), who deserves it if only because she was exposed to many different urban cultures: she was born on Staten Island, New York, grew up in Tilburg (at that time a non-city in the south of Holland), attended the University of Utrecht (a very old, typically European city in the center of Holland), and presently lives in Boston, where she works in the international department of a software company. In a sense she embodies today's flexible and multi-centered society, and she knows firsthand the crucial difference between cities with and cities without a vigorous urbanity.

# Introduction: Intuitions of Urbanity

## Urban Preferences

Many of us, who are not plagued by an anti-urban, bucolic animus but rather enjoy the hectic life in a large town, have their favorite city, or maybe a few favorite cities. We may not actually live in the city of our preference, but we want to visit it regularly, since we immediately feel at home in it. There is, certainly in the Western world, a rich variety to choose from: New York, San Francisco, Boston, Montreal, London, Edinburgh, Amsterdam, Paris, Munich, Vienna, Rome, Florence, Madrid, Barcelona, and, probably soon again, Berlin, St. Petersburg, Budapest, Prague. The choice is not reasoned, is in fact rather irrational. And to those who do not share our preference, the choice is usually quite ununderstandable. It is like a love relationship between persons.

Many also have their distinct dislikes as to cities. Detroit is, probably undeservedly, the cliché example of a generally unloved city. But consensus is rare, if it comes to urban likes and dislikes. Someone who loves to live or dwell in Boston, may abhor Chicago or New York, a true Montrealer can and will not understand how one could ever live a happy life in Toronto, just as a true Amsterdamer would shiver at the thought of having to live in Rotterdam (and vice versa, of course!). Apparently, cities do things to us, to our emotions and to our consciousness. In a sense cities are statements to which we respond positively or negatively. What then is it, that brings these reactions and responses about?

What is it that makes a city like New York so attractive to many, and then, what kind of attraction are we talking about? If one lives and works there, one gradually begins to develop an ambiguous relationship with it. One loves and hates its hectic pace, its noise, its penetrating smell, its chaotic plurality of cultures. If one lives there, one wants to leave, if one has left, one wants to return. This city does something to people, not just functionally in terms of jobs and obligations and practical pursuits, but also, and above all, emotionally. It is an ambiguous love-hatred. In some the love, in others the hatred predominates.

1

But all the same, this city does something to its people. Again, what is it that affects people positively or negatively or both, when they are exposed to New York?

Other cities too have this very strange, ambiguous power over people. It has been said of the Austrian writer, actor, and comedian Helmut Qualtinger (1928–1986) that Vienna was actually his fate: he wanted to run away from it all the time, yet he could not live without it. "When in Vienna," his biographers reported paradoxically, "he experienced a strong feeling of longing—a real *Heimweh*—for Vienna. He lost this feeling, the moment he left the city. Vienna was his fate: he always wanted to flee, yet he also wanted to stay put. He was hooked on the city. Vienna was his drug."[1]

Although this book will heed the undue romanticization of urbanity, the existence of urban fascination cannot be denied. The rather melancholic desire for the big city was probably portrayed most forcefully by Anton Chekhov in his play *The Three Sisters*. The sisters constantly talk and dream about their escape from the small provincial town in which fate had dropped them cruelly some decades ago. They long for a return to Moscow. Actually, the fascinating thing about this play is that the big city with its longed for urbanity plays a crucial role by its very absence.

### New York—A Metaphor of Urbanity

The present study intends to develop a theory of urbanity viewed as the economic and civic culture of cities. But before such a theory is constructed, let us try first to evoke some impressionistic notions of urbanity in order to drive home intuitively what is meant by the concept. Urbanity, we shall see in the course of this book, is fraught with many ambiguities. Let us try to grasp them intuitively first, before they are analyzed and discussed in the more formal setting of the theory. To that purpose I focus on two examples: New York City and Vienna. Other examples could have been taken as well, but New York and Vienna are most illustrative since they contrast nicely in several respects. New York then is taken here as a true metaphor of urbanity. James Weldon Johnson (1871–1938) caught its spirit adequately, when he said, "New York is the most fatally fascinating thing in America. She sits like a witch at the gate of the country."[2]

Lest my conception of New York's urbanity be too pompous and ponderous, let me hasten to add a quotation from Peter Berger. It comes from a paean to New York, a city the author lauds as a signal of transcendence: "Somebody once defined a true metropolis as a place where an individual can march down the street wearing a purple robe and a hat with bells on it, beating a drum and leading an elephant by the leash, and only get casual glances from passers-by. If so, then surely New York is the truest metropolis there is."[3]

The most striking thing about New York—and that is typical of the urbanity of any city—is its ambiguity. To start with, it is as if the whole world concentrates itself in this city, in particular in its core, Manhattan. Already in 1854 the New York preacher Edwin H. Chapin called his city "an epitome of the social world," and he greatly emphasized the ambiguous nature of its cosmopolitanism: "Here you may find not only the finest Saxon culture, but the grossest barbaric degradation."[4]

All nations of the world are somehow represented somewhere in this city. Its cosmopolitanism stands in sharp contrast to any kind of localism or nationalism. Yet, this world is made up of ethnic neighborhoods in which people live and behave like "urban villagers."[5] And even the self-styled cosmopolitan intelligentsia exhibits, if one looks behind its façades, as Tom Wolfe has done inimitably, a great deal of narrow-mindedness and even chauvinism.[6]

All the extremes of humanity, from the sublime to the degenerate, are visibly present and openly exhibited, greedily reported by the media. There are abysmally bad newspapers, not much more than silly tabloids, and there is the *New York Times*, uncrowned emperor of journalism. There are many little orchestras and string-bands, and there is the New York Philharmonic. Off-Broadway theater shows are often substandard, but there are also internationally applauded, standard-setting performances on and off Broadway.

Speaking of the stage, there is of course the Metropolitan Opera at the lonely top of the operatic world, while the musical as an art form has reached great perfection here. But, this is also the place for lots of low camp and murky kitsch. There are many banks, and many churches, tying money and faith together in a typically American way. But it is at the same time a place of destitute poverty and abominable vices. There are huge universities and gigantic hospitals, but there are scores of illiterates and uncared for sick and disabled persons.

This confusing mix of beauty and ugliness, affluence and poverty, literacy and illiteracy, is paired to a nervous rhythm during the day and a tense atmosphere during the evening. This pace and the tensions abate but little during the night in which the silence is constantly disrupted by the sirens of police or firetrucks, and the incessant honking of innumerable taxicabs.

It is, as if Manhattan relaxes only during the weekends, in particular on somewhat sleepy Sunday mornings. One strolls along Fifth Avenue or bikes through Central Park which during the week in daylight is plagued by heavy traffic, during the night by crime. There is no city in which the senses are so intensely tickled and stimulated as in New York. Even the air one breathes is unique: a kind of indescribable "no-stench" that cannot be smelled anywhere else. One either hates this human cauldron at once, or one falls in love with it on first sight— a love, as I said, which in all probability will grow into a strange kind of love-hatred.

Now, what is it that keeps this chaos of events, facts, colors, sounds, smells, cultures, and subcultures together? It often seems as if this metropolis will explode, or fall apart at the seams. This has not happened yet, although the voices that predict an apocalyptic "urbicide"[7] grow in number. For decades now this city seems to balance on the brink of financial disaster and social collapse. However, it has not collapsed until now, it has as of yet not slid off into an all-engulfing socioeconomic and sociocultural chaos.[8]

Apart from the fashionable notion that "the city" does actually not exist—a notion to which I shall take exception later—it could be argued that New York in actual fact consists of many self-organizing subsystems. I am not referring here to the burroughs as administrative units, but rather, on a smaller scale, to distinct, usually ethnic neighborhoods. They constitute in a sense the prime sociocultural components of a large city. Still, even if these neighborhoods procure their own order, this does not explain yet why New York City as a whole, that is as something more than the sum of its components, still exists, has not collapsed.

Perhaps, if we are talking about cities the size of New York, there is some deep truth in the idea of a an urban chaos which by itself institutionalizes into some strange kind of order? What precisely is this underlying order? The concept of urbanity is indispensable, I think, if one wants to answer the question satisfactorily.

## Behind Vienna's Façades

Vienna's urbanity is of a quite different nature. This city and its inhabitants have until recently, in a sense, lived of the past—a culturally rich and politically tragic past. Until the *Anschluss* with Hitler's

Germany in 1938, applauded by the majority of the Viennese, this capital presented a cauldron of seething, progressive, and innovative culture. Politically Vienna had no role to play anymore after the collapse of the Habsburg "Double Monarchy." But in philosophy and the sciences, in music, architecture, design, sculpture, painting, and the performing arts, including social and political satire, Vienna was a true maelstrom of creativity and innovation. It suffices to mention the names of some influential persons and institutions, chosen at random: Freud, Wittgenstein, Carnap, Kraus, Schnitzler, Roth, Zweig, Musil, Mahler, Schönberg, Berg, Loos, Klimt, the *Wiener Kreis*, the *Wiener Werkstätte*, the *Secession*, and so on. The list could be continued easily and fill a complete page.

Not all but most of this seems to belong to the past now. Vienna today is a city for tourists and congress participants. Hardly any capital in Europe resembles a museum as much as Vienna does. The flauntingly grand Hofburg in the inner city, a posh hotel like the Imperial, the Burgtheater, the Staatsoper, the Wiener Philharmoniker and the many museums all live off the famous past of the decades prior to the 1930s. It gives this city and its inhabitants a melancholic tinge. Books on Vienna, written by outsiders, such as Schorske's celebrated *Fin-de-Siècle Vienna* (1981) and *Wittgenstein's Vienna* (1973) by Janik and Toulmin add to this museumlike melancholy. The Viennese know very well that the fame of their city's culture is vastly overdrawn, and in any case a matter of history, but they will not easily say so in public. They, in fact, love to maintain their façades behind which they conceal things that strangers do not have to know.

There is in all probability no city in which the Goffmanean game of front stage and back stage is played as skillfully as in the Viennese middle class. In the drawing rooms of the bourgeoisie social intercourse is courteous and playfully civilized: "Küss die Hand, gnädige Frau," "Grüss Gott, Herr Doktor," or even "Herr Hofrat" and "Herr Medizinalrat." But behind the drawing room, in the kitchen or the spatially separated daily living quarters, one relapses into a whining, drawling, nasally complaining dialect, filled with uncouth curses, usually of the anal sort. Then and there it is, as if the company which shortly before in the reception room had been addressed with elaborate expressions of kindness and friendship, is despised intensely, if not hated with a passion. In Viennese argot this is called: "durch die Cacao ziehen"—"to draw through the cocoa." Freud undoubtedly had a psychoanalytic explanation for this expression.

Elegance is the concept which suggests itself, when one encounters the Viennese in their front stage performances. Their coziness—the proverbial Viennese *Gemütlichkeit*—which is exhibited in particular in their wine-drinking bouts in a *Heurige* somewhere in the Vienna Woods, is in most cases but pretence. The bourgeois Viennese is most of the time himself only, if he can complain and gossip. Hilde Spiel, who fled from the Nazi hordes just in time, lived in England for many years, and returned to Vienna in the beginning of the 1970s, remarked in a very critical book on Vienna and the Viennese: "Grouching and grousing, moping and nagging—these are favorite pastimes in Vienna."[9]

Characteristic also is the elaborate network of corridors and tunnels deeply under the surface of the city. The probably apocryphal story is told that several of them have been closed hermetically by thick walls, because they contain still active pestilential bacilli. In this underworld there is also a gigantic sewer system which played a well-nigh mythical role in the "classic" motion picture about postwar Vienna, *The Third Man*. In any case, when the bourgeois Viennese drop their masks of coziness and bonhomie in daily social life, it is as if the odious smells of an netherworld of resentment arise. Usually, the vapors of a seemingly endemic anti-Semitism complete the stench.

Naturally, the building technique of providing modern bank and office buildings with reconstructed, (semi-) old façades is applied gratefully in present-day Vienna. Something similar is also done in (semi-) avant-garde architecture. The renowned and notorious Hundertwasserhaus, for example, is an apartment building in the social housing sector of Vienna. It was designed and painted by the bizarre painter Friedensreich Hundertwasser. In the otherwise very dull neighborhood this odd structure possesses a kind of Disney World quality.

All of this is, it seems, enough to loathe Vienna and the Viennese. That, however, would be a grave mistake. The picture sketched up till now is very incomplete. Vienna and the Viennese have several other, quite different qualities which are endearing and captivating. There is, to begin with, the rich humor, interspersed with self-derision and self-criticism. It is a subtle kind of humor which remains hidden, if one only visits museumlike Vienna with its Sachertorte and Lippizaner. Actually, one must understand the Viennese dialect in order to catch the often sardonic and melancholic substance of these jokes. That is not easy because this dialect is far removed from High German. The above-mentioned Helmut Qualtinger who incidentally at the end of his life played a small role in the motion picture *The Name of the Rose*, stands as a model for this type of Viennese humor. His irony, often bordering on cynical sarcasm, is expressed best in his performance of the "black songs" of G. Rühm and H. C. Artmann. The texts in juicy dialect which often deal with the odd qualities of the Viennese, are not sung in the conventional way. Rather he spits them out.

Qualtinger stood in a rich tradition with celebrated names like Johann Nestroy and Ödön von Horváth. The dreaded literary critic and writer Karl Kraus was as much part of this tradition. Should we not also add Sigmund Freud to it? Did his psychoanalysis not reveal the unconscious as a subterranean sewer system of the soul, as a demonic force behind or beneath the scenes of the conscious? He himself and certainly most of his followers made the fateful mistake to apply this typical Viennese analysis to all of mankind.

There is yet another saving grace in the museumlike façade culture of Vienna. As no other urban culture, Viennese culture has always managed to sublimate dirtiness, distastefulness, ugliness, mustiness, the uncouth, and the unworthy. It happens in particular in the arts. In the music of Vienna, for example, the dark and the threatening, the vulgar and the coarse are sublimated aesthetically. In the music of Mozart, and even more so in that of Schubert, there are seemingly superficial melodies and rhythms, but behind and beneath this music there is a demonic current at work. If this drift pushes the music to the brink of vulgarity and even kitsch, it is immediately kept under control and sublimated into harmonies and rhythms of the highest quality.

Maybe, Mahler stands out in this in particular. Often his scores border on baseness, vulgarity, tastelessness, and kitsch, complemented by anxiety, bitterness, and even resentful hatred. But these qualities are only touched on and then immediately sublimated in music of the highest order. If one does not know Vienna behind the façades, one will not really understand this music. Incidentally, it is not at all amazing that Leonard Bernstein, a great musician and a very American one at that, fell in love with Vienna and the *Wiener Philharmoniker* at the end of his life. He was, in the core of his being, vulgar, common, if not *kitschig*. Together with the seemingly very bourgeois *Philharmoniker*, in all probability the only orchestra in the world that has managed to keep female musicians out of its ranks (until February 1997, that is), he produced maybe the best Mahler performances of the last quarter of this century. Somehow, there must have been an "elective affinity" between Bernstein and Vienna.

The lover of this music, cannot but love Vienna and the Viennese. Yet, at the same time this city and its culture are pathogenic also. The Viennese are the first to know this, certainly, if they belong to the younger generations. To them belongs the immense task of elevating this city and its culture above the museumlike traditions from a golden past. What needs to be done is to revitalize urbanity into an invigorating and electrifying city culture which fits a world that is vastly different from the one populated by Mahler, Freud, Klimt, Wittgenstein, and the likes of them. There are many indications that this is indeed happening—a cultural rejuvenation that set in during the 1980s. This happy trend, it may be expected, will be reinforced by the opening of formerly communist Central and Eastern Europe.

## Urbanity's Ambiguity

Both examples, New York City and Vienna, illustrate the fact that urbanity should not be viewed in too idyllic and romantic a fashion. Urbanity is a very ambiguous phenomenon. As to New York, ugliness, destitution, and crime are as much part of it, as are beauty, affluence, and self-sacrificing charity. The big city is as much a place of peace-loving humanism and humanitarianism, as it is a place of crime, vice, and violence. François Barré emphasized the latter, when he wrote: "The urbanity of a modern city is not a substitution for social peace. Its violence—in what it produces, its driving force, its numbers, its anger and its reappropriations—is real. It is as present under the paving stones as at the top of public buildings. The strident wailing of police car sirens in New York is a vital element in the urbanity of that brutal, sumptuous city."[10]

As to Vienna, the tale of this city's culture demonstrates the weight of a golden past in which an extremely rich and vital urbanity colored the city and its inhabitants. Yet, much of this culture consisted of sublimations of unsavory qualities hidden behind the façades of civilization. Ever since the war this culture has borne a museumlike quality. It is, as we have seen, the task of the younger generations to liberate themselves from this past and work towards an urban culture that fits the demands of a world which increasingly develops into a global system. It is a task, as we shall see at the end of this book, which actually confronts every modern city that aspires to develop and maintain a vital, contemporary urbanity.

In any case, both examples illustrate the fact that urban culture is not necessarily a nice and friendly phenomenon. Culture—organizational, regional, national, and urban culture—is typically human in that it contains all the dimensions of the human condition—the low and ugly as much as the sublime and beautiful. The darker side of culture is often forgotten or consciously covered up. This happens in particular in the vogue of "corporate culture" which more often than not serves PR-interests first.

In general, the notion of culture evokes rather soft and agreeable connotations. Such a conception of culture is far too naive and simple. Culture covers the evil and the good, the beautiful and the ugly, the sublime and the base components of the human condition, and more often than not these moral and aesthetic opposites are not neatly separated from one another. In fact, it makes sense to emphasize its demonic nature—the notion of the demonic taken in its original, Greek meaning. The idea of a *daimon* in antiquity pertained to a nonrational force, a source of nonrational vitality. It may come to the surface disguised either as rationality or as irrationality. Axiologically, the demonic is neither good and positive, nor bad and negative. It is not beyond good and evil, like in Nietzsche's immoralism, but rather prior to good and evil, like in an axiologically neutral amoralism. The demonic a priori of culture is energy, an electrifying force which stimulates individuals as well as collectivities to engage in all sorts of actions and activities which might turn out to be good or evil, ugly or beautiful, sublime or base, or, most likely, mixtures of these opposites. As such, it was originally not automatically tied to the satanic, as happened in Judaism and in Christianity.[11]

For social scientists it is difficult to grasp this demonic essence of culture. Of all the social theorists Pareto touched on it and came closest to a sociological interpretation of it, when he wrote about the nonrational "residues" of human action. They resemble instincts, but are better labelled as impulses. People, Pareto argued, are primarily driven by these impulses which they then rationalize ex post facto by numerous "derivations." People invent and pass on such rationalizations in order to give their behavior the appearance of morality and rationality. There is indeed something "demonic" in the ancient Greek sense in the many actions and rationalizations which Pareto collected, described and interpreted in his at times bizarre "Treatise on General Sociology."[12]

The demonic, nonrational nature of urban culture is very visible in a city like New York, in its, at first view, chaotic nature—its nervous pace, its mixture of beauty and ugliness, affluence and poverty, virtues and vices, sophistications and stupidities. In fact, each city with a strong and lively urbanity is in this originally Greek sense of the word, a demonic place. Vienna shares this demonic ambiguity, albeit in a completely different juxtaposition of good and evil, beauty and ugliness, sublimity and baseness. Urbanity is a city's cultural energy which is, in principle, axiologically neutral. It may produce wonders of human creativity and inventiveness, but also, and at the same time, abysses of misery and destitution. Although, the remainder of this book will focus mainly on the "positive" sides of urbanity, we ought not to forget its shadowy dimensions.

## Leading Concepts

In sheer numbers the socioscientific literature on the city is by now immense. In fact, one can speak of a true urbanological discourse. Yet, this discourse is, if one distances oneself from it for a moment, somewhat one-sided in that the cultural dimensions of the city are generally treated in a stepmotherly fashion. And if it is discussed, as for instance in the case of Simmel, Wirth, Mumford, and Jacobs, it generally lacks theoretical sophistication. There is, I believe, a need for a more or less systematic and comprehensive theory of urban culture. The concept of urbanity is, I am convinced, indispensable for such a theory.

Urban historians and urban anthropologists are by the very nature of their disciplines prone to focus on culture, but their accounts are often very descriptive, lacking (usually on purpose!) theoretical interpretations and generalizations. In many instances these anthropological and historical accounts are quite useful and helpful, but to the theoretically inclined reader they often lack heuristic power. Most specialists in the field of social urban studies tend to neglect the cultural dimensions of the city. Urban economists, urban sociologists and specialists of urban design and urban planning are predominantly occupied by the spatial morphology, the political power structures, and the quantitative economic and social parameters of cities. Again, many useful data and insights may be gained from their studies, but urbanity is clearly not at the center of their interests.

Most contemporary organizational studies have by now gone beyond these morphological, structural, and quantitative dimensions, and focus on the axiological and qualitative aspects of organizations. It is called organizational or corporate culture. Much of it may be faddish, yet there is a legitimate core in it: organizations do have their own history and identity, and the people that make them up are axiologically acting, thinking and feeling creatures. They are driven - often intuitively and nonrationally—by values, norms, and meanings. That indeed may be called "culture." In contrast, most urbanologists are still thinking and writing on the rather superficial level of morphological structures and socioeconomic functions, neglecting the qualitative and deeper structures of urban culture. In fact, this has become a kind of paradigm which allegedly separates "normal" from "abnormal" science. Thus, a serious student of urban economics, urban sociology or urban planning and design knows better than to quote favorably such cultural analysts of the city as Wirth, Simmel, Mumford, or Jacobs, lest he be treated as an academic outcast by the pundits of the urbanological discourse.

In contrast, I believe that Simmel, Wirth, Mumford, and Jacobs pioneered in the identification of urbanity as a legitimate object of scientific analysis and research. They admittedly failed to provide their interpretations with a systematic theory based on sound conceptualizations. In this essay, I shall try to construct a theory of urbanity which is (as is the case in other publications of mine) mainly based upon some theorems of "classic" sociology, in particular upon the Weberian brand of cultural sociology. I believe that this kind of sociology enables us to bring urban culture into a sound theoretical perspective. However, as in the other publications, in this book I shall not engage in an exercise of exegesis of Max Weber and other "classics." They rather will function as the conceptual giants on whose shoulders I stand in order to look at reality—urban culture in this case—from a better vantage point than that of the mainstream of present day urban studies. The two leading and intertwined concepts in this theoretical exercise are, in conjunction with the central concept *urbanity*, *economic culture*, and *civic culture*.[13]

Urbanity, I shall argue, is a typically Western species of the genus economic and civic culture. As such it is comparable to and closely related with the Protestant ethic. In fact, both urbanity and the Protestant ethic stood at the cradle of Western capitalism and beyond that of Western modernity. The Western bias of the present volume is obvious, and will hopefully become plausible during the course of the ensuing argument. I have not sought for any fashionable excuses for or relativizations of this bias. The bias, however, holds historical ground. It was during the Middle Ages that trading cities emerged in Western Europe, and it was within these Western cities that an urban culture—urbanity—emerged which was and remained unique for Western civilization.

Naturally, there have been rather large cities far beyond the Western world. They were also much older than their European counterparts. But none of them developed the kind of urban culture which in this essay is called urbanity. Yet, the question is legitimate and will be debated later, if today, in the state of late modernity, we are not in the process of erecting urban conglomerates—sometimes called unaesthetically "conurbations" or "megalopolises"—that are increasingly devoid of the electrifying energy, called urbanity.

Urbanity, it will be argued throughout this essay, is a specimen of what may be called "economic culture." The concept must be clarified, in particular since it may easily suggest a Marxist connotation. Economic culture is definitely not meant in the sense of an *Überbau*, a superstructure which legitimates an economic *Unterbau*, an infrastructure of forces and means of production, on which it depends well-nigh passively. The concept refers rather to the Weberian notion of an "elective affinity" between a set of values, norms and meanings on the one hand and particular economic structures and processes on the other. Weber's well-known argument about the elective affinity between the "Protestant Ethic" and the "Spirit of Capitalism" serves as an example of an economic culture.

Weber emphasized by way of contrast the positive elective affinity between rational Puritanism and the mentality needed for a successful capitalism. Calvin and the Puritans never had the intention to stimulate the capitalist economy, but their rational and initially antimagical ethos did foster unintendedly the early trade capitalism in the cities of Western Europe.[14] The work ethic, elaborately discussed by Weber, was the hard core of this peculiar elective affinity. In particular through this ethic Puritanism provided capitalism with its electrifying and stimulating ideology. However, the capitalist pursuits affected the Puritan ethic in its turn. It secularized its religious contents, to such an extent that Catholics, Jews, and agnostics absorbed its work ethic unconsciously, when they engaged actively in capitalist pursuits.

Though less interested in urbanization, Weber's contemporary and self-proclaimed rival, the historical economist Werner Sombart, also elaborated a rather extensive theory of economic culture which he too placed within the context of capitalism. For example, he started his noteworthy study of the (early) capitalist bourgeoisie with a discussion of the cultural dimensions of economic life. Like Weber, he employed the awkward concept *Geist*, when in fact he was writing about culture—that is, economic culture.[15]

We will see later that, prior to Puritanism, namely approximately from the ninth and tenth century on, urbanity began to develop a positive relationship with trade capitalism which in its turn put a heavy stamp on the culture of merchant cities. There was a true elective affinity between urbanity and capitalism which, in fact, laid the historical foundations for the emergence of the Protestantism of the sixteenth century. The values, norms and meanings, the institutions like city hall, the guild, the university, and so forth, were components of a distinct urban culture that was closely tied to an economic system which became increasingly capitalist. In this sense, urban culture was indeed an economic culture.

But urbanity was also and simultaneously a political phenomenon. Or, in other words, urbanity is not just an economic but also and at the very same time a civic culture. It served as the mental and behavioral mold for the political actions of the urban dwellers in the merchant cities. These merchants did not merely engage in trade but gathered, mainly through their economic success, considerable amounts of power also. In fact, the nobility and even the church became very soon economically dependent upon the riches of the urban merchants, artisans and service experts like lawyers and bankers who formed the core of the rising bourgeoisie. The bourgeoisie used this power to free itself from the bonds of feudalism in order to erect a political system which was more in line with their economic and social interest. A new political phenomenon began to emerge: citizenship as the collection of civil rights which enabled the inhabitants of a city to participate actively in the urban political arena.

In this way the burghers of the emergent trading cities of Western Europe developed gradually into a rather vigorous, socioeconomic class with its own political, economic, and social interests. It enabled them to compete successfully with the leading powers of medieval society which they would eventually supersede. Impressive city halls in the center of these urban settlements testified to the newly gained independence and power.

Naturally, these merchants began to develop also their own, specifically bourgeois style of life, which forged them into a status group—a *Stand*—which again competed successfully with the other traditional status groups of medieval society, the nobility, the clergy and the peasantry. They erected their very own cultural institutions, those of learning in the first place, but those of the arts and leisure as well. This combination of class and *Stand*, and the antifeudal, pristinely democratic power formation, gave urbanity the distinct character of a civic culture.

It is in this sense that we shall call urbanity an economic and civic culture. During the course of the argument these concepts will acquire more heuristic substance.

## Notes

1. Michael Kehlmann, Georg Biron, *Der Qualtinger, ein Porträt* (Wien: Verlag Kremayr & Schieriau, 1987), 182. My translation.
2. Quoted in Jim Sleeper, "Looking At Our City," *Dissent* (Special Issue: "In Search of New York," Fall 1987), 419.
3. Peter L. Berger, "New York City 1976: A Signal of Transcendence", in Peter L. Berger, *Facing up to Modernity* (Harmondsworth, U.K.: Penguin Books, [1977] 1979), 265.
4. Edwin H. Chapin, *Humanity in the City* (New York: Arno Press, [1854] 1974), 18.
5. Herbert J. Gans, *The Urban Villagers* (New York: Free Press, [1962] 1969).
6. Cf. Tom Wolfe, *Radical Chic & Mau-Mauing the Flak Catchers* (New York: Farrar, Straus and Giroux, [1970] 1987).
7. Jim Sleeper, "Our City," 425.
8. Cf. Janny Scott, "Forget Good, Bad and Ugly: New York Is the Place to Be," *New York Times*, 3 July 1994, pp. 1 and 26.
9. Hilde Spiel, *Vienna's Golden Autumn 1866-1938* (New York: Weidenfeld and Nicolson, 1987), 33. She adds the following observation: "In accordance with their schizophrenic disposition, these grumblers, grousers and apparent harborers of ill-will towards their fellow human beings have always shown the greatest respect for those who have made their way in life, who have acquired fame, or wealth, or titles whose status seemed to rub off on those who addressed them as "Herr Doktor" or "Herr Baron." Ibid., 33.
10. François Barré, "The Desire for Urbanity", in *Architectural Design*, vol. 11/12 (1980), 7. The whole issue is devoted to urbanity, but lacks a theoretical explanation of the concept.
11. Cf. G. van der Leeuw, *Religion in Essence and Manifestation* (New York: Harper & Row, [1933] 1963), vol. 1, ch. 15, 134–140. Also K. Hammer, "Exkurs: Das Dämonische bei Mozart," in *W. A. Mozart: Eine theologische Deutung,* (Zürich: EVZ Verlag, 1964), 79–81.
12. Vilfredo Pareto, *The Mind and Society: A Treatise on General Sociology* (New York: Dover Publications, [1935] 1963), vol. I: "Non-Logical Conduct."
13. There is no monograph yet on the concept of economic culture. See, however, Peter L. Berger, *The Capitalist Revolution* (New York: Basic Books, 1986), pp. 7f., 10f., 24-27, 73. The by now classic statement on civic culture is Gabriel A. Almond, Sidney Verba, *The Civic Culture: Political Attitudes and Democracy in Five Nations* (Princeton, NJ: Princeton University Press, 1963). The authors find a combination of citizen activity and passivity, and of influence and deference characteristic of a civic culture. Activity and influence, it may be added, will be more prominent than passivity and deference, when a civic culture is in the process of emerging. When it has reached a certain stage of development, routinization will set in and passivity and deference will balance activity and influence. This has certainly happened in the case of urbanity.

14. The words "initially antimagical" were used on purpose, since Puritanism too returned to magical forms of thought and behavior soon. See in particular Keith Thomas, *Religion and the Decline of Magic* (New York: Charles Scribner's Sons, 1971), 177–282.

15. Werner Sombart, "Der Geist im Wirtschaftsleben," in *Der Bourgeois* (München-Leipzig: Duncker & Humblot, [1913] 1923), 1–11. See also *passim*. A well-known anthropological example of an economic culture is the *kula* ring of the Trobrianders, described by Bronislaw Malinowski. Cf. Michael W. Young, ed., "The Kula," in *The Ethnography of Malinowski: The Trobriand Islands 1915-18* (London: Routledge & Kegan Paul, 1979), 159–242.

# 1

# Urbanity: Origins and Ramifications

## Restrictions of the Argument

This book focuses on the city as a sociocultural phenomenon, in particular as it developed since roughly the end of the Middle Ages in Western Europe. This imposes some distinct restrictions on the argument. To begin with, this is mainly a study of Western cities. The argument will be made later that the great cities of ancient India, ancient China, Babylonia, pre-Columbian Mexico, and Peru may have been true cities in the quantitative and morphological sense of the word. But, they lacked a distinct economic and civic culture which could have forged their inhabitants into specific social bonds, thereby molding them into true citizens, as happened in many late medieval and early modern cities of Europe. I am fully aware of the Western bias that lies at the foundation of this theoretical point of departure. Yet, I am not prepared to abandon the notion of this typically Western, urban culture for the sake of liberal-minded multiculturalism. Also, the accusation of "cultural Imperialism" cannot convince me, as it is too obviously ideological. It is simply a historical fact that urbanity is in origin and nature a Western phenomenon, just as the sonata, or sociology, or the nation-state is.

However, I am prepared to concede that detailed comparative analyses of contemporary cities outside the Western European and North American orbit might yield a considerable relativization of this Western bias. Modernization and modernity have by now become *mondial* phenomena, thus elements of urbanity may well have spread over the world, in company with such originally Western phenomena as democracy and capitalism. And the other way around, many Western cities have declined in urbanity and begin to resemble the bazaar cities of the former, pre-modern Middle and Far East. Los Angeles, as we will see in chapter 4, has already been called "the capital of the Third

World." Non-Western cultures have, of course, their very own histories and possess their very own cultural characteristics. Comparative studies of contemporary urban cultures would certainly soften the Western bias. And indeed, it would be a fascinating challenge to subject cities like Istanbul, Cairo, Osaka, Djakarta, Singapore, Rio de Janeiro, and Santiago to detailed empirical analyses with a central focus on their respective urban cultures. It would be of similar interest to study the respective urban cultures of contemporary cities and metropolises in Africa. Such studies might even yield important results for their policies of urban renewal. However, one of the restrictions of this study is that it will not and cannot be comparative in the sense of detailed and methodologically refined analyses of present-day non-Western cities, for the simple reason that this would transcend the limits and possibilities of this theoretical treatise.

The American reader might draw the conclusion that this essay is too Eurocentric to be applicable to American cities. This, however, would be a restriction I cannot and will not accept. I am the last to belittle the cultural differences between Europe and America, and thus between the urbanity of American cities and that of European cities. However, I am convinced that this depends on the level of theoretical generalization that one allows oneself to operate upon. On a low level of generalization "Europe," "the European city," "America," and "the American city" do not exist. In view of particular cities these concepts present unmanageable generalities. But it is like walking in a forest with so many idiosyncratic, mutually different trees and bushes that one is unable to "see" the forest. But, from the altitude of a helicopter—on a higher level of generalization—these individual differences blur; the structural contours of the forest as a whole—as a gestalt—emerge. There is obviously a limit to this generalization: the helicopter can fly to such an altitude that even the forest as a whole disappears from sight. Admittedly, my theoretical helicopter flies on a high altitude, but is still, I trust, capable of getting the European and American brands of urbanity into focus as specimens of a phenomenon that historically emerged in Western Europe at roughly the end of the Middle Ages.

On an acceptable level of generalization American and European cities appear to have much in common, despite admittedly numerous differences. They are comparable, if they are economically vital and politically influential centers of economic (capitalist) activities, artistic performances and innovations, scientific education and research, scores of public and private organizations that are consciously or unconsciously driven by a civic spirit. All of this should occur within the context of democratic political structures. If these conditions are present—and they are present in many American and European cities—they exhibit, albeit in different shades and gradations, urbanity.

Naturally, there are American cities that are blatantly devoid of urbanity as a viable economic and civic culture. These cities lack the main characteristics that the present theory attributes to urbanity. But such cities do exist in Europe as well. The city of Rotterdam, for example, which contains the largest harbor in the world, direly lacked urbanity up until the 1980s, mainly due to the destruction of its center by the Germans at the beginning of World War II, and bad urban planning in the years after the war.[1] The lack of urbanity is not a matter of Americanism but the result of bad urban planning, and bad urban planning has occurred and still occurs on both sides of the Atlantic. The point is rather, that these American and European cities-without-urbanity stand in need of revitalization, and a lively and vigorous urbanity is, according to the present theory, the essence and core of such an urban renewal and revitalization. Rotterdam, for example, went through a remarkable regeneration during the past decade. Its urbanity remains vastly different from that of Amsterdam but that is the result of their historically determined, different economic functions. In any case, the revitalization of Rotterdam's urbanity which is far from completion, is the result of good planning and sound policy on the part of an enlightened city government. We will return to this subject at the end of this book.

The present theory of urbanity deals with the historical origins and developments of Western European cities and their urban culture. Yet, the essay should not be read as a historical study in the sense of a detailed and methodologically refined historical account and analysis.[2] The main objective is the construction of a *sociological* theory of urbanity. A detailed discussion of the history of the Western city, beginning with the Greek *polis* and the cities of the Roman Empire, and covering the history of urban development in Europe and North America, would lead us too far astray. And after all, there are several rather outstanding studies of urban history, many of which were gratefully used in the preparation of this book.

## Symbolic Infrastructure

However, the most important limitation of this study I've yet to mention. I am less interested in the city as a spatial, quantitative, and material entity whose morphology, demographic density, economic productivity, logistic infrastructure, and various social and economic services could be measured statistically. Needless to say these metric dimensions of the city are essential. Urban design and urban policy cannot be effective without a detailed analysis of these quantitative and metric parameters. Thus, it stands to reason that they have been the main target of most contemporary urban studies.

However, this study will ignore them on purpose. Rather, it searches, as it were, behind these physical and quantitative features for the *symbolic infrastructure* of the city. What is it that ties these countless actions and interactions, these vastly different groups and individuals, these organizations and institutions, together into something called "urban life"? Cities can be huge conglomerates, millions of people thrown together haphazardly, without common bonds and sentiments, without a shared sense of a collective, urban identity. Such cities lack a symbolic infrastructure.

Cities, however, can also represent collective economic, social, and political interests on the basis of which the inhabitants share certain norms and values, certain sentiments, a collective identity, and a sense of civic pride. Such cities possess a symbolic infrastructure, comparable to the organizational culture of an industrial or commercial firm. The symbolic infrastructure of a city is its urban culture, its urbanity. It is predominantly and intrinsically an economic and a civic culture.

As to the cities of Europe and North America, their symbolic infrastructure has a distinct historical origin, namely in the late medieval and early modern trade cities of northern Italy and northern Europe. Venice first, but Ghent, Bruges, Cologne, and above all Lübeck soon after were the urban vanguards of influential economic, sociocultural, and political changes in Europe. Many other cities would follow suit. This was, in fact, the cradle of modernization and modernity. Here a new mode of trade (capitalism), new modes of production (craftsmanship first, manufacturing next, and then industry), new socioeconomic bonds of solidarity (the bourgeoisie), and new cultural institutions (professional and higher education; the arts, crafts, and sciences) were forged.

Soon, these growingly affluent cities acquired political stamina and developed into rather influential powers. This would have been impossible if these cities had been faceless conglomerates, if they had lacked a vigorous symbolic infrastructure, if they had not developed a vital and inspiring urbanity. "A city," Daniel Bell once wrote, "is not only a place but a state of mind, a symbol of a distinctive style of life whose major attributes are variety and excitement; a city also presents a sense of scale that dwarfs any single effort to encompass its meaning."[3] These words are, incidentally, so much in agreement with the basic tenet of the present study, that I placed them as leading epigraph at the beginning of this book.

## Urbanity-Urbanism

The concepts of urbanity and urbanism occur frequently in urbanological discourse. They are usually not defined, nor mutually distinguished. In order to be useful scientifically, such concepts actually ought to be defined explicitly. Yet, it is in the nature of most concepts referring to culture that formal definitions offered in advance are of little heuristic value.

For instance, it does not make much sense to begin a treatise in the sociology of religion with a detailed and learned exposition about the possible and most useful definitions of the religious phenomenon. It is better to gradually build up the conceptualization in question, to discuss its various components as coherently as possible. At the end of such an exposition, one may want to sum it all up in a concise and formal definition. Often, however, this will not be really necessary: the essence and contours of the phenomenon have become apparent and clear anyhow.

Meanwhile, it does make sense for a start to look briefly at the lexicographic meaning of the concepts *urbanity* and *urbanism*. Urbanity is usually seen as a synonym of suavity: a refined politeness or courtesy. An urbane person is someone who knows his manners. It comes close to civility, derived from the Latin *civilitas*. The concept which is used to denote urban culture, is in most dictionaries: urbanism, as in Wirth's "Urbanism as a way of life." However, gradually urbanity also acquired the meaning of urban culture, thus becoming synonymous to urbanism.

Since most concepts ending with -ism refer to morally inspired ideologies, such as Catholicism, Protestantism, Marxism, modernism, functionalism, nudism, etc., and most concepts ending with -ity refer to culture as a state of mind and a connected style of life (ethnicity, masculinity, femininity, vanity, etc.), it may be preferable to employ urbanity instead of urbanism, if one refers to the cultural dimensions and the symbolic infrastructure of cities. It is, of course, just a matter of words and thus not of great importance, but it should be kept in mind that in this book, the concept urbanity is preferable to that of urbanism. The concept of urbanism, as used in this book, refers rather to urban philosophies and ideologies, such as those of Howard, or Wright, or Le Corbusier.

## The Concept of Culture

It is no longer true that a confusingly large variety of definitions of culture are current in social sciences. If one, for instance, is cognizant of today's discussions and publications about corporate or organizational culture, a kind of common notion of culture, emerges instantly. In general, culture is understood to be the combination of a few elements. I summarize them briefly for clarity's sake.

To begin with, culture is the invisible reality of mutually related *meanings, values, and norms*. These are passed on from generation to generation through enculturation and thus constitute a *tradition* which transcends the flow of generations. Certainly, in a fully modernized society in which most traditions are no longer sacred and magically taboo, these meanings, values, and norms will be subjected to often rapid and radical changes. Yet, even today, individuals or generations do not invent their very own meanings, values, and norms, each time they have to act in and upon the world. In fact, large portions of them are stored up in tradition and are taken for granted. They represent a "normal" state of affairs. They constitute normalcy in the sense of "this is the way we do things around here." This leads to the second element of culture.

Culture is the totality of ways of thinking, feeling, and acting of the members of a group. Durkheim coined a concise definition of this: *des manières d'agir, de penser et de sentir*—ways, or patterns of doing, thinking, and feeling. And he adds to this definition that these patterns are, in a sense, exterior to the individual and endowed with a coercive power which they impose upon the individual.[4] A technical term for such patterns of behavior is *institutions*. Culture, thus, is the totality of institutions of a group of people. These institutions are naturally closely tied to the values, norms, and meanings. In fact, the latter are patterned, are institutionalized. And that is precisely what the culture of a collectivity of human beings is—the institutionalized and traditional set of meanings, values, and norms.

This is also what renders them empirical. Culture—that is, the sum of invisible and in that sense nonempirical meanings, values, and norms—becomes empirically visible and researchable in the traditional patterns of behavior which mold the acting, thinking, and feeling of individual actors. Culture is empirically "real," because it "exists" in behavior, in actions and interactions. At the same time, culture is as much psychologically "subjective" (thinking, feeling) as it is socio-logically "objective" (doing).

Thirdly, these patterns of behavior, these institutions, provide the members of the group a shared sense of *identity*: "these are the ways we think, feel, and do things around here," "these are our manners"—that is, the *modi operandi* and lifestyles which are typical of a specific group. These observable patterns of behavior, these institutions, also enable outsiders to identify and typify the collectivity: "such and such are their institutions: typically intellectuals, typically farmers, typically politicians, typically urbanites." That is to say, culture provides individuals with a shared identity. If the definitions of the collectivity's culture by outsiders coincide with the definitions of the members themselves, the sense of collective identity will be strengthened. If this is not the case, that sense will be weakened, depending on the power and the authority of those outsiders. In fact, a collectivity may be called a group in the sociological sense of the word only, if its members do share a sense of collective identity caused by and couched in shared values, norms, and meanings.

Thus, whenever and wherever people, for whatever reason, do things together, they will constitute a group, because they begin to develop common patterns of behavior which are passed on to newcomers (tradition). A shared sense of identity, a sort of solidarity emerges in the process. Durkheim distinguished analytically between two types of solidarity: in a relatively small society with a relatively low degree of division of labor solidarity tends to be "mechanical" in that it is couched firmly in a taken-for-granted tradition; in a relatively large society with a relatively high degree of specialization solidarity tends to be "organic" in that it depends on the functional necessity of the specialists to cooperate.

As we shall see in greater detail later, urbanity shares all of these characteristics of culture, although its type of solidarity is modern and functional and can be typified after Durkheim as an "organic solidarity." This in rather sharp distinction to the solidarities of clans, extended families, castes, feudal estates, and most religious communities which are to be defined as being inherently "mechanical."

## Urbanity's Social Foundation

The core of the sociology of knowledge is the search for the social foundations of ideas, sentiments, values, norms, and meanings. As Karl Mannheim in particular claimed, culture does not float around freely and abstractly in thin air but is always tied to specific groups in specific situations with specific material interests. He was quite deterministic in this, unlike Max Weber who also tied culture to specific socioeconomic strata (classes, status groups) in society but did so in terms of elective affinities. He was, in other words, interested in the (usually unintended) fit between culture and socioeconomic strata.

If we generalize this basic notion of the sociology of knowledge, we could view the cultural evolution of the human race as a succession of various sociological loci or home-bases for the meanings, values, and norms that have directed and controlled human behavior. Thus, from early times on, the nuclear family, in whatever shape and format, must almost certainly have been the primeval social foundation of culture formation. This base was then broadened, we may assume safely, into the extended family, including the deceased ancestors. Having become sedentary, the land of the ancestors and the possession of land was added to this sociological home base of culture. Religion (e.g., notions of joining the ancestors after death) and magic (e.g., fertility rites and medical practices) penetrated deeply into sedentary, agrarian culture.

Beyond such familial, clanlike bonds, ethnic ties and ethnic castes emerged as powerful home-bases of culture formation. Then it is but a short distance towards the primordial notion of race, or nation, or people (*Volk*) as the mystical and often metaphysical collection of common blood ties that forge people together in, at times, extremely exclusive and closed bonds of (predominantly "mechanical") solidarity. In many instances this led to a metaphysical enclosure of culture which impeded economic and social development and progress. Monotheism did in fact break through these enclosing barriers, certainly when it fiercely attacked religious metaphysics and magical nonrationalities, as was the case in the prophetic tradition of ancient Judaism and in Calvinism. The bulk of Judeo-Christian and Islamic monotheism, however, maintained close ties with magic and metaphysics and its organizations, like churches and scores of religious organizations. They functioned in terms of the sociology of knowledge as important home-bases for values, norms, and meanings.

The interesting and fascinating fact about urbanity is that it was not at all founded and based upon such irrational (religious, magical, and metaphysical) factors like family, church, caste, race, and soil. From roughly the tenth and eleventh century on (it started, as we shall see, in Italy, and in particular Venice), inhabitants of European cities began to group together in their common trading and artisan ventures, joined soon by service experts, such as lawyers, bankers, insurance agents, and so on. Not the ties of family and religion, not the possession and long-time habitation of a piece of land, not the belonging by birth to caste or race, but the very rational economic interests in early capitalist trade, and equally rational political interests in autonomy vis-à-vis the ruling feudal forces and in a pristine form of democracy drove these city dwellers together. These rational and intertwined interests laid the foundation for an urban economic and civic culture, based on a typically "organic" type of solidarity.

These burghers did not constitute a closed caste or ethnic group, but an internally as well as externally open group of people whose social bonds were forged primarily by their common economic and political interests. Here, in these burghers, we encounter the first vestiges of modernity. In comparison with their primordial predecessors (family, clan, caste, race, etc.) their physical and social mobility, their rational calculations of costs and profits, their increasing cosmopolitanism and internationalism testified to a completely different world, a completely different mentality, a completely different style of life.

Moreover, for the first time in history, a real class, an urban class, emerged. Unlike the caste or the status group (estate, *Stand*), into which one was born and out of which one would eventually die, this urban class was a relatively open configuration. That is, one's socioeconomic position in the urban class structure was, in principle, not ascribed but achieved. There was ample room for social mobility. That is initially because, as we will see shortly, soon enough socioeconomic inequalities arose in these early modern urban societies. In any case, whoever engaged successfully in trade and craftsmanship, and later in manufacture and industry, became a member of this urban class which soon began to differentiate into lower-, middle-, and upper-middle classes. For the first time in history the city itself became the social foundation of culture formation, and the focus of a new type of solidarity.

This was truly a historical event. The urban merchants and artisans, and the representatives of allied services, such as bankers, lawyers, teachers, transporters, and so on, gradually developed their own collective values, norms and meanings, their own patterns of behavior, their own *modi operandi*, their own life styles—urban patterns, city manners. It was, in short, their own identifiable culture: urbanity. In contrast to most cultures of previous times and in other parts of the world, with the possible exception of the ancient Greek *polis*, this was a rational, an economic culture. And as these burghers began to develop their very own, increasingly forceful political power, this urban culture became a civic culture as well. This economic and civic culture of the early modern European cities was one of the most influential driving forces behind the modernization of the world. This point will be taken up again and further elaborated in the next chapter.

## City = Oikos + Market

If we conceive of the city, somewhat superficially, as a relatively large collection of houses, buildings, and streets exerting functions that transcend the routines of daily social life, such as the defense against hostile attacks, and the administration of surrounding rural regions, then cities existed some six thousand years ago. In this superficial sense, cities are a *mondial* and very old phenomenon. In Mesopotamia archaeologists found the remainders of walled fortresses which they have dated 4000 B.C.[5] Historians demonstrated that relatively large and influential cities were quite normal long ago in various Asian civilizations.[6] Thus, as a physical and morphologically distinct phenomenon the city is a globally dispersed and rather ancient phenomenon.

However, urbanity as a distinctly urban economic and civic culture which gives the inhabitants of a city a sense of collective identity and consists of a distinct type of solidarity, has been limited in time and location. If we leave the ancient Greek *polis* out of the discussion for clarity's sake,[7] we may conclude that urbanity emerged at the end of the Middle Ages and during the Renaissance in Europe, contributed to the process of modernization (the rise of technology and the sciences, the rise of high capitalism, the rise of the nation state), and was then modified again by this very process. In short, historically and sociologically we ought to distinguish between cities with and without a distinct urban culture, that is, urbanity. But it is imperative then to define the city more precisely.

Max Weber's definition of the city is, I think, still useful.[8] He emphasized that morphology and quantitative size—the amounts of houses and inhabitants—are irrelevant for such a definition. There are, in fact, small cities and large villages. He then singled out two elements which separate cities from villages: *oikos* and *market*.

Often, cities developed from citadels which rulers—in medieval Europe, usually bishops—erected and maintained in the defense and the administration of their territory. These citadels and administrative centers, usually quite small in size, were often characterized by strong social bonds of a familial nature. The ruler—either belonging to the nobility or to the higher clergy, or in some cases both—occupied the position of a *pater familias*. They were a kind of artificial extended family, a kind of home. Weber, therefore, used the Greek concept of *oikos* (house) to define these medieval citadels as social systems. Weber characterized the specific authority of such an *oikos* as being patrimonial.

But a habitat that functions as a military stronghold and administrative center is, as such, not quite a city in the sociological sense of the word, even if it is a system with patrimonial social bonds. Such citadels become true cities, if they harbor tradesmen and craftsmen, and in their wake service experts like bankers, insurance brokers, lawyers, and medical doctors, who primarily work for a *market*. Cities in the sociological sense, in other words, are not just garrisons and administrative centers under the patrimonial care of a ruler, rather they are trading, manufacturing, and servicing centers in which people work and produce for a market—directly, as in the case of merchants, craftsmen, and bankers, as well as indirectly, as in the case of teachers, preachers, and administrators.

Initially, this market was physically restricted to the city's center, where farmers, artisans, and craftsmen would sell their products. The market was located on the square in front of the church. The German word for market is *Messe* which is reminiscent of the holy mass. After the mass, the town's people would gather in front of the church, the farmers would sell or barter their produce, the craftsmen their products. This, incidentally, proves that there was, in actual fact, no social and economic gap between the city and the country. The city and its surrounding country needed each other mutually. Their respective interests, in other words, intersected. This would always be the case in the further development of city and country.[9]

Soon, however, the market would become a wide and rather abstract phenomenon. The merchants of the Hanseatic League virtually treated all of Europe, from Bruges to Novgorod, from Lübeck to Venice as their market. The search for new markets became an urgent drive within the urban economic culture of Europe. It led to daring voyages of discovery far beyond the borders of the European continent.

In sum, a citadel and administrative center can, according to Weber, only be called a city in the sociological sense of the word, if it is not only a social system, an *oikos*, but above all an economic system, a market, or better still, a center of market activities.

Pirenne argued that various Roman fortresses in Europe incorporated this double function already, but that this radically changed once again around the ninth century.[10] Due to an economic crisis, which he attributed in particular to the loss of the Mediterranean to Islamic forces, these cities began to lose their market functions. In the Carolingian era they were actually reduced to garrisons or episcopal administrative centers without much economic activity, and certainly without an economically active and energetic class of merchants and craftsmen. The church cashed in on this politically: "When the disappearance of trade, in the ninth century, annihilated the last vestiges of city life and put an end to what still remained of a municipal population, the influence of the bishops, already so extensive, became unrivalled. Henceforward the towns were entirely under their control."[11]

Thus, it was not before the eleventh century, according to Pirenne, that the European economy, in particular that of the cities, began to reemerge strongly, due to the decline of Islamic power within the Mediterranean orbit. Naturally, in this orbit it were the cities that took the lead in this economic revitalization. In particular Venice which, because of its close commercial ties with Constantinople, had never lost its economic vigor, went ahead and developed rapidly into a powerful center of quite lively trade relations.[12]

Yet, the ninth and tenth centuries, aptly called "the crucible of Europe" by Geoffrey Barraclough, were decisive for the reemergence of the cities. After the death of Charlemagne Europe fell apart and was attacked from all sides—the Vikings from the north, the Magyars from the east, and the Saracens from the south. Every castle, village, and town was on its own, and the lack of political authority created a void which was filled by countless feudal arrangements between lords and serfs.[13] In Italy, Barraclough argues, the successful merchant cities emancipated themselves from the counts and counties in the land and developed into city-states. An astounding economic revival occurred in the eleventh century, with Venice in the nearly unrivalled lead.[14]

The economic and civic culture of these Italian city-states were well developed by the thirteenth century, as was testified by an historian in an illustrative book on the power and imagination of the city-states of Renaissance Italy. "Political feeling in the Italian cities around 1300," he claims, "was rooted in a passionate attachment to place: a city and its environs. Along the banks of the Arno and near the Po, in the Veneto as in Liguria, citizens had a first and fervent allegiance to their own cities, to the local shaping of their own political destinies, and this feeling survived in the Renaissance.... The intensity of local feeling made for a hundred states rather than one."[15]

The same author adds, however, that there was also much discord and conflict in these cities. There is indeed, and this has to be kept in mind constantly, no reason for a romanticization of their urbanity: "Conspiracy, insurrections, mass exile, the vengeful razing of houses, the penchant for physical assault on public officials, or the readiness of men to imperil their souls."[16] In order to avoid chaos and maintain a degree of urban authority many cities instituted the "podestal government." A *podestà* was a magistrate who had to be able to transcend the many factions of a city-state—often "a nobleman from another province, practiced in arms or in law, and experienced in public life. Chosen by an ad hoc electoral commission or by a selection of the leading communal officials, he might be subject to the approval of the commune's legislative council."[17] Incidentally, the autobiography of Benvenuto Cellini (1500–1571) testifies vividly to the incredible degree of violence and danger to which the Italian cities had declined come the sixteenth century. In comparison, most of today's metropolises are havens of safety.[18]

From the twelfth and thirteenth centuries onward, other cities, first and foremost the trading and harbor cities in northwestern Europe (e.g., Ghent, Bruges, Cologne, and Lübeck), followed suit. After the Viking raids, which had crippled them for such a long time, had ended in the tenth century, these cities slowly regained their economic stamina. From the eleventh century onwards, they not only strengthened and cultivated their trades and crafts, but also their own culture and above all their political autonomy. Increasingly and in fact quite rapidly cities developed into forces to reckon with. Their economic and civic culture provided them with stamina, strength, and confidence.

This point is of crucial importance to the present argument. Unlike cities in Asia which in many cases were specimens of the *oikos*-plus-market but lacked an economic and civic culture, many European cities became, from the tenth and eleventh centuries onwards, foci of economic and political power, forging their very own type of "organic" solidarity among their inhabitants, forging, above all, their very own type of urban identity. These trading cities soon set the economic, sociocultural, and political standards in Europe.

Those garrisons and administrative centers that did not catch up with this evolution, declined rapidly in prosperity and influence, and faded away into little, irrelevant towns. The standard-setting cities were, in fact, not mere centers of trades, crafts, and related services, but distinct *urban communities* based on a city-centered solidarity. Weber called this a specifically urban *Gemeindeverband*—communal association.[19] That is, as socioeconomically and politically diverse as they have been internally, the burghers of these cities still experienced and maintained a sense of community which was not based, as had been the case up till then, upon the solidarity of familial, clannish, religious ties, neither on the bonds of estate, race, or caste, nor on the possession of land. This solidarity was borne by the city itself as a socioeconomic and political entity. It was first and foremost a rational community of interests.

Naturally, urban authority could no longer be patrimonial and restricted to clergy and nobility, as it had been in the medieval days, when cities still functioned mainly as garrisons and administrative centers. The Italian podestal government was not a viable option for the powerful trade cities of northwestern Europe. As an economically strong and thus politically powerful class, the successful merchants, artisans, and allied professionals gradually usurped the administrative powers from the nobility and clergy. They installed an elected council as the urban government, consisting of notable merchants and allied service providers. They were often called *consules* or councillors.[20] It was in these cities that democracy—that is, democratic participation and democratic control of power—emerged. This urban democracy was, incidentally, less a utopian ideal, than a necessary corollary of economic and sociocultural developments. As a result, economic culture was linked to civic culture.

From the tenth and eleventh centuries onwards, the burghers of several economically successful cities began to join forces against the still dominant patrimonial powers of the nobility and clergy. They demanded their share in the decision making power of their city. Increasingly, they aspired to take over the city's command altogether. This was called a *coniuratio*.[21] It was in a sense a kind of revolutionary act of fraternization, in which influential burghers combined forces in order to defend their economic and political interests against the ruling feudal forces. However, such a nearly conspiratory act did not always have to occur in actual fact. More often than not, the gradual increase of power and autonomy of the new class of burghers—the bourgeoisie—had to be accepted by the ruling feudal estates as an inevitable fact. Many members of the ruling estates became financially and economically dependent on the increasingly prosperous bourgeoisie.

If ever there was a case of historical necessity, it was this rise of bourgeois power and autonomy in the merchant cities of northwestern Europe. In most cases a kind of sharing of power was arranged with the clergy and nobility through peaceful, if not always easy, negotiations. In any case, gradually the burghers of the economically vital cities received their city rights and citizen rights, their own courts, and an ever firmer grip on the urban administration. It was indeed a development of revolutionary proportions.

## The *Hansa*-An Excursus

The word *Hansa* has a double original meaning. It referred to a franchise for which merchants had to pay in order to engage in trade within a certain city or territory. It also referred to an association of merchants of a particular city or of a group of cities, the association being the "owner" of the franchise. In the German Hanseatic League (ca. 1150– 1669) such trade franchises had to be paid to the monarch of the German Holy Roman Empire.

After the twelfth century, three leagues of Hanseatic cities emerged. There was, since the first quarter of the thirteenth century, the Flemish Hansa of London—a league of Flemish cities, led by Bruges and Ypers— that had the right of trade with England and Scotland. It declined rather soon at the end of the thirteenth century. Second, in Flanders and northern France there was also the Hanseatic League of Seventeen Cities in which, among others, Ghent, Brussels, Louvain, and Amiens participated. Its focus was on trade with Italy and on the annual fair at Champagne. When the latter declined, the League of Seventeen Cities declined too. Again, this was at the end of the thirteenth century.[22]

Meanwhile the German Hanseatic League, led by Lübeck, had come to prominence. Its palmy days were the fourteenth and fifteenth centuries in which it reigned economically from London and Ghent, where it had important offices, and from the cities at the Dutch Zuyder Zee, to Gotland, the Baltic ports, and Novgorod in Russia. Its ships—specifically built for intensive trading[23]—dominated the Baltic Sea and the North Sea, and ventured as far south as the Bay of Biscaye and the ports of Portugal. On land the Hanseatic merchants travelled all over northern Europe, from Ghent and Bruges to Tallin and Novgorod. They also covered much of southern Germany and northern Italy.

Decline set in from the sixteenth century onward. Several causes were at work in this decline. There was, to begin with, much internal discord and strife. Lübeck had a hard time maintaining its primacy against the aspirations of equally powerful cities like Cologne in the west and Tallin and Novgorod in the east. Second, there was an ongoing conflict, mounting to a real war, with the kings of Denmark who loathed the power of the league in general and of Lübeck in particular in and around the Baltic Sea. Third, there were the increasingly powerful non-Hanseatic cities of Holland, Amsterdam in particular, that regained sovereignty over the North Sea first and soon also began to penetrate into the Baltic Sea. Fourth, the cities in southern Germany began to prosper and then resented their dependence on the north German cities. Finally, the sovereigns of the Holy Roman Empire, who at first fostered the Hanseatic League, gradually lost their grip on these powerful merchants and thus turned against them politically.[24]

Yet, despite these ills and weaknesses, the German Hanseatic League exhibited a surprisingly common, transnational urban culture. To begin with, these Hanseatic cities possessed a remarkable combination of localism and cosmopolitanism. In the beginning, these merchants would travel on land or over sea in groups in order to protect themselves against pirates and brigands. They were very mobile,[25] and rarely at home, yet very much attached to their city of origin. This combination of localism and cosmopolitanism was maintained, when successful merchants began to send their agents abroad while they ran their business from the main office, the *skrive-kamere*—the writing room.[26]

The Hanseatic culture was a civic culture. Leading merchants took up positions in their urban government, as mayor, alderman, or member of the city council. The old Roman title of *consul* was even introduced again. Soon, of course, an urban elite would manifest itself: the patriciate.

In these Hanseatic cities the relations between men and women fundamentally changed. It would be too much to speak of true emancipation, since women would not share the legal rights of men; they were also excluded from political positions in the government of the city. However, in business, men and women worked together closely as partners. It was normal for a widow to take over the executive position of her deceased husband. Thus the continuity of the family business was insured.[27]

Actually, it was the state of mind of these Hanseatic burghers which was most striking. It had, in fact, all the basic elements of modernity. Schildhauer summed it up handsomely:

> New attitudes emerged over this period in the Hanseatic merchant: reliance on his own strength, the knowledge that he could achieve something on the basis of his

own abilities, a willingness to take risks coupled with a dose of considered reason, and a hunger for authority. He adopted a constructive approach to life. His political horizons were broadened by far-flung trade links, travels which taught him much about his world, about the ways of foreign peoples, foreign towns. Alongside other influential burghers he set the tone for a new urban culture and a trend for progress. It was completely new to hold human labour in such high esteem. The monetary economy developed by the merchant was reflected in the use now made of time, measured in terms of work. The evolution of a professional ethic among merchants and other urban trades reveals the basic transformations that were occurring within feudal society, particularly from the thirteenth and fourteenth century onwards. With the merchants and the urban bourgeoisie, a force had been born which would be able to confront the princes and lords, and even the foreign kings.[28]

Lübeck managed to impose its own dialect as the leading language on the other cities of the German Hanseatic League.[29] Yet, it has been claimed that many merchants in this league made efforts to master the tongues of their foreign trading partners, particularly the Nordic languages, Russian, English, and French. Some even tried to conduct conversations in Estonian and tried to prevent their Dutch competitors from learning the languages of the Baltic region. Regretfully, no clues have been offered as to how they accomplished this.[30] In any case, we may safely assume that these cosmopolitan merchants managed to understand each other beyond their often vastly different languages. In any case, they all spoke the same language—the language of trade, profit, market opportunities, and competitions, that is, the language of trade capitalism.

The Hansa exerted a great influence on literature and played a crucial role in the founding of urban schools and universities.[31] It was, one should not forget, the period of the Reformation and Renaissance Humanism. The invention of book printing enabled these spiritual forces to spread their ideas extensively. Next to the Luther translation of the Bible, a popular legend and bourgeois satire like "Reynard the Fox," and later that of "Till Eulenspiegel," were read widely in the orbit of the Hanseatic League. Such popular literature had political meanings, as it implicitly ridiculed early absolutist monarchic rule. But its function was definitely also to help the bourgeois class forge its very own identity.[32]

In sum, in the Hanseatic League we find all the features and trimmings of urbanity, both in their positive and negative dimensions. The Hansa, which in a sense was the first European economic community, definitively illustrates that, if there ever was a common, typically European culture behind or beneath vast differences in language, religion, ethnicity, politics, and socioeconomic circumstances, it was urbanity.

## Weber's Comparison

Weber asked a question which is typical of his brand of sociology—a sociology molded by the logic of *Kulturwissenschaft*[33]: why is it that European rather than Asian cities functioned as the breeding and feeding ground of a bourgeoisie which generated its very own culture and its very own economic and political power—a power, needless to add, which was crucial to the emergence of high capitalism in the Western world? The ancient Near East, ancient India, and ancient China did have cities which often were, like in Europe, big and influential citadels and administrative centers. Many also harbored early capitalist activities in trade and crafts. Their administrative systems and their civilizations were very sophisticated, in many respects more so than had been the case in contemporary, medieval Europe. Yet, they were in actual fact "bazaar cities,"[34] market places without an *oikos*, without any trace of a *Gemeindeverband*. It was therefore not in these Eastern "bazaars" but in Western cities that from the ninth and tenth centuries onwards the bourgeoisie emerged as a capitalist class with economic and political power, and, most importantly, with its very own culture, that is, its very own urbanity as a civic and economic culture.

Weber invites us to focus on two crucial factors.[35] First, in the cities of Europe, the burghers were able to arm themselves. Ever since the heyday of feudalism, there had been regular conscription, not just of the agrarian but also of the urban populations. These enlisted men possessed their own weapons. Weber even used Marxist terminology to emphasize the importance of this fact: these "soldiers" were the owners of the means of production. The production was defense, but of course also, potentially, political power. Urban men in the West were armed men and derived a considerable measure of power from this fact.

In ancient Egypt, Mesopotamia, China, and India, soldiers, in contrast, never possessed their military means of production, and thus remained powerless. They were enlisted by princely armies which were, unlike their European counterparts, centrally organized and controlled. These enlisted men were armed by their princes, whenever their armies had to come into action. Weber explains this remarkable difference by the fact that in these regions the regulation of the large rivers which overflowed regularly, and the irrigation of the surrounding agrarian lands when the water in the rivers were low, had to be organized centrally by means of a relatively massive bureaucracy. (Needless to say that this bureaucracy was not legal-rational but patrimonial by nature.)

In short, the large rivers caused the emergence and maintenance of a strongly bureaucratized and centralized government, whose military power as well had to be centralized radically. Naturally, the means of military production—the arms—remained in the hands of their possessors; they were not handed over to the producers.

Compared to this, the armed burghers in the cities of medieval Europe which, like the rest of medieval society, lacked strong centralized and bureaucratized powers, actually had easy access to power. In most cases, there was, as we saw before, no real need for a *coniuratio*.

Religion and magic, are the second factors that Weber emphasized in answer to the question why evolution towards a powerful bourgeoisie (the initiator and bearer of the development towards high capitalism) occurred in Europe rather than elsewhere. In the civilizations of ancient Asia urban people were unable to establish a cultic community, since they adhered to magically closed groups, such as families, clans, or castes. They were, so to say, trapped by very restricted religious-magical bonds controlled by strong taboos. In China, these were, above all, the bonds of ancestor worship; in India, the bonds of inherited castes. City dwellers first and foremost experienced and maintained a solidarity within these bonds—the clan, the extended family, the ancestors, the fellow caste members. Thus they could and did not identify with the city as a *Gemeindeverband*. As a result, an urban fraternization, let alone a political *coniuratio* against the powers that ruled, was simply impossible.

In contrast, within the orbit of the East, medieval cities were in fact cultic communities with the church physically and sociologically at their center. Episcopal cities were indeed more than mere administrative centers, as Pirenne had argued. They were, of course, religious centers as well. However, Weber added that in contrast to the metaphysical irrationalities of Eastern religions, Christianity possessed, despite much irrationality in doctrines and rituals, an ancient and inherently rational core. Despite the tenacity of magic in medieval Christianity,[36] a pervasive process of *rationalization* viewed by Weber in terms of disenchantment—that is, of decline of magic—[37]laid at the foundation of Judeo-Christian civilization.

The prophets of ancient Judaism, Weber argued, destroyed magic, not by denying its existence but by branding it as something diabolic and objectionable. At the end of the Middle Ages this was taken up again by Puritanism and its inherent rational view of life and the world, based on an "innerworldly asceticism" (Weber). Next, in early Christianity the miracle of Pentecost meant to establish a fraternization of people of all walks of life in the Christian spirit, while the rejection of circumcision meant to proclaim a universal brotherhood of mankind. Both removed the magical boundaries between families, clans, ethnic populations, and races. This, Weber emphasized, opened the way to the rise of the Western city and its specific type of solidarity based upon rational interests.

Yet, we may not forget that in the Middle Ages much of this rationality was lost again, in particular among the rural masses outside the cities.[38] Indeed, the economic resurgence of the cities, as described by Pirenne, was necessary in order to restore a level of rationality which in its turn would foster economic success and political emancipation. Both the Reformation, which contributed so much to the disenchantment of Roman Catholic metaphysics and mysticism, and Renaissance Humanism, which adopted so much rationality from Greco-Roman antiquity, prospered in this urban environment. They in their turn strengthened urban rationality.

In any case, the burghers of these cities united themselves in order to defend, promote, and maintain their common material and cultural interests over against the dominant forces of medieval feudalism. This was indeed a rational kind of solidarity which broke the largely irrational bonds of family, clan, race, estate, caste, and soil.

### Inequality and Conflict

Before we discuss the rationality of this urban solidarity further, we ought to focus on the fact, briefly mentioned before, that urbanity, like any other type of culture, has never been a matter of complete consensus and harmony. There is, in other words, no historical ground for a naive romanticization of urbanity as the seedbed of urban consensus and solidarity. On the contrary, its history testified many times of grave internal conflicts due to basic socioeconomic and sociocultural inequalities and cleavages. In fact, strife and inequity have been characteristic of urbanity almost from its very inception in the ninth and tenth centuries.

One should bear in mind, to begin with, that the merchants, artisans, and allied service experts began to identify themselves with their cities, and that they did so initially within the sociopolitical context of a still rigidly traditional and patrimonially authoritarian society. Feudal society kept people divided within mutually separated estates, and it stands to reason that the leaders and leading families in particular among these urbanites adopted much of the mentality and lifestyle of the ruling estates of feudal society, especially the nobility. In fact, even when the bourgeoisie had developed into a true socioeconomic class, the relatively small upper-middle class would soon emulate the noble estate of feudalism and develop a seminoble lifestyle and culture. They constituted the wealthy and powerful *patriciate*. This patriciate consisting of a restricted number of upper-class families, developed gradually into a hereditary ruling class or semi-estate with many properties within and often also outside the walls of the city. These properties functioned as insurance against possible setbacks in trade which, of course, remained their prime business—a notoriously risky business, certainly in the days prior to the large, well-organized Hanseatic trade firms.

Below this powerful and wealthy upper class there was a relatively prosperous middle class of artisans and service men. Unlike the estate society of feudalism, the class society of these cities knew social mobility, upwards as well as downwards. It stimulated energies and the working ethic of the bourgeoisie, not in the least within the ranks of the vulnerable middle class. There was, however, a lower-middle class of craftsmen without any property and without much power and influence. Their existence was rather precarious and their economic dependence on the higher echelons of the bourgeoisie considerable. In their situation there was not much to look forward to in the city.

The situation was even grimmer for the proletariat at the bottom of urban society, often recruited from amidst the rural serfs who had fled the ties of feudal bondage. They were free men, if they managed to stay in the city for one hundred and one days. "Town air brings freedom," as the saying went. Indeed, the personal bondage of feudalism was absent within the walls of the city. Yet, it is questionable whether the debts and financial dependence to which the proletariat almost invariably was subjected, were really less oppressive than the feudal bonds between lords and serfs.[39]

It is against this background of basic socioeconomic uncertainty that one must view the emergence of the guilds. They functioned not only as interest groups that guarded the new entries to their occupations and watched over their segments of the market. They also constituted associations of mutual assistance, "friendly societies" that offered their members a degree of social security.[40]

Thus, beyond and often in contrast to the stratification of feudal estates, to which the individual belonged by birth (ascription) and within which one was, apart from exceptions (marriage of females, military and ecclesiastic careers), caught for life, an alternative stratification of socioeconomic classes began to emerge.[41] In the early days of these European cities with their newly acquired wealth, power, and independence, belonging to the bourgeois class was still very much a matter of achievement rather than ascription. Unlike the estate system (let alone the caste system), the class system was based on social mobility and in this sense was an open system. Soon, however, ascription and immobility would penetrate the class system too. This was particularly observable, when the patriciate acquired hereditary power and the guilds ossified into rigid and closed private-interest organizations. Needless to add that in the end, during the past two centuries, the Industrial Revolution and the rise of high capitalism added to this rigidification of the class system.

In any case, this class system was in origin a typically urban phenomenon. If the clergy and the nobility continued to view and treat the bourgeoisie (condescendingly up until the French Revolution) as the Third Estate, the burghers themselves acted rather as a socioeconomic class, the membership of which was in principle (if not always in fact) not based on family descent and allied privileges, but on the results of one's socioeconomic and political performance.

This class of merchants, craftsmen, lawyers, and bankers was at home in the city, and their mentality and lifestyle were from the start very much urban. If they still were an estate—the Third Estate—it had been their urban culture, that is, urbanity, which had given them estate features. If in the *ancien régime* noblemen lived urban lives, it was predominantly in the capital, where the monarchy was, that they conducted their affairs and led their often luxurious lives. Indeed, here they could live their lives, entangled in scores of *liaisons dangereuses*, always threatened by the emptiness of *l'ennui*.[42]

## An Aesthetic Ethos

These cities of Europe were not merely places in which profits were made, services rendered, political affairs conducted. The focus was not exclusively on material welfare and political dominance. On the contrary, it was within the socioeconomic and political orbit of these European cities that the bourgeoisie began to (re)discover the power of the human mind, the beauty of the human body, the strength of the human will, the vitality of nature, and the capriciousness of history. In fact, the Renaissance and its great influence on the spectacular developments in the arts and sciences would have been impossible in bazaar-cities direly lacking in urbanity. Not just Lübeck, but all European cities with urbanity fitted Thomas Mann's definition of the city as "a spiritual form of life."[43] Indeed, the unity of urbanity and humanism is crucial and essential.

Our language still testifies to this dimension of urbanity: an urbane person is a well-mannered, well-educated, and civilized individual who as an autonomous, "inner-directed" personality knows what he wants, and above all what his capabilities and limits are. Indeed, the emergence and the development of urbanity have been the heart of what Norbert Elias has called "the process of civilization."[44]

With an ever growing self-confidence the bourgeoisie began, since the eleventh century, to experiment with and to promote humanist values which were juxtaposed to the religious and political values of the feudal tradition. The undisputed center of the medieval city had always been the church. From the Renaissance on, educational institutions, like the typically Renaissance-styled Latin School in which Greek, Latin, classical culture, mathematics, and the natural sciences were taught, and the university in particular, began to compete with the primacy of the church and the ecclesiastic schools and theological faculties. Their inherent humanist culture penetrated gradually and deeply into the core of urban culture. From the Enlightenment on, the university pushed the church, step by step, from the center to the peripheries of urban society and culture.

At this point, we must address another rather paradoxical dimension of urbanity. In its aesthetic component urbanity harbors a self-destructive force. Particularly in its artistic pursuits the bourgeoisie has tried time and again to transcend itself, to elevate itself beyond the mundane level of trade, craftsmanship, production, consumption, profits and market strategies. In Daniel Bell's phrase, this is one of the main cultural contradictions of capitalism.[45] In urbanity there is an essentially nonpolitical, purely aesthetic, and nonrational impulse of de-bourgeoisification, often bordering on self-hatred and self-contempt. Bourgeois artists have almost always been antibourgeois.

The Bohemian of the nineteenth and twentieth centuries is the archetype of this aversion directed against the bourgeoisie. Bohemians may flirt with Marxism as a welcome political and anticapitalist ideology, but in the end most of them realize that they are caught in a dilemma. Artists may impulsively dislike or even hate the bourgeoisie and its capitalist mode of production, yet they could not survive, materially as well as artistically, without an audience (of bourgeois background and with bourgeois money) and without the working of the capitalist market (cf., the international trade of modern art).[46] As to the latter, this century has demonstrated that the quality of the arts does not necessarily improve, when the market is eliminated, as in communism, or neutralized, as in the welfare state. What remains, is a non-rational antibourgeois and anticapitalist animus, an aesthetic impulse towards de-bourgeoisification.

Thomas Mann described this contradiction in the above-mentioned Lübeck address of 1926. He argued that he himself was a bourgeois storyteller (*ein bürgerlicher Erzähler*) who in his life always told just one story: the history of de-bourgeoisification (*Entbürgerlichung*). This "de-bourgeoisification" has brought about *not* the Marxist but the artist who flies towards freedom and irony. The fruit of an artist prone to fly out, up and away, is, according to Mann, "a bourgeois humanity which maintains itself in irony—an irony that in its artistic endeavors transcends all classes."[47] This aesthetic de-bourgeoisification is, of course, unthinkable outside the urban orbit. In fact, it demonstrates once more the ambiguity of urbanity: a bourgeois culture imbued with an antibourgeois animus. This testifies to urbanity's openness and flexibility which always has been and still is its strength as well as its weakness.

## The Public and the Private

The *polis* of ancient Greece was in the Weberian sense a city, since it functioned as garrison and administrative center and as a marketplace as well. It was, in addition, an urban community based on democratic autonomy. The *polis* was an autocephalous city-state. A well-known restriction of its democracy was, of course, that only free and propertied males could actively participate in its economic and political affairs. Resident aliens, slaves, and women were excluded. Moreover, the *polis* conducted its economic and political affairs within the notoriously rigid fetters of the slave system.

In comparison, all citizens of the early modern European cities were in principle, if not always in actual fact, eligible to positions of political power. They threw off the shackles of serfdom, and generally enjoyed an infinitely greater freedom than their feudal ancestors. They fruitfully put the urban liberties and opportunities to use in their political, economic, and artistic pursuits and endeavors. Within such ramifications, the market could function much better, at least as long as the guilds were not ossified yet into rather closed private interest organizations.

When Aristotle defined man as a *zoon politikon*, he meant to say that man ought to be viewed first and foremost as a being that can only live fully and survive honorably within the context of a *polis*, a sociocultural and political context. Unlike the animal, man is a polis-being. And unlike the animal, Aristotle continued, man is endowed with the capacity for speech. Animals produce sounds, when they experience pain or pleasure. It is the surplus strength of human language to express notions of advantage and disadvantage, justice and injustice, good and evil, beauty and ugliness. A collectivity of people endowed with language constitutes a household, a society, a state, and these are in essence moral communities.

Since the whole always precedes the parts, Aristotle went on to explain, society and state have precedence over the family household and the individuals therein. This is proven by the simple fact that an isolated individual would sooner or later perish. We do depend on others: "A man who cannot live in society, or who has no need to do so because he is self-sufficient, is either a beast or a god; he is no part of a state. All human beings, then, are endowed by nature with the social instinct."[48]

Thus, in the relationship between the public and the collective on the one hand and the private and the individual on the other Aristotle gave precedence to the former. That was typical of his time and society. Hannah Arendt, and Jürgen Habermas after her, drew attention to the fact that in the social thought of those days two spheres were distinguished and juxtaposed: the *idion* which is the own, the familiar, the private, and the *koinon* which stands for the common, the collective, the public. The former is the sphere of the family and the household— the *oikos*. It is the sphere of coercive labor within a strict division of labor and duties between men, women, children, and slaves. This is also the realm of biological necessities. In short, the *idion* and the *oikos* are the realm of coercion and absence of true freedom.

The *koinon*, on the contrary, is the *polis*, the city-state as community in which free male adults can enjoy their democratic citizen rights and engage in political debates. If anywhere, it is here that the individual can optimally develop his personality. It is not the sphere of labor and coercion, but the realm of contemplation, discussion, communication, meaningful action. Indeed, here action is free and symbolic—not labor but work, not behavior but communicative action, symbolic interaction.[49]

Since the late medieval and early modern cities of Europe had abandoned the feudal system of serfdom, they offered, even more so than the Greek *polis*, opportunities to individual citizens to pursue their material interests, to realize their rights and liberties, and to develop their personalities. To many of them, having turned their backs on the bondage of feudalism, their urban economic and political pursuits were experienced, to use Arendt's terminology, as work and action instead of labor and behavior.

Again, this was not so for propertyless artisans and the early urban proletariat. Certainly later, when the Industrial Revolution set in, a working class and proletariat emerged for which economic participation meant hard "labor" and often totally meaningless "behavior," while any meaningful political participation (i.e., suffrage) remained illusory for quite a long time. Needless to say the position of women was far from ideal as well.

Yet, despite all this the world had changed fundamentally in these early modern cities: in principle there was, for the majority of city dwellers, a strong bond between the public-and-collective on the one hand and the private-and-individual on the other. The former, the urban *Gemeindeverband*, had a distinct precedence over the latter, as had been the case in the Greek *polis*. The inhabitants of the economically successful and politically powerful Hanseatic cities, for example, shared a sense of pride and collective identity. They experienced their city as a meaningful *Gemeindeverband*, as a true *nomos*. Each of them was supposed to contribute to it according to his capacities. In this way each of them made a difference.

In this sense, the early modern European city with a vital economic and civic culture constituted a revived *polis*, a meaningful, ordered collectivity, a *nomos*.[50] (Incidentally, in view of all this Weber should have used the Greek word *koinon* rather than *oikos* in his definition of the city which we discussed previously.)

For the free citizen of the Greek city-state, or of the European bourgeois city, "society" was not an abstract, alienating and coercive "social structure" in which one had to play various unconnected and bureaucratically organized roles. If there was any societal awareness at all—a sort of sociological consciousness—it was defined in terms of a *koinon*, a common and public sphere of solidarity in which work and communication were experienced prereflectively.

This stands in sociological contrast to our current state of affairs. We live in an abstract society in which we experience—if we can experience it at all—freedom and authenticity in the private sphere of small groups, like the nuclear family or the peer group, and of many flexible, self-construed networks. Not the *idion* but the *koinon*—the realm of societal organizations—is viewed as the realm of coercion and alienation, of "labor" and "behavior." Man after the Industrial Revolution is not a *zoon politikon* but a *homo sociologicus*. In a somewhat romantic vein Ralf Dahrendorf described the plight of this "sociological man" as such: "society is the alienated figure of the individual, *homo sociologicus*, a shadow that has run away from its originator in order to return as its master."[51] This is indeed a structural transformation to which we shall return in the next chapter. It had a profound impact on the city and on urbanity. It constituted a gradual polarization of the public and the private, the collective and the individual, the objective and the subjective. This polarization is the heart of modernization and modernity.

The Greek city-state and the early modern European bourgeois city still managed to maintain an (often delicate) balance between the public and the private realm, while the former held precedence over the latter. As we shall see later, the modernization which at first was fed and fostered by the emergent bourgeois city, disturbed the balance and reversed the priority.

In the sixteenth century Martin Luther had already set the tone for it with his theory of the two realms. It led him to the construction of a fateful anthropological dichotomy: the human being as free subject and conditioned object, as unique individual and general social being. Authenticity, he believed, lies in the subjective and individual component of the dichotomy. Referring to the royal ruler, the elector of the German state he lived in, Luther formulated the dichotomy in his inimitably clear manner as follows: "I said time and again that one should distinguish official function and personality. These are totally different human beings, the ones who are called Hans or Martin, and those who are called elector or Doctor and preacher."[52] And: "Each individual human being has on earth two personalities: one for himself, bound to nobody but God alone, but also a worldly personality, through which he is bound to other people."[53]

In his above-mentioned dissertation on the structural transformation of the public realm, Habermas argued that in the days of absolutism the public sphere functioned as a stage on which the private sphere was exhibited for all to see. The public realm thus degenerated into a theater in which the private is shamelessly exhibited. For example, in

Versailles the bedroom of Louis XIV functioned as a kind of theater in which people, upon official invitation, could witness the *coucher* and *lever* of the monarch. This eventually led to "the fall of public man"[54] and the rise of pervasive subjectivism.[55]

In this process cities began to lose their power and were gradually outstripped and superseded by the nation-state. Werner Sombart has argued convincingly that the big European capitals of the seventeenth and eighteenth centuries had degenerated to mere places of consumption. Here members of the nobility, court dignitaries, rich merchants and manufacturers, prosperous professionals, and members of the higher clergy lived in order to bathe in luxuries. They were, by and large, nonproductive people who attracted a host of servants who parasitically lived off of this luxury.

In contrast, economically active and productive trading cities with centers of craft and home manufacturing, Sombart concluded, remained small in size and politically insignificant. The absolutist court was the motor of this nonproductive system which had to be financed by heavy taxation of the urban bourgeoisie, the rural gentry, and the peasants in the country. Above all, this parasitical system was kept afloat by mercantilism, set up and maintained by the state. In all of this the cities had, according to Sombart, hardly any role to play. Needless to add, their urbanity as an economic and civic culture simultaneously withered away in this process of decline.[56]

## Urbanity Summarized

Let us, for the sake of clarity, summarize the main elements of the historical phenomenon of urbanity. To begin with, urbanity was first and foremost a form of rational solidarity—a mutual reliance of burghers, a kind of secularized economic covenant which was not based upon family ties, possession of land and adherence to soil, religious convictions, caste, or estate membership. For the first time in history solidarity was based primarily on very rational, economic interests and not on traditional, irrational, and confining bonds. This is what was implied, when we called urbanity an economic culture.

Second, urbanity was characterized by a narrow bond between the private and the public spheres of life. They flowed, as it were, together into an urban community with a distinct social structure, the middle class. This class functioned as the firm power base from which citizens could actively participate in democratic urban institutions. Not all citizens were, in actual fact, able to participate politically, like the urban proletariat that grew in numbers and eventually incorporated a power-less underclass that only through class action—the labor movement of the nineteenth and twentieth centuries—would reappropriate their citizens' right to participate in the democratic decision-making process (i.e., universal suffrage). Others would not be interested in such active participation, leaving "politics" to the politicians.[57] Urbanity is certainly not an "activist" type of culture. In any case, in principle and certainly in origin, urbanity presented a historically unique type of civic culture.

Third, urbanity was the worldview and ethos of the bourgeoisie as a socioeconomic class. As such, urbanity presented a more or less coherent set of values, norms, and meanings—the bourgeois style of life—which were structured in typically urban institutions like the guilds, primary and secondary schools, the university, organized arts and crafts, many artistic groups and companies, and, of course, various political bodies of urban democracy. In all of this a typically urban and bourgeois mentality and identity prevailed. At the center of civic virtues stood undoubtedly a work ethic which paired hard work with creative initiatives. At the same time, material interests were not separated from spiritual and aesthetic refinements. Various types of schools and higher learning, the arts and artists, museums, universities, theaters, amateur choirs, and the like were intrinsic parts of urbanity.

Fourth, urbanity was, from the start, not simply a localistic but a very cosmopolitan kind of culture as well. It had the intrinsic tendency to transcend the limits and boundaries of particular cities, regions, and nations. During the process of modernization, as we shall see in more detail in the next chapter, this feature of urbanity would be reinforced. Its gradual generalization would eventually lead to its virtual disappearance in the context of a fully modern, centralized nation-state. Here we witness an intrinsic component of urbanity which, as an unintended consequence, would eventually come to foster anticivic tendencies.

Fifth, urbanity was a creative force that promoted and helped to institutionalize the sciences and the arts. Urbanity was the seedbed par excellence for Renaissance humanism and Enlightenment rationalism. Above all, it gave shape and substance to a specific bourgeois culture which, however, carried its own contradictory forces, the seeds of its own destruction: the aesthetic and artistic desire and urge to transcend, if not destroy, the bourgeoisie itself with its despised and hated relentless pursuit of material, capitalist interests and its equally hated, at times obnoxious, self-sufficiency. That is, an important component of urbanity turned out to propound an antieconomic, bohemian style of life.

In sum, as these characteristics demonstrate, urbanity is wrought with ambiguities and contradictions, some of which carry the seeds of destruction. We will further discuss and interpret them in the next chapter.

## Notes

1. This critique of the postwar planning of downtown Rotterdam is common wisdom in this city today. It was not shared by Mumford who in the 1950s visited the area and then lauded its layout. Cf., "A Walk Through Rotterdam," in Lewis Mumford, *The Highway and the City* (New York: A Harvest Book, [1957] 1963), pp. 31–41.
2. See e.g., Mark Girouard, *Cities and People: A Social and Architectural History* (New Haven, CT: Yale University Press, 1985).
3. Daniel Bell, *The Cultural Contradictions of Capitalism* (London: Heinemann, [1976] 1979), p. 106.
4. Émile Durkheim, *Les Règles de la Méthode Sociologique* (Paris, [1895] 1947), p. 5.
5. Compare V. Gordon Childe, *Man Makes Himself* (New York: Mentor Books, [1936] 1951), p. 35: "Actually in the Near East the Bronze Age is characterized by populous cities wherein secondary industries and foreign trade are conducted on a considerable scale. A regular army of craftsmen, merchants, transport workers, and also officials, clerks, soldiers, and priests is supported by the surplus foodstuffs produced by cultivators, herdsmen and hunters. The cities are incomparably larger and more populous than neolithic villages."
6. Compare G. Sjoberg, *The Preindustrial City* (New York: n.p., 1960).
7. It is still worthwhile to read the classic study of N. D. Fustel de Coulanges, *The Ancient City*, (Garden City, NY: Doubleday Anchor Books, [1864] n.d.).
8. I made use of the German edition of "Economy and Society" where the large essay on the city can be found—see Max Weber, "Die nichtlegitieme Herrschaft (Typologie der Städte)," in *Wirtschaft und Gesellschaft*, ch. 9, section 7, 2d vol. (Berlin: Duncker & Humblot, 1964), pp. 923–1033. Also very relevant is his posthumously published series of lectures "Economic History" in Max Weber, *Wirtschaftsgeschichte* (Berlin: Duncker & Humblot, 1958), in particular ch. 7, pp. 270–289, where Weber links the emergence of capitalism to the rise of European cities.
9. Compare W. Abel, "Wandlungen in der Beziehung von Stadt und Umland," in *Die Stadt als Lebensform* (Berlin: Colloquium Verlag, 1970), pp. 153–162.
10. Henri Pirenne, *Medieval Cities: Their Origins and the Revival of Trade* (Princeton, NJ: Princeton University Press, [1925] 1974).
11. Pirenne, ibid., p. 65.
12. Compare Fritz Rörig, *The Medieval Town* (Berkeley and Los Angeles: University of California Press, [1955] 1967), pp. 15–18.
13. Marc Bloch, *Feudal Society*, vol. 1: "The Growth of Ties of Dependence," (Chicago: University of Chicago Press, 1970), pp. 3–58.
14. Geoffrey Barraclough, *The Crucible of Europe: The Ninth and Tenth Centuries in European History* (Berkeley and Los Angeles: University of California Press, 1976), p. 102f.
15. Lauro Martines, *Power and Imagination: City-States in Renaissance Italy* (New York: Alfred Knopf, 1979), p. 111.

16. Ibid., p. 112. By the fourteenth century urban conflict and discord had reached dangerous proportions. It is against this background that one should read Remigio de Girolami's treatise *De bono communi*, written with Florence's political turmoil of 1302 as backdrop. Fra Girolami argues that the good of the community should be placed above that of the individual. "*De bono communi,*" Martines writes, "is a passionate condemnation of factionalism and selfish men. The insistence upon citizenship in effect accuses Florentines of having shed their humanity in their tearing up of the commune. Against a background of war and ruthless faction, Remigio hailed the united community and the supremacy of the state, which alone made possible the conditions for the exercise of virtue." Ibid., p. 128. Girolami ridicules the corruption in his beloved city "Firenze." Just as the French said "fi, fi," when they smelled an hideous odor, "the citizens of Florence must be aware that the perfume of her fame had been transformed into the evil stench of infamy." Charles T. Davis, "An Early Florentine Political Theorist: Fra Remigio de Girolami," in *Proceedings of the American Philosophical Society* 104, no. 6 (December 1960): 668.

17. Martines, *Power and Imagination*, p. 42. Incidently, Western European medieval cities did not, apart from Italy, develop into autonomous city-states but rather negotiated a *modus vivendi* with their surrounding feudal lords, the barons and the counts. The count of Flanders played Ghent, Bruges, Ypres, and Lille skillfully against the barons who were feudally subject to him. Cf. Gianfranco Poggi, *The Development of the Modern State* (London: Hutchinsons & Co, 1978), pp. 40–41.

18. Cellini began his autobiography *Vita di Benvenuto Cellini*, 1558, in Florence. The first edition came out in 1728. The first English translation by J. A. Symonds, *The Life of B. Cellini Written By Himself*, appeared in 1888 and had numerous reprints. I used the well-illustrated Dutch translation, *Het leven van Benvenuto Cellini door hemzelf verteld* (Amsterdam: Querido, 1969). Historically this autobiography appears to be unreliable. However, sociologically it is very illustrative, as it gives a colorful impression of urban life and culture in Renaissance Italy.

19. Weber, *Wirtschaftsgeschichte*, pp. 273–274.

20. Rörig, *The Medieval Town*, p. 26.

21. On *coniuratio* see Weber, *Wirtschaftsgeschichte*, and Rörig, ibid.

22. The two short-lived Flemish Hanseatic Leagues are usually forgotten in historical accounts of the Hansa. For information about them I used the Dutch encyclopedia *Grote Winkler Prins*, ninth edition, vol. 11 (Amsterdam and Antwerp: Elsevier, 1991), s.v. "hanze," p. 54f.

23. The typical merchant ship was the *coggo*, the "Kogge," or "cock ship" which had, for those days, an exceptionally large loading capacity.

24. The rise and decline of the German Hanseatic League is described in detail by Philippe Dollinger in *La Hanse (XIIe–XVIIe siècles)* (Paris: Aubier, 1964). I used the German translation of Marga and Hans Krabusch, *Die Hanse* (Stuttgart: Alfred Kröner Verlag, [1976] 1981).

25. There was a popular expression that said *koplude* (merchants) are *loplude* (walking people). Schildhauer, *The Hansa: History and Culture*, translated from German by K. Vanovitch (Leipzig: Edition Leipzig, 1985), p. 104.

26. Rörig, *The Medieval Town*, p. 41. Rörig correctly calls this a rationalization: "No longer did the merchant's strength lie in travelling around with his colleagues, but in the degree of organization in his own concern. Thus purely individualistic characteristics emerged which had distinct effects of a social nature going beyond the sphere of commerce. At the end of the thirteenth-century Lübeck

as a result of the organizational advances made by its merchants, went through a period of the greatest economic prosperity." Ibid., p. 45f.

27. Schildhauer, *The Hansa*, p. 107.
28. Ibid., p. 108.
29. Dollinger, *La Hanse*, p. 342.
30. Schildhauer, *The Hansa*, p. 104. He refers to W. Stieda, "Zu den Sprach-kenntnissen der Hanseaten," in *Hansische Geschichtsblätter*, 1884, p. 157ff.
31. Dollinger, *La Hanse*, p. 344–349. On architecture, see pp. 349–355.
32. See my study *Reality in a Looking-Glass* (London: Routledge & Kegan Paul, 1982), in particular pp. 83–86: "Till Eulenspiegel-A Powerful Bourgeois Legend."
33. See in particular Heinrich Rickert, *Kulturwissenschaft und Naturwissenschaft* (Stuttgart: Philipp Reclam, Jr., [1898] 1986). I gave a brief exposition of his neo-Kantian methodology which influenced Weber's methodology profoundly, in the appendix to my *On Clichés* (London: Routledge & Kegan Paul, 1979), pp. 106–113.
34. See, for the concept of bazaar-city or bazaar, John L. Myres, *Mediterranean Culture*, The Frazer Lecture 1943 (Cambridge: University Press, 1944), p. 15. Myres uses the concept synonymously with Rostovtseff's concept of "caravan-city." He contrasts them with the "sanctuary-city"—the "hieropolis"—which offers for the spirit what the "bazaar-city" provides for material needs. Yet he is unable to adjudicate a community creating force to the "sanctuary city."
35. Weber, *Wirtschaftsgeschichte*, pp. 275–277.
36. This was described in great detail for England by Keith Thomas, *Religion and the Decline of Magic*, passim.
37. Weber called rationalization "the disenchantment of the world" which literally means de-magicization. This was, according to him, a process of rationalization, since he viewed magic as an irrational phenomenon. It is, however, questionable, if it is correct to label magic as irrational. There is an inherent functional rationality at work in all, vastly different forms of magic. This is not the place to discuss this point in further detail. Cf. Bronislaw Malinowski, *Magic, Science and Religion, and Other Essays* (Garden City, NY: Doubleday Anchor Books, [1948] 1954).
38. I discussed this type of irrationality in my study of premodern folly, *Reality in a Looking-Glass* (London: Routledge & Kegan Paul, 1982).
39. In this brief discussion of urban inequalities I made particular use of Rörig, *The Medieval Town*, pp. 20–28.
40. Compare A. Black, *Guilds and Civil Society in European Political Thought from the 12th Century to the Present* (London: Methuen & Co., 1984).
41. The well-known argument of Marx that the class system was not absent in medieval society but in fact superseded and obfuscated by the estate system, makes much sense. There is, however, no need to discuss the point in greater detail here.
42. Sombart gives a lively portrait of the luxurious, idle, and conspicuous lifestyle of the urban nobility and the higher bourgeoisie during the *ancien régime* in Werner Sombart, *Liebe, Luxus und Kapitalismus* (München: Deutscher Taschenbuch Verlag, [1912] 1967). See also Norbert Elias, *Die höfische Gesellschaft* (Darmstadt: Luchterhand Verlag, [1969] 1975). With the nineteenth century, melancholy and tedium had become grave upper-class illnesses. Cf. César Grana, *Modernity and its Discontent*, 1964 (New York: Harper Torchbooks, 1967). See also Wolf Lepenies, *Melancholie und Gesellschaft* (Frankfurt am Main: Suhrkamp Verlag, 1969).

43. Thomas Mann, *Lübeck als geistige Lebensform* (Lübeck: Otto Quitzow Verlag, 1926).

44. Norbert Elias, *Ueber den Prozess der Zivilisation*, two volumes (Bern and München: Francke Verlag, [1936] 1969). Elias is mainly interested in the process of state formation. A brief discussion of the rise of European cities since the eleventh century can be found in the second volume, pp. 58–67.

45. Daniel Bell, *Cultural Contradictions*, passim.

46. Compare Arnold Gehlen, *Zeit-Bilder: Zur Soziologie und Ästhetik der modernen Malerei* (Frankfurt am Main: Vittorio Klostermann, [1960] 1986), pp. 226–233.

47. Mann, *Lübeck*, p. 54f.

48. I used the translation of J. Warrington, *Aristotle's Politics and Athenian Constitution* (London: J. M. Dent, 1959), p. 8.

49. See Hanna Arendt, *The Human Condition* (Garden City, NY: Doubleday Anchor Books, 1959), in particular chapter 2: "The Public and the Private Realm," pp. 23–73. See also Jürgen Habermas, *Strukturwandel der Öffentlichkeit* (Berlin and Neuwied: Luchterhand, [1962] 1971), in particular chapter 5: "Sozialer Strukturwandel der Öffentlichkeit," pp. 172–217.

50. For the Greek concept of *nomos* as a meaningful order see Peter L. Berger, Hansfried Kellner 1962, "Marriage and the Construction of Reality," in Peter L. Berger, *Facing up to Modernity* (Harmondsworth, UK: [1977] 1979), pp. 27–48. Cf. also Émile Durkheim's concept of *anomie*.

51. Ralf Dahrendorf, *Homo Sociologicus* (Köln and Opladen: Westdeutscher Verlag, [1958] 1964), p. 34. My translation.

52. Quoted from F. Lau, *Luthers Lehre von den beiden Reichen* (Berlin: Luthertum Heft 8, 1953), p. 30. My translation.

53. Quoted from Harald Diem, *Luthers Lehre von den zwei Reichen* (München: n.p., 1938), p. 28. My translation.

54. Richard Sennett, *The Fall of Public Man* (Cambridge: Cambridge University Press, [1974] 1977).

55. Compare Arnold Gehlen, *Die Seele im technischen Zeitalter* (Hamburg: Rowohlt, [1949] 1957). Also Christopher Lasch, *The Culture of Narcissism* (London: Abacus, Sphere Books Ltd., [1979] 1980).

56. Sombart, *Liebe*, passim.

57. Almond and Verba also emphasized the fact that civic culture is not just characterized by active participation and political influence of citizens. Passivity and deference are as much part of a democratic civic culture. Cf. *The Civic Culture*, pp. 440–476. "In the civic culture participant political orientations combine with and do not replace subject and parochial political orientations. Individuals become participants in the political process, but they do not give up their orientations as subjects nor as parochials," ibid., p. 31f. This quiescent component adjudicated to the civic culture by Almond and Verba, flies, of course, in the ideological face of the activism of the 1960s and 1970s. There is, however, little historical ground for its denial.

# 2

# Abstract Urbanity:
# The Modernization of Urban Culture

## Rationalization and Modernity

European cities and their inherent urbanity have been crucial, it was argued in the first chapter, to the process of modernization. These cities were, so to speak, the sociological seedbeds for modernity, yet they, in turn, changed under the impact of modernization. Urban culture in particular was affected by modernization. It stands to reason that a more detailed discussion of this curious and rather complex interaction between modernization and urbanization, between urbanity and modernity is in order.

Often, modernization is employed as a kind of umbrella concept that covers several processes such as secularization, urbanization, industrialization, democratization, and the increasing dominance of science, technology, and bureaucracy. Such a conceptual hodgepodge is, of course, not very helpful heuristically. Hence most social theorists have tried to reduce the notion of modernization to one or the other structural transformation of society, polity, economy, and personality—a transformation that underlies and links, as it were, these various processes. So-called classic theorists came up with several basic changes of structure, like the transition from aristocratic to democratic conditions of existence (Tocqueville), from mechanical to organic solidarity (Durkheim), from status to contract (Maine), from *Gemeinschaft* to *Gesellschaft* (Tönnies). Others focused on one basic process of change which influenced and fostered the various processes mentioned above. Thus, Marx saw all of history as an unceasing development of exploitation which would reach its apex and apocalyptic end in bourgeois capitalism, whereas Weber viewed history as an often capricious rationalization which reached previously unknown proportions in the capitalist, industrial, and bureaucratic society.

Mannheim argued that this rationalization was an uneven process, since it indeed meant an increase of functional rationality, but simultaneously a proportional decrease of substantial rationality. This became very problematic, in his point of view, in the twentieth century, the celebrated age of planning. Without sufficient substantial (value-) rationality, planning could impossibly develop into a planning for freedom.[1] It would thus prepare the road towards what Tocqueville had called the tyranny with velvet gloves, and what Weber dubbed the iron cage.

Most of these (ideal-typical) theories of modernization of the "classic" social theorists were sociopsychological in that they tried to cover and interpret not only the transformations of societal, political, economic, and cultural structures but the alterations of human consciousness, experiences and attitudes as well.[2] As Arnold Gehlen phrased it, during the Industrial Revolution man crossed a *Kulturschwelle*, a cultural threshold. This basic transformation that began roughly at the end of the Middle Ages and is still taking place today, is comparable, Gehlen claimed, to the Neolithic revolution—the first threshold mankind crossed.[3] That is, not only did man's sociocultural and natural environment change radically under the impact of industry, science, and bureaucracy (according to Gehlen the threefold inner core of modernization), but his consciousness, his ways of looking at reality, his ways of thinking and feeling all began to change fundamentally as well. It was indeed a structural transformation.

Weber thought similarly, when he defined rationalization as an *Entzauberung der Welt*, as a disenchantment, a de-magicization of the world. Prior to modernization, the world—nature, society, culture, history—was seen and experienced as a *Zaubergarten*, as an enchanted garden, in which mysterious and unpredictable things happened all the time. Modern man, in contrast, lives in a rational world in which everything is calculated, planned, and predicted rationally. This world is not ruled by fate and contingency, but by rational calculus and rational planning.[4]

Urbanization and urbanity are intrinsically related to all of this. For instance, Weber showed that the maintenance of family ties and the worship of ancestors were essential components of the ancient Chinese "enchanted garden."[5] They were a restraining factor in the development of urbanity, as they also inhibited existing forms of early capitalist trade from developing into high capitalism. In contrast, as we saw in the former chapter, European urbanity could emerge in a society in which not ties of blood (family) and soil (burial grounds of the ancestors), but Christian *brotherhood* exerted a primary rationalizing influence on the merchants of various European cities. In these cities a rational and secular kind of solidarity began to emerge—the solidarity of shared economic and political interests. Urbanity as a primarily functional-rational solidarity exerted from the eleventh century on, joined by the rational work ethic of Protestantism after the sixteenth century, a decisive influence on the spectacular rise of capitalism and the further modernization of the Western world.

In what was probably his most profound study—a sociological theory of the division of labor—Durkheim in fact analyzed the gradual modernization of solidarity.[6] To him, solidarity was a sociological a priori: without it a society as a more or less coherent whole of individuals and their actions and interactions, would be completely impossible. Solidarity was to be seen, Durkheim felt, as the basic mortar that keeps the societal walls and buildings standing erect and solid. Division of labor, even the most simple one, will enhance the production of the material means of existence, and thereby cause the growth of a population. If demographic density increases, again, the division of labor will increase. If, for whatever reasons, this division of labor becomes massive, causing the emergence of many specialisms and subspecialisms, as was the case in Europe—initially at the end of the Middle Ages, and then rather massively during the Industrial Revolution— solidarity will be altered structurally. Consequently, the social order itself will be transformed, since solidarity is its main source of cohesion.

If, as in the case of small bands of nonsedentary hunters, tasks are not yet divided into innumerable specialisms and subspecialisms, societal order will consist of the mutual attraction of the similar: "like" attracts "like". This type of solidarity may continue to keep societies together, even when they are in a more advanced stage of division of labor: people with shared kinship bonds, collectively maintained religious convictions, rituals, and magical taboos, shared traditional patterns of stratification, and so on. Solidarity based on the principle "like-attracts-like" is generally transmitted from generation to generation, becomes traditional, and is experienced in a taken-for-granted fashion as being natural. Durkheim, therefore, called it *mechanical solidarity*. If, however, the division of labor increases rapidly and extensively—causing the emergence of a complex structure of specialisms and subspecialisms belonging to separate sectors and subsectors in which predefined roles and subroles ought to be played—solidarity will change in character altogether. "Like" will no longer attract "like" within the taken-for-granted context of "natural" groups, but "unlike" will have to co-operate with "unlike" within a rational and often abstract structure of tasks and subtasks, each of which must possess its own contracted rights and responsibilities. Thus, not the "natural" ties of blood and soil, but various "rational" social contracts constitute the foundations of this modern type of solidarity. It should be noted that this modern type of solidarity is no longer based upon unity but rather upon differences and differentiations.[7]

In this typically modern system, solidarity actually reigns for the sake of efficiency. The various tasks and specialisms in such a rationalized system depend on each other functionally, comparable to the various organs of a biological system which need each other, which cannot function without each other. Durkheim, therefore, dubbed this rational type of societal mortar *organic solidarity*. Since this concept is easily confused with a notion like *Gemeinschaft* which in fact means the exact opposite, it may be better to substitute the term *functional rationality*. In accordance with that we could then replace mechanical solidarity with *traditional solidarity*. After the discussion in chapter 1, it will be obvious that urbanity is a prime example of Durkheim's functional solidarity.

In his various analyses of modernization, Weber also paid due attention to structural differentiation. Yet, his prime interest and focus was a different one. As we just saw, he interpreted modernization primarily as an expanding rationalization which penetrated ever deeper into social structure and man's consciousness. He was, in particular, preoccupied by the spread of functional rationality, which he called *Zweckrationalität*, that is, means-end rationality. This type of rationality, he argued, tended to supersede substantial rationality, which he called *Wertrationalität*, or value-rationality. It was in particular Karl Mannheim who put this supersedure of substantial rationality by functional rationality in the center of his analysis and interpretation of modernization.[8]

Weber saw rationalizing tendencies in many, often radically different cultures but they were generally nipped in the bud by nonrational patterns of thought and action, in particular by magic which Weber always viewed as the antirational force *par excellence* (quite erroneously, I believe, because most magic was and is to all intents and purposes rather functionally rational[9]). According to Weber, the world remained an enchanted garden until it became radically rationalized under the impact of the sciences and technology, of bureaucracy and particularly the capitalist mode of production.

However, Weber did not argue in a linear, evolutionary manner. Long before rationalization got hold of European societies there had been, as it were, pockets of antimagical rationalization in history. In Greek and Roman antiquity rather "modern" trends of thought and action were definitely present, yet mostly surrounded and constantly penetrated by supernatural, mythological, and magical forms of thought. It was, however, in the prophetic Judaism of ancient Israel that an uncompromising attack upon magical and mythological forms of thought was launched.[10]

Weber viewed prophetic Judaism as a rationalizing and indeed secularizing force, since the world and history were radically disenchanted here. This rationalization went underground in the rabbinical Judaism of the diaspora, and in the Roman Catholic Church of the Middle Ages. It reemerged again in Calvinism which was, to all intents and purposes, opposed to any kind of magic. To the prophets of ancient Israel of the sixth century B.C. and the Calvinists of the sixteenth and seventeenth centuries, nothing in the world could be sacred since only a radically transcendent God was holy. Nature, including human nature such as sexuality, and societal institutions, such as the monarchy or the state, were not and could not be sacred, and thus ought not to be sanctified and adulated. They are a secular reality for which human beings bear responsibility (stewardship)—a "neutral" field of possibilities to be realized by men.

We find here the beginnings of the Enlightenment ideology of the "makeability"—*Machbarkeit*—of the world. As to those prophets and Calvinists, they believed and preached that only one reality was sacred within the here-and-now: the deeds of Yahweh/God with his chosen people, that is, history as eschatology, that is, as a history of salvation.[11] This is crucial: not things, institutions, and human beings but events—time, history—are declared sacred. This is one of the most seminal sources of the Enlightenment ideology of progress.[12]

Yet, during the Enlightenment rational secularization radicalized in the direction of humanism: man makes, constructs the world no longer as if it were a divine mission, but does so in accordance with his own design and wishes. Progress is longed for not eschatologically in the faithful hope of reaching eternal salvation, but rationally in the calculated expectation of acquiring earthly equality, justice, and happiness. Rationalization thus led to the emergence of Rationalism as a godless religion. This rationalism was soon paired to the eudaemonistic search for happiness and the generally good life—a far cry, of course, from the Puritan work ethic, but a definite reappropriation of certain strains of the moral thought of antiquity.[13]

The most interesting part of Weber's theory of the disenchantment of the world is when he imputes causality to religion. From a rather simplistically rationalist point of view, religion is often seen as an irrational force. In contrast, to Weber, religion—certainly the great world religions—has in fact contributed to the rationalization of the world. It did so in a dual manner. First, religion was itself substantially rational in that it tried to present a coherent worldview—"an assumed structure of reality"—and an ethos—"an approved style of life" (Geertz).[14] Worldview and ethos were both couched in fundamental values. (Compare the concept "value-rationality.") The great world religions, in particular monotheistic Islam, Judaism, and Christianity, have always presented reality—nature, society, history—as a coherent gestalt, that is, as an understandable cosmos, rather than an incomprehensible chaos. These religions produced theories, schools of thought and learning, religious teachers, preachers, and lawyers who contributed to the rationalization of the world since they produced meaningful thoughts, values, and norms, and above all doctrines and theories.

Second, religions founded upon an unrelenting faith in monotheistic revelation contributed (unintentionally though) to the emergence of an antimagical, scientific worldview, in which reality is seen and experienced as a secular reality to be conquered, to be worked upon, to be made and remade by man. Yet, this rationalization in the end turned against religion and against magic: the value-rationality of religion was steadily overhauled by the rationality of science and the functional rationality of magic was overtaken by the rationality of modern technology.

Since science is not fit to create and maintain value-rationality, and to offer its "believers" promises of salvation, the modern world is dominated by just one specific type of rationality: the functional one. A truly modern society is very strong in its functional rationality, in its perfection of means, methods, procedures, instruments to be used for the realization of particular ends. If there are values at play here, it is the "thin" values of efficiency and effectiveness.[15]

The steady weakening of substantial rationality, or value-rationality, has led to a strange paradox: since a well-developed value-rationality is needed in order to set clear goals and formulate clear ends, we may well end up with explicit and even sophisticated methods, procedures, and instruments, but very vague, abstract, and generalized goals to apply them to. In fact, the means and methods themselves may eventually become goals and ends in themselves.[16] In that case rationalization turns into its exact opposite and easily causes the reemergence of premodern, magical forms of thought and action (astrology, paramedical medicine, New Age philosophies, etc.)

Modernization is thus viewed as a gradual increase in functional rationality and the gradual supersedure of substantial rationality by it. This may again easily lead to the re-emergence of irrationality. One should bear in mind here that the expanding structural differentiation, which Durkheim emphasized in his theory of modernization, almost automatically affected the values, norms, and meanings in case. In order to "cover" increasingly expanding functional structures, their specialisms and subspecialisms, the related values, norms, and meanings have to be stretched like rubber bands.

For example, Christian values, norms, and meanings can be very concrete and "fundamentalistic" as long as the church is located geographically, sociologically, and psychologically in the center of rural society. However, in a radically industrialized urban society with a very complex social structure of innumerable, rather autonomous sectors, disciplines, and roles, the Christian church can no longer be the center. If it wants to maintain itself socially and culturally, it will have to accommodate its doctrine, it will have to put secular water into its religious wine. But then it will simultaneously be subjected to cultural inflation, so to speak. In other words, these culturally inflationary values, norms, and meanings will be less and less concrete and "fundamentalistic," and ever more general, abstract, secular, and uncommitted—in short: modern.[17]

Obviously, such general and vague values, norms, and meanings will loosen their original institutional ties and begin to float about freely and attach themselves to different institutional networks, where they will lack the commitment which they previously engendered and solicited, in premodern, strongly institutionalized conditions. As Gehlen, Schelsky, and Giddens have argued, the individual is thrown back upon his or her subjectivity, where experiences are being processed in reflexivity. The modern Self is, as it were, permanently reflecting upon and about itself.[18]

We should add, however, that in line with structural differentiation culture too is compartmentalized. Within particular structural niches and within particular groups, such as religious sects, peer groups, and youth gangs, values, norms, and meanings may very well be concrete, committing, and even imposing. They are concrete, and they do commit people in an ad hoc manner, often satisfying distinct interests. They may thus bind people together and provide them with a moral commitment. Yet, that may last for as long as they feel fit to be together and committed.

In fact, modernity is typically institutionalized weakly, no longer founded on a rock of traditional and venerable institutions, like the church, the extended family, the university, the state, the corporation, let alone the city! Actually, individualized and ad hoc networks are more important and functional today than traditional institutions are. These networks represent a weak, or thin institutionalization, in contrast to the traditional institutions which were the products of a rather strong, or thick institutionalization.

However, the institutions have not disappeared. The family, the church, the university, the state, and the city continue to exist, but they do so in a rather abstract manner that arouses only weak feelings of commitment and solidarity.[19] Fully modernized individuals do adhere to values, norms, and meanings which are general, abstract, and rather thin these days. If they are still able to command moral commitments, these commitments lie within loosely institutionalized and flexible networks which often cross the borders of the traditional institutions. The result is a society which is infinitely more pluralistic and flexible than traditional societies that were based upon venerable and venerated, often magically tabooed institutions.

It stands to reason after what has been said that urbanity serves as the environment in which these late modern developments are facilitated. In fact, as we will see shortly, the development of urbanity ran parallel to these processes of modernization; it even influenced them heavily. But before this is discussed in more detail, we ought to focus first on still another dimension of modernization which pertains strongly to the economic and civic culture of cities.

## Polarization and Mediation of the Private and the Public

In urbanity, as we saw in the first chapter, the public and the private relate to one another in a rather delicate manner. Mediating structures are essential to the vitality of urbanity. Now modernization is a process in which this delicate relationship between the private and the public alters dramatically. It is actually endangered, since modernization entails, to a certain extent, an ever expanding polarization between the private and the public; the individual and the collective; the micro-structures—such as the nuclear family; and the macrostructures—such as the state or the multinational corporation. In the process, intermediary, or mediating, structures—in particular the many voluntary associations of civil society which mediate between these opposites and function as buffers against unmitigated power—tend to atrophy.[20]

In democratic societies, the individual is increasingly exposed directly to the abstract and highly differentiated megastructures of modern society, and in particular to their (often Tocquevilleanly soft) coercion and control. Totalitarian systems are much more radical in this. They absorb the mediating structures by subjecting them to the dictates of the single party and the bureaucratic control of the state. But they do so at the cost of individual citizens and their material interests and civic liberties.

Something similar happened in the radical welfare states of Western Europe, although unlike totalitarian states they have always left sufficient room for individuals and their particular interests and liberties. In the welfare state, as the next chapter will demonstrate, the polarization of the collective and the individual, the public and the private, became well-nigh endemic to the system. In this respect, welfare states are, sociologically speaking, more advanced in modernity than those industrialized nations that managed to maintain viable and vital intermediary structures, or those industrial nations that maintained a strictly centralized, totalitarian control.

In pre-industrial societies, individuals are surrounded by cultural institutions and societal organizations which stand between them and the bodies of government and administration, which constitute the very cornerstones of a vital civil society.[21] For instance, in the United States of America visited by Tocqueville in the first half of the nineteenth century, not just the family, but also the neighborhood, the voluntary association, the school, the professional organization and the church functioned collectively as a buffer between the individual and the state— or whatever there was in terms of government and administration.

The Netherlands prior to the 1960s present a clear example as well. It was the heyday of (re-)pillarization.[22] Organizations in such crucial fields as education, communications, health, and leisure activities were still solidly founded upon religious and humanistic worldviews. They constituted a rather massive field of intermediary structures that maintained a large degree of autonomy vis-à-vis the state and exerted a large degree of authority and control over the individuals belonging to these pillars. Since the 1960s these organizations maintained their independence and autonomy legally, yet were in actual fact absorbed by the rapidly expanding welfare state. As a result, they increasingly lost their intermediary character and functions, thereby contributing to the widening gap between the public and the private spheres of life.

Sociologically, mediating structures are the soil that nurtures the values, norms, and meanings of a society, and keeps them vital and vigorous. As confining and coercive as they may actually be, they do provide life with a sense of taken-for-granted meaning and direction. They are the structural parameters of the *community*, the concrete relations of mutual solidarity. That is, they provide the concept of society with content and meaning: society as *nomos*, that is, as a meaningful and valuable gestalt. In contrast, in late modernity the notion of society stands for an abstract sociological entity like "the social system," or "social structure," or "societal structures." It no longer refers to concrete relations, organizations, and institutions as components of a coherent lifeworld. In late modernity, people live as rather isolated individuals in flexible, lowly or thinly institutionalized networks in which values, norms, and meanings are attracted and applied in an ad hoc manner just as the interests and necessities of the moment demand. Of course, the Durkheimian threat of anomie hovers over this abstract society incessantly.

Today, much of the interactions between men and organizations are electronic, guided by wonderful (nearly neo-magical) gadgets such as word processors, computer networks, faxes, modems, and so on. Communication—if it can still be called this—acquires three predominant characteristics: it can be quick, massive, and repetitive. It does guarantee more freedom and liberty, albeit a freedom and a liberty that is potentially couched in anomie. Due to the electronic revolution, the world has once again come closer to the haunting visions of Franz Kafka.[23]

## Civil Society and Urbanity

In the previous chapter we have seen how urbanity, from its early start in the eleventh century, hatched the basic components of modernization, in particular a rather new, namely functional-rational type of solidarity that emerged within its context. At the end of the same chapter, I also argued that urbanity itself was, in turn, subjected to the modernization that it nurtured. This again changed its nature and functions drastically.

Originally, urbanity lacked any severe polarization of the public and the private. On the contrary, the *koinon* and the *idion*, the public and the private were closely linked. The professional guilds, in particular, functioned, prior to their degeneration into compartmentalized and closed interest groups, as vital intermediary structures, as vocational associations which constituted a concrete societal foundation for the values, norms, and meanings of urbanity. This changed steadily, however, during the ensuing process of modernization.

Take, for example, the fate of the street and the neighborhood in fully modernized cities. The more an urban society begins to modernize, the more its streets are transformed into functional traffic arteries through which people move and are moved from here to there. In the process, such streets lose vital social functions. They are, for example, no longer public spaces in which people interact, in which children play, and for which inhabitants feel a taken-for-granted kind of responsibility and commitment. This is no longer "their street," and "their neighborhood" as the spatial setting of a collectively experienced identity. The street and the neighborhood as spaces in which public man (Richard Sennett's term) presents himself and engages in meaningful interactions, have become alienated spaces which are now deemed the special responsibility of public authorities. If there are still children living in such a street—more likely than not their parents have moved with them to the suburbs—the space between the houses is no longer safe enough to play in. Adults too live and interact behind, no longer in front of, their front doors. The street is no longer a space for the exchange of gossip and small talk, let alone for festivals and barbecues. The private and the public have become separated spheres, mediated only through the functions and the functionaries of the state.

A Dutch sociologist took one such street in the city of Utrecht as an object of a detailed qualitative investigation. He reconstructed its history, and interviewed the old and the new people living there. It was a late-nineteenth-century street in a working-class neighborhood. His picture of this street (he called it a portrait), of its transformation after the 1950s in particular, is lively and impressive. Before the young adults began to move out and the new people started to move in, this street was not a traffic artery but a relatively close community. The street is rather narrow, so people could talk and converse with each other across the street. Children could be watched by adults while playing, which, of course, heightened the sense of security. Prior to the welfare state, poverty in the street was indeed grim, but it did create a strong sense of solidarity, an obvious component of the vital culture of poverty. That has changed radically: "The people living here are no longer poor. They do not need each other that much anymore as in former days. The car in front of their house accentuates their independence, their freedom of movement. If they want to, they are on the camping place outside the city in no time."[24]

Affluence and the provisions of the Dutch welfare state, the author seems to imply, were a mixed blessing. They did away with abject poverty and desolation, but they also fostered a socially centrifugal tendency which affected the quality of solidarity. The younger residents withdrew to their own private lives and interests, had fewer children than their parents, and tried to move from the street altogether the moment they could afford a better house or apartment elsewhere. Their places were then taken by migrants from Turkey or Morocco, by students, and by young nurses. The change is described as follows: "The solidarity of the first years of this street which was caused and fed by poverty and indigence, is gradually atrophied and in the end exchanged for a preoccupation with one's own nuclear family and one's own person. This preoccupation is easier to maintain and easier to satisfy. What can be seen next, is a nuclear family that is self-sufficient and that turns its back to the street."[25]

The centrifugal withdrawal to the private abodes of the *idion*, enjoyed and fostered often in suburban dwellings, and the anomic consequences thereof for the street as a social system could not have been better formulated. The result of all of this is, of course, another step towards the demise of urbanity. What we witness here, as in a laboratory setting, is the gradual generalization and neutralization of urbanity—the emergence of an abstract urbanity.[26]

We saw before that the ability to differentiate between the public and the private, as had occurred in the Greek *polis*, could be viewed as a first impulse towards modernization. However, as long as both keep bearing on each other through mediating structures, there is little chance for the emergence of a fully modernized, or late modern, abstract society. However, the developments of most Western European societies towards a centralized welfare state demonstrated that the gradual separation and polarization of the public and the private, and in its wake the gradual loss of autonomy of mediating structures, have indeed brought about an abstract society which again adversely affected urbanity. We return to this later, when we discuss urbanity and the welfare state. At this point, however, we must reemphasize the importance of the polarization and separation of the public and the private in modernized cities.

The German urban sociologist H. P. Bahrdt argued that in cities the public (*Öffentlichkeit*) and the private (*Privatheit*) always tend to grow apart, while still maintaining a mutual relationship: "A public and a private sphere are formed which maintain a close interaction, without destroying the polarity."[27] However, Bahrdt then adds an observation which, in my view, is adequate only in the case of fully modernized cities and not, as he claims, of cities in general. In cities, he claims, the polarity of the public and the private causes the gradual loss of influence and relevance of intermediary associations. This, in fact, would render a city more urban: "The life spheres which can be characterized neither as "public" nor as "private," lose significance. The stronger the polarity and interaction between the public and private spheres have taken shape, the more "citylike," sociologically speaking, the life of a habitat will be."[28]

Historically, this observation can hardly be justified. It has to be turned around. As we have seen before, as of the tenth and eleventh centuries, the trading cities of Europe began to develop into "citylike" habitats, that is, into habitats with urbanity because their inhabitants banded together, with or without a revolutionary act of *coniuratio*. They forged a historically new kind of solidarity—the functionally rational solidarity of an economic and civic culture—based on scores of intermediary organizations and institutions. Not ties of blood or religion, neither the possession of land or a particular *territorium*, nor the ascribed membership of feudal estates forged these merchants, craftsmen, and allied service experts into "city people." Shared economic interests and common social actions conducted in scores of larger and smaller organizations that functioned as vital intermediary structures, were the parameters of urbanity as an economic and civic culture. Thus, an urban community emerged which was open, cosmopolitan, and rational. Once again, this community should not be romanticized as a "warm" *Gemeinschaft*, as it was riddled with socioeconomic and political conflicts and cultural contradicitions. Yet, it was the economic and political interests they shared vis-à-vis the late medieval, feudal powers which bound and held these urbanites together.

Within the context of an emerging economic and civic culture, the public and the private could develop as distinct spheres of life which were yet indissolubly linked together through intermediary structures—the ever-more powerful guilds, but also such typical urban organizations and institutions as the school, the university, the hospital, the orphanage, the poor house, and so on. Unlike the religious, charitable institutions of the Middle Ages, these organizations began, after the eleventh century, to develop and prosper as typically urban public-private partnerships.

Thus, the public and the private realized their fruitful mutual interaction in the increasingly massive societal field of associations and organizations. It is this intermediary field—*civil society, bürgerliche Gesellschaft,* in the original sense of the word—which provided cities with politically, economically, and sociologically energizing urbanity.

However, as we shall see in the next chapter, together with the rise of the centralized nation-state which reigned from the absolutist monarchies of the seventeenth and eighteenth centuries until the welfare states of the twentieth century, cities gradually lost their political autonomy and their economic and sociocultural vitality and stamina. Today, cities, particularly within the regime of an interventionist welfare state, are subjected to a rather sharp polarization and even separation of the public and the private spheres, and thus to a gradual atrophy of the intermediary field. Civil society's associations and organizations, even if they are autonomous legally, are entangled in a web of state regulations, and smothered by state subsidies and the bureaucratic rules and controls attached to them. At the very same time individual citizens calculate their private interests foremost, and tend to use the associations and organizations of civil society only if they foster these private interests.

In a sense, this is a *centrifugal* process which weakens civil society considerably. Yet, it is, of course, not just the interventionist welfare state that exerted centrifugal force on civil society and thus contributed to the emergence of a generalized, vague, and abstract urbanity. There is, as we have seen, in modernization itself a differentiating and centrifugal tendency which becomes apparent and visible in particular in late modern cities and metropolitan areas. It has led to the emergence of the late modern, fragmented city of which contemporary Los Angeles is perhaps the most illustrative example (discussed further in chapter 4). As to interventionist and centralized welfare state it is, I shall argue in the next chapter, a typically modern project. The project has failed and is, ever since the 1980s, in revision. The post-welfare state era is a late modern era, and Los Angeles may well be, as postmodernists argue, its exemplary city—a city with a very abstract kind of urbanity, or perhaps, devoid of urbanity. We return to all this at a later stage in our discussion.

One thing is clear by now, come the 1980s urbanity had lost much of its former stamina and power. In many European and American cities it has become rather general, neutral, and abstract, if it has not evaporated entirely. The question then emerges, whether this must be accepted as part of a fateful historical development, or if this ought to be the special focus and subject of late modern urban policies. This, too, deserves more discussion.

## Cultural Pluriformity and Urbanity

Urbanity, I argued repeatedly, is wrought with ambiguities and contradictions. The most important contradiction is the fact that it bears the seeds of its own decline. This is, among others, illustrated by its intrinsic cultural pluriformity. From the start, early modern cities with urbanity were characterized by their openness towards outsiders, strangers, and aliens. In particular the feudal serfs from rural communities could relatively easily obtain freedom and citizenship within the walls of these merchant cities. Again, this should not be romanticized. Very soon the guilds erected protective walls around their own interests in order to prevent outsiders and strangers from entering their part of the urban market. The initially open market, so essential for a vital economy, was closed again.

When, after the eighteenth century, these guilds declined, and industrialization began to alter the world of production and consumption radically, people from many different economic, social, and cultural walks of life took up their residences in the cities. More than ever before in history, the industrializing cities became the sources of the wealth of nations.[29] They exerted a magnetic attraction on scores of people who had only one thing in common—the desire to flee rural destitution and to become successful in life. The city was, and actually still is, the only viable context for this desire. Needless to say, the industrial cities of the nineteenth century were simultaneously the seedbeds for exploitation, deprivation, and poverty. In the slums, a culture of poverty emerged as an relatively autonomous kind of culture which increasingly lost touch with urbanity-at-large. Or phrased differently, urbanity fragmented along class lines. In the twentieth century yet another fragmentation of urban culture occurred.

Prior to this century, most European and North American cities were relatively homogeneous in ethnic and national composition. Apart from Jewish neighborhoods or ghettos the main differentiation between urban inhabitants ran along class lines. In the second half of the nineteenth and in the twentieth centuries, however, first the North American cities, then, particularly after World War II, the cities of Western Europe as well, began to differentiate in terms of ethnicity and nationality. Next to and often intersecting class stratification, emerged the differentiation according to national and ethnic origins, giving rise to a multicultural urban population.[30]

Naturally, urbanity was affected by this ethnic and national pluralization. In fact the economic and civic culture of the city, as it emerged after the eleventh century and functioned up until the rise of industrialism, lost much if not all of its primacy in most ethnic subcultures which more often than not shared the culture of poverty of the urban working class of the nineteenth century. In fact, in these industrial, multicultural cities ethnicity began to gain primacy over urbanity.

*E pluribus unum* is the motto of the United States—unity through pluriformity. It led to the ideology of "the melting pot" in which all the different subcultures were to be forged into an allegedly united American culture. The ideology obviously emphasized the *unum* more than the *e pluribus*. Not just in actual fact, but also normatively, democracy is not and should not be a melting pot in which cultural differences are wiped out through a massive and thorough assimilation to dominant values and norms which are necessarily the values and norms of the politically and socioeconomically dominant forces. Moreover, due to the previously discussed process of modernization these values and norms have grown abstract, vague, and neutral, and are thus not very fit to forge any unity in the existing pluriformity.[31] In fact, they have to compete with the norms and values of the ethnic subcultures which are usually far from vague, general, and abstract.

Instead, one could view society, it has been suggested, as a mosaic in which distinct and distinguishable parts somehow, like a chaos that organizes itself, form a whole, some sort of pluriform gestalt. However, if a society is characterized by centrifugal tendencies, that is, if there is, for whatever reason, a disintegration of the intermediary field of associations and organizations, cultural plurality will not at all lead to a pluriform unity but rather to a state of anomic "balkanization" which, of course, in the end weakens civil society. Ethnic groups will then cherish their own culture as the ultimate symbolic expression of their own material interests at the expense of the commonwealth of the city-at-large. This is condoned by the ideology of multiculturalism which, in a sense, is the exact opposite of the melting-pot ideology.

Often ethnic subcultures are not functionally rational and abstract but, on the contrary, driven by the value-rationality of traditional family ties, historical and national roots, traditional organizations, and religious convictions and allegiances. It may even lead to divisive dual ethics: "outsiders" are treated and encountered differently than "insiders." In such a situation, multiculturality is not an attractive option for life in the city. When urbanity itself has lost the power to bind people together—as in a common but rational bond of identification and solidarity—because its values and norms have grown abstract, expressions of ethnicity easily fill the void, and become all the more attractive as viable alternatives. They offer a strong, if compartmentalized and divisive, experience of belonging, solidarity, and shared identity. They may even foster a sensation of power, as illusory as this power often is at the end of the day. Later, I shall argue that only the revitalization of intermediary structures in our cities, together with a revitalization of urbanity to be expected in its wake, may prevent the progress of such disintegrating forces, without smothering the cultural plurality that the ethnic mosaic has to offer.

## Modernity's Anti-Urban Nemesis

There is yet another ambiguity in urbanity that deserves closer attention. Throughout history, there have been apparent tensions between the city and the surrounding countryside. Economically, the two have always been mutually dependent, but socially and culturally the relationship was wrought with distrust and, at times, even disgust. In ancient Judaism the *am ha'aretz*, that is, the rural people, were looked down upon as primitives caught and shackled by heathen, magical beliefs. Likewise, in the eyes of the clergy in medieval administrative cities, the countryside was seen as an ever-present source of covert and, at times, even overt paganism and magic. For instance, the recurrent festivals of fools, often celebrated irreverently within or immediately outside the church, the early modern urban fools' societies, and also the gargoyles under the roofs of the cathedrals, testified to a persistent paganism that had its main source of existence in the premodern countryside.[32] In fact, persistent (late) medieval paganism was a rural, not urban, phenomenon.[33] Yet, the early modern merchants, craftsmen, and allied service producers employed it jokingly and teasingly in their rather wild festivals of fools and the various exploits of their fools' societies.

This might well have been the origin of the typically urban preju-
dice that peasants and farmers are rude, uncivilized, and ignorant. In-
versely, the city—certainly the rich and wealthy city—presented, from
the point of view of the countryside, a bewildering panacea of perni-
cious immorality and arrogant presumption, a cauldron of dubious ideas
and styles of life, a decadent Babylon, or even a sinful Sodom and
Gomorrah. It also led to the idea that urban people, estranged from
nature, live unnatural and unhealthy lives.

However, the anti-urban animus was and still is not just a rural phenomenon but also, and maybe even primarily, an urban one. Urban
anti-urbanity was fostered by the process of modernization. The modernization of urbanity, we saw before, meant a gradual generalization
of its values, norms, and meanings. Its worldview and ethos became
free-floating and disengaged itself from the main urban class, the bourgeoisie, and even from the city itself. This abstract urbanity lost much
of its vigor and stamina, and progressively lacked the actual power to
forge and maintain a collective sense of identity and solidarity.

The merchant, the craftsman, or the lawyer and banker in the
Hanseatic city of Lübeck in the sixteenth century could still draw pride
and a distinct sense of belonging and identity from his urban citizenship. In the nineteenth and certainly in the twentieth century this had
become impossible. When Thomas Mann gave his previously mentioned address in commemoration of the 700th birthday of Lübeck's
city rights, he called himself "son of this city" and addressed the audience with "my dear fellow burghers." But these words, spoken in 1926,
sounded quite artificial. It is known that he saw himself in those days
primarily as a German but upon Hitler's rise to power he discovered,
much to his chagrin, that this was an illusion. He eventually fled to
America and became an American citizen, but felt himself ever since a
global citizen, a "world burgher." That, of course, is a very modern but
quite abstract sense of identity and solidarity.

The modernization of urbanity has contributed to the growing estrangement from the city and from its urbanity on the part of the inhabitants. The more modern and abstract urbanity grew, the wider the
anti-urban animus spread within and outside the cities. Often, this estrangement was voiced in rather romantic and irrational tones. The
rejection of the city's functional rationality and its abstract solidarity
consisted usually of the same components: romantic notions about
nature (or, in contemporary terminology, the environment), about medieval society, about rural village life, about *Gemeinschaft* and its al-

legedly strong solidarity. It is the romantic nostalgia for the lost Garden of Eden.

The romantic critique of the big city as a heartless and cold world[34]in which there is more solitude than solidarity, and in which freedom engenders estrangement, was of course voiced astutely in the nineteenth and twentieth centuries but could be heard long before the era of romanticism. In 1625, to give just one telling, yet rare, example, Francis Bacon aired his critique of city life in his short essay on friendship:

> But little doe Men perceive, what Solitude is, and how farre it extendeth. For a Crowd is not Company; And Faces are but a Gallery of Pictures; And Talke but a Tinckling Cymball, where there is no Love. The Latin Adage meeteth it a little; Magna Civitas, Magna solitudo; Because in a great Towne, Friends are scattered; So that there is not that Fellowship, for the most Part, which is in lesse Neighbourhoods. But we may goe further, and affirme most truly; that it is a meere, and miserable Solitude, to want true Friends; without which the World is but a Wildernesse.[35]

The romantic critique of and revolt against the city and its culture were, for the most part, verbalized eloquently and expressed artistically by academics and artists. The Enlightenment of the eighteenth century was still predominantly an urban worldview and ethos. Although such revolutionary values as *liberté, égalité et fraternité* were quite general in their intention (they referred to the nation France, not to its capital Paris), they were yet the values employed by the urban bourgeoisie revolting against the fetters and shackles of *ancien régime* absolutism. But, as is often forgotten, the French Revolution affected the countryside as much as the cities of France. Georges Lefebvre emphasized correctly that much of the revolution was a rural affair.[36]Yet, its epicenter was solidly urban and metropolitan. In a sense, this revolution was heir to the late medieval *coniuratio*—an urban plot of the bourgeoisie, joined by the urban proletariat against the two leading estates of absolutism, the clergy and above all the nobility.

Soon it became clear, however, how general and abstract these revolutionary values actually were, how much they functioned as the empty slogans and clichés of a new repression and tyranny. The generalized and abstract reason of the Enlightenment, put on a metaphysical pedestal by the Jacobins, began to terrorize people, making a mockery of liberty, equality, and solidarity. Next, this in origin urban rationalism—a popularized version of Rousseau's philosophy—was felt to have alienated itself too much from Nature. Also the functional rationality of urbanity was sensed to be too far removed from the traditional bonds of solidarity in the family, the neighborhood, the church, the region and, above all, the nation.

This was voiced by the romantic call for a return to nature, the family, the (particularly Roman Catholic) church, and the nation.[37] Emotions and desires, aspirations and motives could allegedly not develop to their fullest potential within the rational chill of a generalized and abstract urbanity. Not in an urban environment but in nature and in one or the other form of *Gemeinschaft* men and women were supposed to fully develop and explore their talents and capabilities. In short, the pursuit of happiness could allegedly not be successful within a solidly urban context.

Needless to say, this kind of romantic anti-urbanity presented itself often as a conservative, if not reactionary ideology. That became particularly apparent in the German concept of *Volk*, eulogized by various romantic philosophers. It penetrated deeply into the German youth movement up until the 1930s and was then brought to its racist extremes by the Nazis. But even Rousseau's philosophy which is often presented as a progressive and even revolutionary ideology, contains, if scrutinized closely, quite an anti-modern and therefore anti-urban agenda. In that typically modern dilemma between the general (collective) will and the particular (individual) will Rousseau's followers opted generally for the prevalence of the former as far as society and the state were concerned. This is, as has been observed many times, a totalitarian streak.[38] As to the individual and his particular will, he referred them to the illusions of Nature and naturalness. It was and still is a very strong anti-urban ideology.

Quite informative in this respect are the recurrent utopian projects that set out to transform sociocultural life into a *commune*. From Tolstoy and Thoreau to the commune movement of the 1960s and 1970s such visions of society have indeed been strongly anti-urban. The French sociologists Danièle Léger and Bertrand Hervieu, for instance, discussed various neorural utopias that have emerged from the political movement of 1968 in France. They demonstrated how these neorurals, as they called them, turned their back on radical Marxist politics and ended up with a rather vaguely romantic and anarchistic kind of philosophy. This ideology was strongly anti-institutional, somewhat akin to anarchism, and, needless to say, strongly anti-urban. It all adds up to a rather regressive ideology full of gnostic (Manichaeistic) notions, ideas, and sentiments.[39] Anti-urbanity is intrinsically linked to antimodernity.

In comparison, the Commune of Paris (1871) was, in fact, very urban indeed. It was the intention of these *communards* to transform Paris into an autonomous city-state in which the people would devote themselves to noncapitalistic pursuits on the basis of liberty, democracy, and solidarity. The reason why this truly urban movement remained unsuccessful and why it could not bring about a vital urbanity, was its rather zealous anticapitalism. By that the Commune of Paris, as much as it could have saved urbanity as a civic culture, destroyed it as an economic culture.[40]

However, it would be quite mistaken to think present-day anti-urbanity were exclusively romantically antirational and rurally regressive. On the contrary, today one finds the most vigorous and influential anti-urbanity among the self-proclaimed progressive, rational, and technocratic city planners and city designers, among neo-positivistic (ahistorical, operationalistic, one-sidedly quantitative) socioscientific urbanologists, and like-minded civil servants in governmental agencies responsible for urban (re)development.

If one skims through the reports, journals, articles, and books on urban planning and urban (re)development, one is struck by the predominant one-dimensionality of thought. Not just houses, as Le Corbusier once said, but total cities are viewed as "machines" for the use of people who allegedly act and behave like "machines." These are, apart from recent exceptions which will be discussed in the last chapter, cities designed rationally on the drawing board and, if materialized in real cities, usually devoid of any trace of urbanity—dead places, like cemeteries. In particular Le Corbusier's well-known urban design philosophy is apt to nip urbanity in the bud.[41]

During the negotiations about India's independence in 1947, Punjab lost its capital Lahore to the newly established muslim state Pakistan. The province was in need of a new administrative center. Under the supervision of President Nehru himself, this new city was set up at the feet of the Himalaya and named Chandigarh. Nehru, who had met Le Corbusier and learned about his wish to build a city according to his own philosophy, saw to it that the famous architect from France received the unique chance to design and build the city of his dreams.

Under Le Corbusier's supervision his nephew Pierre Jeanneret, the British architect-couple Maxwell Fry and Jane Drew, and a few Indian architects set out to construct from scratch a city according to Le Corbusier's Radiant City philosophy: many open spaces and squares, much green spots, separation of traffic, living, working, and recreation functions, and all this within a grid-shaped infrastructure. The city was initially planned for a population of 500,000 and would not in any way conceivable resemble other Indian towns and cities. Chandigarh was the typical product of modern urban design couched in the rationality of the drawing board, tinged with a touch of megalomania. Or, as Fishman formulated it in a kinder fashion: "He [Le Corbusier] ignored the social context and created isolated monuments to his own genius.[42]

Something interesting happened, not previewed by Le Corbusier and his staff— truly an unintended consequence. The many native construction workers, attracted from the countryside, built their huts round and about the construction sites. However, after a building was finished, they would not remove their huts. On the contrary, more of such huts and semi-permanent tents were erected by other migrants, often relatives, who had fled rural poverty and tried their fortune within this emerging big city. By now more than 700,000 people live, work, travel, and recreate in and between the houses and buildings of Chandigarh. Shantytown structures are scattered between often colossal concrete buildings which gives the place a much more Indian than Corbusierean appearance.

It is because of these chaotic shantytown structures, and of course not because of the typically Western drawing board rationality underlying Le Corbusier's initial plan, that Chandigarh after all turned out to be a relatively successful urban project. It should be borne in mind, however, that the project was never finished in the spirit of the original plan. As it is now, Chandigarh presents a kind of Corbusier mausoleum.[43]

Much to his disappointment, Le Corbusier never received the chance to build his kind of city within the Western hemisphere. He designed many grand plans but they never left the drawing board. It might well have been a blessing, because his philosophy was inimical to any sort and degree of urbanity. This stands to reason, when the basic functions of a city—traffic, work, social life, and recreation—are spatially kept separate. Such a functional-spatial differentiation precludes the emergence of a vital economic and civic culture. In fact, it is even questionable if Le Corbusier's cities could have developed into bazaars!

We would deviate from the core of our discussion too much, if we would also discuss the urban visions of Frank Lloyd Wright (Broadacre City) and Ebenezer Howard (Garden City), whose social philosophies of urban design were, for vastly different reasons, also antagonistic to urbanity.[44] It suffices to conclude that until recently much of modern city planning has been quite devastating as far as urban culture is concerned.[45] This has been the case in particular, as we shall see in the next chapter, under the regime of a welfare state in which housing and urban (re)development are the prime targets of governmental policy. Before we turn to the subject of (anti-)urbanity and the welfare state, we should, in conclusion, briefly enumerate the specific problems cities face when they lack urbanity.

## Cities With and Without Urbanity

Historically, cities without a vigorous urbanity have actually been quite normal. Throughout the ages urban conglomerates, sometimes quite large in size, have existed in which many people lived and worked without identifying themselves at all with the city as a social and cultural entity. They have been called aptly bazaar cities. It was, as we saw, in Europe that as of the tenth and eleventh centuries people began to cooperate and interact economically, politically, and socioculturally as the inhabitants of a city which developed gradually beyond an *oikos*-plus-market into the carrier of a collective identity. The city thus became the focus of social cohesion, collective pride, and, above all, political power.

Yet, urbanity—the economic and civic culture of early modern urban capitalism—which initially contributed so much to the take-off of modernization, modernized itself during the ensuing centuries. If there was in fully modernized cities urbanity at all, it was an abstract urbanity. That is, it generalized into vague forms of identity and solidarity. At the end of this development, first in the context of a centralized nation-state such as the welfare state, next in the late modern, differentiated and fragmented society, we are confronted with the problem of cities (often metropoles of unheard of sizes) without urbanity.

In order to realize fully the problems that cities without urbanity encounter, we must briefly enumerate once more the sociocultural, political, and economic advantages of urbanity. It gave, to begin with, birth to a previously unknown opportunity for people to advance in life socially and economically through bonds of solidarity which were infinitely more open and flexible than the traditional bonds of blood, land, religion, and magic. The urban bonds were primarily functionally rational networks, borne by common material interests. Urbanity was a previously unknown economic and civic culture which combined liberty and mutual responsibility, openness and cohesiveness, local identification and cosmopolitanism.

It was indeed an ideal cultural setting for the advancement of trade and manufacturing, of the arts and sciences, and of industrial developments and technology. Urbanity is also the bearer of a work ethic which was stimulated and reinforced by the fact that the stratification according to socioeconomic classes left infinitely more room for social mobility than the estate system of feudal society, based as it was upon the stalemate of pedigree descent. Urbanity was, in the words of Thomas

Mann, "a spiritual form of life" which paired solidarity to what Georg Simmel once called *Verstandesherrschaft*, that is , the rule of reason. This rational solidarity, Simmel argued, found its economic expression in a monetary economy. In his monumental study *Philosophie des Geldes* (1900)—a somewhat misleading title for an intellectually powerful book—Simmel demonstrated convincingly to which degree rationalization, money, and city were in fact intertwined. His argument can be found summarized in his famous, much criticized, yet much quoted and intensively read essay, "The Metropolis and Mental Life (1903).[46]

This originally European urbanity soon became a source of sociocultural, economic, and political energies. It stimulated urban democracy, urban social life, urban economy, the arts, the sciences, technology. Cities with urbanity took the lead, leaving those without it far behind. In such vital cities not just the market place, but also cultural institutions such as universities, vocational schools, museums, concert halls, theaters, zoological and botanical gardens, etc. eventually sprang up, prospered, and provided the urban community with an identifiable face and above all with pride.

These cities with urbanity soon developed into influential centers of political activity and developments which caused the emergence of urbanity as a civic culture and the seedbed of participatory democracy. The spectacular development of Western societies since the late Middle Ages is to be greatly attributed not just to cities but to their urbanity, that is, their vigorous economic and civic culture. Jane Jacobs is right, when she claims that cities are the main source of the wealth of nations.[47] However, we should add that not all cities have been in the past or will be in the future the wells of welfare and prosperity. It is only the cities with urbanity that can function as the prime motors of development—as pluralistic, abstract, and thus modern this urbanity will be.

After this list of advantages of urbanity it is not difficult to list the obvious disadvantages of the lack of an economic and civic culture. If, for example, Western cities modernize radically in the direction of fragmented social and cultural systems, cities will become quite similar to the big cities of ancient China and India. Not Manhattan, as many romantic or neorural anti-urbanites often claim, but Calcutta is the bugbear of contemporary metropolises: a vast urban conglomerate without a trace of overarching urbanity. Perhaps Los Angeles comes close to this urban nightmare. However, this very non-European metropolis presents, in terms of urbanity, an intriguing puzzle to which we will return later.

To begin with, cities without urbanity are actually no longer marketplaces but bazaars in which, in an incoherent manner, scores of merchandise and services are bought and sold. Particular interests, promoted and defended by various interest groups and their lobbies, not the general interest of the urban commonwealth, take the lead in such a bazaar situation. If there is not total chaos in Western cities without urbanity, it is because a penetrating kind of administrative bureaucracy spins intricate webs of regulation and control around the burghers, the urban institutions and organizations, and in particular their economic activities.

Together with the bureaucrats who oftentimes assume an anti-customer, patrimonial attitude, the various experts in the profit and nonprofit services tend to keep the urban population in an often paternalistic tutelage. This alliance of bureaucrats and service producers, and the ensuing bondage of the citizens whom they are supposed to serve, can be observed most clearly in those countries in which the welfare state has been developed extensively and intensively. Needless to say, this is not a vital civic culture.

Cities without urbanity not only lose their coherence and unity of material interests, but also their most important source of energy, their vitality and resourcefulness. Severe social problems are met in a bureaucratic manner (installation of committees manned by civil servants, producers, and social scientists who then produce reports). They are not confronted by ingenuity and daring policies which are urgently needed to solve them. Politically, cities without urbanity are rendered defenseless vis-à-vis the bureaucracies in the capital from where the nation is primarily run, or vis-à-vis city hall which in many respects dominates the metropolitan area.

There are indeed many, often loud complaints about the lack of real power on the part of local administrators, but when the problems become insurmountable, many a city hall official cries loudly for federal assistance. A considerable part of these complaints is realistic, since apart from exceptional big-city mayors who have a powerful administrative machinery at their command, local administrators do indeed often lack political clout and sufficient financial resources. Yet, much of it is also due to an intrinsic urban weakness: the absence of a vital economic and civic culture.

The gradual drifting apart of the public and the private is also significant. Bureaucrats and politicians dwell in the often very generalized and abstract abodes of urban policymaking, where they deal with charts and maps and models, not with real people. Their counterparts in the city are the powerful organizations and institutions. There is often a mutual dependence between these two parties. Meanwhile, as to the urban inhabitants, the burghers in the original sense of that word, they are inclined strongly to withdraw to their private abodes, tending to the minutia of their daily routines, if they have not yet abandoned the city altogether.

Cities without urbanity are rationalized and abstract places in that they no longer constitute an urban commonwealth but rather a sum of differentiated functions and divided subcultures. Such cities are in the minds, plans, and policies of urban policymakers cut up into various, semi-autonomous sectors which stand for specific functions. That is, in the head of many an urban policymaker dwells *un petit Corbusier*! Thus, there are housing facilities, shopping malls, hospital complexes, university buildings, hotels with and without meeting and conference facilities, recreation zones, industrial sites, traffic arteries, structures, infrastructures, and so on. In short, a massive functional differentiation, usually combined with scale enlargements, tied to rational economies of scale. One thing, however, is usually absent in the minds of these urban policymakers: the city itself.

In a city without urbanity, the monetary economy, which according to Simmel is typical of the true city, changes into pure commerce, land speculation, and greed. The economic sphere is then kept separate from the social and the cultural. It pledges allegiance only to the world of political power. When in the evening and during the weekend bureaucracy and commerce come to rest, these cities—in particular their downtown section where the heart of urbanity ought to throb—are deserted, transformed into dead and dreary places. Streets are ghostly rows of buildings from which all life seems to have been sapped. The sense of unsafety is sharpened—indeed urban space, devoid of urbanity, is very vulnerable to aggression and criminality.

Cities without urbanity have the tendency to degenerate gradually into places of consumption rather than production. It is not first and foremost the consumption of luxury by a small elite, as in the big cities of the *ancien régime*, described so vividly by Werner Sombart, as we saw before. The difference lies in the levels of prosperity which have reached, historically speaking, unprecedented heights and depths in many Western cities, and which, despite much urban poverty, has spread out broadly over the massive middle class. It is, above all, the consumption of private and, in particular, also public services that stand at the core of urban functions. Indeed, modern cities are predominantly habitats of consumption and service, and this, of course, affects the very essence of urbanity as an economic and civic culture.

Cities offer private facilities, such as banking or legal assistance, but also and especially public services, such as schools, health care, elder care, housing, transportation, energy provisions, and so on. In fact, in an intensive and extensive welfare state, services which formerly had been the prerogative of private, urban initiatives, have been adopted by public authorities, adding to the rift between public and private, and thereby acerbating the weakness of the lack of urbanity.

Meanwhile, public and private organizations have (re-)discovered the relevance of a vital corporate culture. Likewise, cities should once again become aware of the relevance of urbanity to their success as the nodal points of democracy and of the regional and national economy.

## Notes

1. Karl Mannheim, *Man and Society in an Age of Reconstruction*, translated by E. Shils (London: Routledge & Kegan Paul, [1940] 1960, 10th ed.).
2. See Anthony Giddens, *Modernity and Self: Identity-Self and Society in the Late Modern Age* (Cambridge: Polity Press, 1991). Also Anthony Giddens, *The Consequences of Modernity* (Cambridge: Polity Press, 1990).
3. Arnold Gehlen, *Die Seele im technischen Zeitalter*, passim.
4. Weber's ideas about rationalization are developed in his essays on the sociology of religion, and occur throughout his publications. However, they were expressed in a comprehensive manner in a series of lectures on economic history which he delivered at the end of his life. Cf. Max Weber, *Wirtschaftsgeschichte* (Berlin: Duncker & Humblot, [1921] 1958). Cf. also his intellectual swan song "Wissenschaft als Beruf" in *From Max Weber: Essays in Sociology*, translated, edited, and introduced by H. H. Gerth and C. Wright Mills (New York: Oxford University Press; a Galaxy Book, [1946] 1962), pp. 129–159.
5. Max Weber, *Die Wirtschaftsethik der Weltreligionen*, part 1: *Konfuzianismus und Taoismus* (Tübingen: J.C.B.Mohr-Siebeck, [1920] 1963), pp. 276–536.
6. Émile Durkheim, *De la Division du Travail Social* (Paris: Presses Universitaires de France, [1893] 1960).
7. The ideal-typical nature of Durkheim's theory of solidarity should be kept in mind. Mechanical solidarity in a unified community is, of course, a constructed type which hardly occurred in real history in a pure form. Even the closest knit community knows differentiations of sorts. Carl Becker emphasized this point correctly, when he wrote: "We thus look in vain for the social solidarity, the psychological uniformity, of the primitive community. What we see is differentiation, the multiplication of distinctions, a greater complexity, an increased instability." Carl Becker, *Progress and Power* (New York: Vintage Books, [1935] 1949), p. 54. Likewise, the organic solidarity of modern society is never completely devoid of unities and unifications. Here too, Durkheim's concept of organic solidarity is an intentionally overdrawn ideal-type.
8. Compare Karl Mannheim, *Man and Society*, in particular pp. 51–58. See also Anton C. Zijderveld, *On Clichés: The Supersedure of Meaning by Function in Modernity* (London: Routledge & Kegan Paul, 1979).

9. Compare Keith Thomas, *Religion and the Decline of Magic*, in particular pp. 177–282.

10. Max Weber, *Die Wirtschaftsethik der Weltreligionen*, part three: *Das Antike Judentum* (Tübingen: J.C.B.Mohr-Siebeck, [1920] 1963), pp. 1–400. In the fourth section of chapter 1 Weber discusses the position of the cities in ancient Judaism. It would lead us too far astray to deal with this in the present essay. I also omit a further discussion of the ancient notion of "the holy city" which runs from ancient Greece, to ancient Judaism, to Augustine and Calvin. The theology of the city falls outside the scope of this essay. Cf. however Jacques Ellul, *The Meaning of the City* (Grand Rapids: Eerdmans, 1970).

11. Compare Rudolf Bultmann, *History and Eschatology* (Edinburgh: The Edinburgh University Press, 1957).

12. This point could have been stressed more by the otherwise very insightful study of Robert Nisbet, *History of the Idea of Progress* (New York: Basic Books, 1980). The rather fateful consequences of this conception of history as a linear chain of events, opposed to the circular conception of history, as in the myth of the eternal return, was discussed by Mircea Eliade, *Cosmos and History: The Myth of the Eternal Return*, translated by W.R. Trask (New York: Harper & Brothers, [1949] 1959).

13. Compare Peter Gay, *The Enlightenment: An Interpretation: The Rise of Modern Paganism* (New York: Vintage Books, [1966] 1968). To Carl Becker the European "doctrine of progress is the most effective, the most revolutionary and dislocating, since it transforms a deocentric into a homocentric universe, and thereby makes man the measure of all things. By liberating the mind from fear for the gods and the restraints of tradition, it invites men to pursue without inhibitions the call of their desires." Carl Becker, *Progress and Power*, p. 93.

14. Compare Clifford Geertz, "Ethos, World View, and the Analysis of Sacred Symbols," in C. Geertz, *The Interpretation of Cultures* (New York: Basic Books, 1973), pp. 126–142.

15. A rather witty analysis of this type of rationalization is offered by George Ritzer, *The Macdonaldization of the World* (Thousands Oaks, CA: Pine Forge Press, 1993). The functionality of the McDonald's fast food chain is taken as a sociological archetype of modern functional rationality.

16. See for this well-known change of means into ends Jacques Ellul, *The Technological Society*, translated by J. Wilkinson (New York: Vintage Books, [1954] 1964).

17. This was the main argument in my *The Abstract Society* (Garden City, NY: Doubleday, 1970).

18. Cf. Arnold Gehlen, *Die Seele im technischen Zeitalter*; Anthony Giddens, *Modernity and Self-Identity*; Helmuth Schelsky, "Ist die Dauerreflexion institutionalisierbar?" in H. Schelsky, *Auf der Suche nach Wirklichkeit* (Düsseldorf and Köln: Eugen Diederichs Verlag, [1957] 1965), pp. 250–275. See also Richard Sennett, *The Fall of Public Man* (Cambridge: Cambridge University Press, 1974), and Christopher Lasch, *The Culture of Narcissism* (London: Abacus, 1980).

19. There is a postmodernist strain of thought which is inclined to proclaim the end of traditional institutions. See for example the essay by Jean-Marie Guéhenno, *La fin de la démocratie* (Paris: Editions Flammarion, 1994) in which the end of the Western, democratic nation-state is announced.

20. Compare Peter L. Berger and Richard J. Neuhaus, *To Empower People: The Role of Mediating Structures in Public Policy* (Washington, DC: American Enterprise Institute for Public Policy Research, [1977] 1996).

21. This is not the place to engage in a detailed discussion on the merits and demerits of the concept of civil society. See for a critical analysis of the history of this

concept: Adam B. Seligman, *The Idea of Civil Society* (New York: Free Press, 1992).

22. On Dutch pillarization see my article, "History and Recent Development of Dutch Sociological Thought," *Social Research* 33, no. 1 (Spring 1966): 115–131.
23. Compare my essay: "Elektronische Interaktion?" in *Die Elektronische Revolution*, ed. Oskar Schatz (Graz and Köln: Styria Verlag, 1975), pp. 97–115.
24. C.H. Jansen, *De straat—een portret* (Muiderberg: Coutinho, 1978), p. 124. My translation. The author, incidentally, does not romanticize the premodern "culture of poverty." See also Andrew Greeley, *Neighborhood* (New York: Seabury Press, 1977) in which neighborhoods are declared to be "good and necessary things for the life of the city." Ibid., p. 1.
25. Jansen, *De straat*, p. 126.
26. It should be repeated that there is little reason to romanticize the culture of urban poverty. Cf. Paul Harrison, *Inside the Inner City: Life under the Cutting Edge* (Harmondsworth and Middlesex: Penguin Books, [1983] 1985, rev. ed.). The author's political *parti pris* does count for some imbalanced judgments and opinions. Cf. for example: "In a socialist economy, change can be planned so that full employment is maintained." Ibid., p. 78.
27. H. P. Bahrdt, *Die moderne Grossstadt* (Hamburg: Wegner Verlag, [1961] 1972), p. 60. My translation.
28. Ibid., p. 60. My translation.
29. See Jane Jacobs, *Cities and the Wealth of Nations* (Harmondsworth and Middlesex: Penguin Books, [1984] 1985).
30. The literature on ethnicity is by now massive. This is not the place to discuss the concept critically. See, for example, *Ethnicity: Theory and Experience*, Nathan Glazer, edited by Daniel P. Moynihan (Cambridge, MA: Harvard University Press, 1975). For social and ethnic stratification see among many other studies Tamotsu Shibutani and Kian M. Kwan, *Ethnic Stratification: A Comparative Analysis* (New York: Macmillan, 1965).
31. I am fully aware of the philosophical and moral complications of all this. However, my essay cannot cover the rather massive moral-philosophical discussion on these issues. See in particular the interesting debate in Charles Taylor, *Multiculturalism and "The Politics of Recognition,"* with commentaries by Amy Gutmann, edited by Steven C. Rockefeller, Michael Walzer, and Susan Wolf (Princeton, NJ: Princeton University Press, 1992).
32. See my *Reality in a Looking-Glass*, (London: Routledge & Kegan Paul, 1982). Also Ronald Sheridan and Anne Ross, *Gargoyles & Grotesques: Paganism in the Medieval Church* (Boston: New York Graphic Society, 1975).
33. See in particular Nathalie Zemon Davies, "The Reasons for Misrule" in *Society and Culture in Early Modern France* (Stanford, CA: Stanford University Press, 1975), pp. 97–123. The Dutch historian Pleij argued that the burghers of these early modern cities experimented with their newly gained bourgeois identity by ridiculing under the disguise of seemingly innocent folly the culture of the feudal knights and priests. See Herman Pleij, *Het gilde van de Blauwe Schuit* (Amsterdam: Meulenhoff, 1979).
34. Compare Edward C. Banfield, *The Unheavenly City: The Nature and the Future of Our Urban Crisis* (Boston, MA: Little, Brown and Company, 1968).
35. Francis Bacon, *Essays* (London: Oxford University Press, [1625] n.d.), p. 107f.
36. Georges Lefebvre, *The Coming of the French Revolution*, translated by R. R. Palmer (Princeton, NJ: Princeton University Press, [1947] 1969), in particular pp. 131–154: "The Peasant Revolution." Also Georges Lefebvre, *The Great Fear of 1789: Rural Panic in Revolutionary France*, translated by J. White (London: Armand Colin, [1932] 1973).

37. See the historical-sociological study of Anthony D. Smith, *National Identity*, (London: Penguin Books, 1991; also Reno, NV: The University of Nevada Press, 1991).

38. See Robert A. Nisbet, *Power and Community* (formerly *The Quest for Community*), (New York: Galaxy Books, Oxford University Press, [1953] 1964). This assessment, I am aware, is debatable, but so is almost everything that is being said about Rousseau and the Rouseaueans.

39. Danièle Léger and Bertrand Hervieu, *Le retour à la nature* (Paris: Editions du Seuil, 1979) and *Des communes pour les temps difficiles: néo-ruraux ou nouveaux moines* (Paris: Le Centurion, 1983).

40. See R. M. Kanter, *Commitment and Community: Communes and Utopias in Sociological Perspective* (Cambridge, MA: Harvard University Press, [1972] 1977).

41. It is hard to assess Le Corbusier correctly and fairly. There is in urbanology some sort of sanctification of him as supposedly one of the greatest architects of this century. This may be correct technically, in particular with regard to his houses and buildings, but seems to me to be questionable sociologically as far as his utopian ideas about urban settings—the Radiant City, the Contemporary City— are concerned. The underlying social and political philosophy is hazardous, to put it mildly. See Robert Fishman, *Urban Utopias in the Twentieth Century: Ebenezer Howard, Frank Lloyd Wright and Le Corbusier* (New York: Basic Books, 1977), pp. 163–263. Le Corbusier believed, Fishman writes, in the centralization of administration and the top-down rule of an authoritarian and technocratic elite, modelled after the centralized management of the army (ibid., p. 181). Like the followers of Sorel, he was an early admirer of Mussolini's type of fascism. During World War II, he openly supported the authoritarian Vichy regime of Pétain. In fact, he had the illusory hope that the collaborators of the Nazis would support his architectural ideas and that they would give him, unlike the prewar administration, orders to realize these plans. When this did not come about, he turned his back to the Vichy administration: "Adieu, cher merdeux Vichy!" (ibid., p. 251). One of his opinions was: "Only a strong program of urbanism—the program of a fascist government—is capable of adapting the modern city to the needs of all" (ibid., p. 224). Yet, as Fishman argues, Le Corbusier was quite inconsistent in this. He actually tried to combine Saint-Simon's emphasis upon the technocratic organization of society by industrial managers with Fourier's sociocratic vision of the *phalanstères* as urban communities for individuals and families. He catered to the powerful elite but was concerned also about the fate of the powerless workers in society (ibid., p. 230f.). Fishman sums his assessment up as follows: "Le Corbusier's social thought is thus a play of opposites: authority and freedom, organization and individuality, mechanization and craftsmanship, planning and spontaneity" (ibid., p. 260).

42. Fishman, *Urban Utopias*, p. 255. See for a critical appraisal of Le Corbusier also Peter Hall, *Cities of Tomorrow*, pp. 203–241: "The City of Towers: The Corbusierian Radiant City—Paris, Chandigarh, Brasilia, London, St. Louis, 1920–1970."

43. See Madhu Sarin, *Urban Planning in the Third World: The Chandigarh Experience* (London: Mansell, 1982).

44. In the Garden City Howard tried to combine and reconcile town and country. Yet, the city he envisaged had very little of the urbanity discussed in this essay. His ideas were picked up in England by a businessman and two millionaires who tried to put Garden City into reality. Two British architects, Barry Parker and Raymond Unwin, built the town Letchworth. The philosophy grew in England into a movement which outgrew Howard. In the 1950s the New Towns in En-

gland were inspired by the Garden City philosophy. See Fishman, *Urban Utopias*, pp. 23–88. Wright, who at heart remained an agrarian, rather anti-urban individual, designed Broadacre City as in fact a non-city. Fishman: "Neither shape nor scale appear recognizably urban: one 'city' may sprawl over 100 square miles without any recognizable center" (ibid., p. 127). Like Le Corbusier's *Ville Radieuse*, Wright's Broadacre City was never built. For Wright's urban utopia see ibid., pp. 90–160.

45. Once the history of urban planning disasters should be written in the vein of Peter Hall's engaging and enlightening *Great Planning Disasters* (London: Weidenfeld and Nicolson, 1980). Quite possibly it has been written already, or is due to appear soon.

46. In *The Sociology of Georg Simmel*, edited and translated by Kurt H. Wolff (New York: Free Press, [1950] 1964), pp. 409–426.

47. Jacobs, *Cities and the Wealth of Nations*.

# 3

# Urbanity and the Interventionist State: An Uneasy Alliance

## Cities and State Formation

Until now, I have, on purpose, discussed the city and urban culture in isolation. We must now focus on the wider societal and, above all, political ramifications of the city and its urbanity. Ever since cities emerged as socioeconomically and politically influential components of post-medieval Europe, there was a very paradoxical and thus complex relationship between them and the emerging nation-states around them. On the one hand, the economic success and the wealth of these early capitalist cities contributed, as we shall see, to the decline of feudal fragmentation and thus to the centralization of power. On the other hand, this centralized power eventually also contributed to the decline of the cities for the simple reason that centralized power, certainly if it aspires to be absolutist, can not condone the competition of urban habitats as rather autonomous city-states.

During the initial phases of centralization, monarchs and princes would marshall the assistance of the wealthy and highly influential bourgeoisie in the city-states. But then, after having been installed safely in the capital as the center of the nation, they would try to curb the autonomy and power of the cities. The absolutist monarchs would, as in France, often politically align themselves with the bourgeoisie in their struggle with the nobility and sometimes the clergy as well, but that was a matter of opportunism rather than an authentic political choice. Above all, the *ancien régime* began to absorb urban culture into the culture of the court. It was no longer urbanity which forged the values and norms, the tastes and styles of life of the bourgeoisie, but the courtly culture in the capital.[1] The bourgeoisie, in particular its higher echelons, modelled their life and culture increasingly after the culture of the palace of the absolutist king. The capital, and particularly the royal court, set the trend for bourgeois culture. This affected urbanity immensely.

The centralization of power towards a nation-state is, as we shall soon see, a complex and hard-to-grasp process. This volume on urbanity cannot, of course, pretend to cover it adequately. From the start, the intention of this volume has been to develop a general and systematic theory of urbanity, not to present a historical account of the rise and decline of cities and urban culture. Empirical historical data are used in order to arrive at a better understanding of this elusive phenomenon which we call "urbanity." For the sake of clarity, it will be necessary to identify, in an ideal-typical manner, some structural singularities of the centralization of power and some structurally distinct phases of development.

Admittedly, to the taste of most historians, such an ideal-typical approach is objectionable as it seems to testify to the state of mind of a *terrible simplificateur*. Yet, one of the basic characteristics of scientific work is the reduction of complexity, the drawing of lines of demarcation in a reality which is infinitely complex in its vast amount of data. In fact, it is rather senseless to merely collect data and record massive amounts of historical facts without trying to make sense out of them, to place them in a broader, more general theoretical frame of reference. The moment one sets out to accomplish the latter, one must draw some firm lines of demarcation.

In this chapter, I shall identify, without any pretention of historical preciseness, some stages in the process of centralization of power, and then relate them to the proper subject of this book: the development of urbanity as a civic and economic culture. We will, briefly, discuss the chaotic stage of post-Carolingian, feudal Europe in which decentralization of power was predominant. Prior to the tenth century, when cities began to emerge as centers of socioeconomic and political power, feudal houses were very busy fighting about territory and competing for dominance. This competition eventually led to the concentration of power within a few dominant houses. This concentration of power culminated in the dominance of one family exerting royal absolutist power in a nation-state with borders which had to be defended and preferably extended. This *ancien régime* of centralized absolutism came to an end in the eighteenth century (cf. the French Revolution) which led to a next stage—the democratic nation-state which competed with surrounding nation-states for hegemony—within Europe and, in terms of colonialism, within the world-at-large.

This stage lasted roughly until the first quarter of the twentieth century, when a structurally different type of centralization began to emerge: the welfare state. It had, as we shall see, its own effect upon cities and their urban culture. In the 1980s the development of centralization entered a new phase again: due to political and economic developments (end of the cold war, an increasingly global market, etc.) and to spectacular developments in (mainly electronic) technology (fax, personal computer and its networks, e-mail, etc.) the borders of the nation-state opened up and gave rise to an influential internationalization, or even globalization of these societies, and of their cities.

In these stages—(1) the initial feudal stage, (2) the absolutist *ancien régime*, (3) the democratic nation-state, (4) the interventionist welfare state, and (5) finally the international and open post-welfare state— cities and urbanity fared differently and experienced different fates. At all stages, there was an uneasy alliance between city and state, between urbanity and national culture.

## Europe at the Crossroads

Popular belief has it that the Roman Empire, internally weakened, collapsed under the onslaught of the Germanic tribes from the North. In fact, however, these tribes adjusted rather well to the culture and polity of the Romans, and were not the forces that brought this Mediterranean realm down. It was the spectacular and rapid emergence of Islam that in the seventh and eighth century put a definitive end to the remnants of the Roman Empire. The Islamic armies occupied the *mare nostrum* of the Romans, split up the East and the West which previously had entertained strong political bonds, commercial exchanges, and cultural ties. Above all, the Muslim onslaught put an end to most merchant activities of the Mediterranean ports—except Venice which managed to maintain its commercial exchanges, in particular with Byzantium. The result was that the balance of economic and political power switched to northern Europe, in particular to the northwest where the Carolingian empire succeeded the fragmented Merovingian state.[2]

Another popular, quite erroneous belief is that Charlemagne's empire took over the political lead of the Roman Empire, that it engendered a strong unified rule over a vast empire, and that it fostered a cultural renaissance, particular in letters and in law. In fact, this empire was economically and politically very weak. The sovereign's resources and budget, for instance, were not kept in order through levied taxes, as was still the case under the Merovingians, but wholly dependent on the revenues of the emperor's own domains, and on the tributes levied on conquered tribes. War booty was also a source of income, albeit partially, as most of it was used for the payment of the armed forces.[3]

As to the governance of this vast empire, there was no administration to speak of. Charlemagne had a small staff of administrators, mostly priests who combined their ecclesiastic duties with some administrative chores. As to the administration of his vast realm, the emperor depended heavily on noblemen who as envoys supervised the old and new territories.[4] These functionaries were not salaried adequately, since the royal budget did not allow for such expenses. They, therefore, had to collect their own revenues from the territories they supervised. This often came down to simple robberies and brutal extortions, a fraction of which would reach the imperial treasury.

A serious political drawback of this situation was the obvious dependence of the allegedly all-powerful emperor on his greatly independent functionaries who rose in economic strength and, above all, in power. This laid the foundation for the fragmentation and decentralization of the empire. The increasingly powerful feudal houses of counts and barons, located in often vast domains, soon began to compete with each other for economic power and political influence. This fierce competition concerned the possession of land, ever more land. Add to this Charlemagne's dependence on the bishops of the church, residing in cities that served as administrative centers, and the picture of political impotence is complete. This contributed, of course, to the rapid dissolution of the Carolingian empire after the death of Charlemagne.

If Pirenne emphasized the rather closed nature of this empire, since it lacked foreign markets and lived, in fact, in economic isolation,[5] Barraclough further argued that this weakly administrated realm could actually only thrive on wars of conquest and expansion. It was merely an expansion of territory, not a search for foreign markets. Consequently crisis set in when these conquests came to a halt:

> The unified structure of the Carolingian state, with counts and bishops spread far and wide and serving the king who was the keystone, was predicated upon success and conquest and expansion. Once conquest ceased, other factors came to the fore without delay, and shaped the course of events.[6]

Charlemagne's son, Louis the Pious, continued his father's reign and was unable to stem the downward spiral of the realm he inherited. But it was obvious that this vast, internally weakened empire could not remain intact. Louis tried initially to avoid partition of the realm but had to yield eventually to the unavoidable. In the Treaty of Verdun (A.D. 843), one son, Pippin, was set aside, and the empire was divided among Louis's three remaining sons: Lothar, Louis, and Charles. The title of emperor was maintained but actually lost most of its substance and meaning:

> Of the three brothers Charles (the son of Louis's second marriage) received the west, Louis (later known as Louis the German) the eastern provinces; the eldest son, Lothar, who already possessed the imperial title, received the belt of country running through the center, from the mouth of the Rhine down to the mountains of Switzerland and Burgundy, and then across the Alps to the Mediterranean coast cast from the mouth of the Rhône to Italy, and the whole of Lombardy and the Italian province. With the constitution of these three kingdoms a chapter of history was at an end: the Carolingian achievement, the vast territorial bloc which we call the "empire," had ceased to exist.[7]

But then disaster befell the partitioned Frankish empire which, paradoxically, contained the seeds of a promising future. This course of events in the ninth and tenth centuries, and not the Carolingian empire which belonged to the past, would shape the future of Europe. This is why Barraclough called these centuries, oft-neglected in historical scholarship, "the crucible of Europe".

On top of the internal tensions, caused by the necessity to set up administrative structures in conquered regions with their own institutions, traditions, and cultural identities, came the external pressure of various invasions. At the end of his reign, Charlemagne was confronted with them. But they would, after his death, roll over his internally weakened empire from all sides in recurrent waves: the *Vikings* from the North, the *Magyars* from the East, and the *Saracens* from the South.[8]

The consequences of these three waves of invasion which occurred simultaneously in the ninth and in most of the tenth centuries, were enormous. To begin with, the former Carolingian empire now broke down definitively into chaos and anarchy. The empire had been quite good in conquest but knew next to nothing about defense. There was no central authority that could coordinate the defense of the many, very long borders, and there were in fact no imperial armies who could do the military job effectively. Peasants in the country, citizens in the towns, and counts and barons in the castles were all on their own and quite mutually dependent upon each other.

This contributed to a penetrating feudalization and decentralization of society.[9] In exchange for military and other services to their lords in the manor or the castle, serfs would receive protection from their lords. In effect, they forfeited their liberty for some degree of security and certainty. These feudal bonds, as Bloch has emphasized, were not only legally, but often also emotionally, strong and therefore functioned as a rather solid defense mechanism against the recurrent onslaught of the invaders. Often castles and fortified cities were the havens to which people from the country would flee in the face of pillaging and murdering invaders. Obviously, these lords, who, again, were vassals to their king and received, when necessary, land and power in exchange for loyalty and service, developed into nodal points of decentralized power and influence. It stands to reason that they would compete among each other for more land and more power. In the end, of course, the few successful among them—as in any fierce competition, the survival of the fittest functioned unashamedly in the chaotic jungle of post-Carolingian, feudal society—would even compete with their sovereign.[10]

Eventually this competition would refoster centralizing tendencies which laid the foundations for the centralized absolutism of the *ancien régime*. But there is still another consequence of the invasions which is relevant to both cities and urbanity. Both Elias and Barraclough have argued convincingly that the Vikings from Denmark and Norway exerted the greatest and the longest lasting influence on Europe, in particular on England and Western Europe. As to mainland Europe, the territories most afflicted in the ninth and tenth centuries were Francia and Burgundy, by and large the kingdoms of Charles and Lothar. With their flexible boats and very skilled warring techniques these Vikings entered deeply into the river-mouths where they pillaged the merchant and fishing towns in particular.

Their hunting grounds covered the north of present Germany, the coasts of England, the coasts of Western Europe from today's Holland to today's Portugal; they even ventured into the Mediterranean, pillaging southern France and Italy. Most remarkable of all was the fact that they often settled in these areas, in particularly England and what came to be called Normandy. Like the Germanic tribes before which adjusted to Roman culture, these Viking settlers also adjusted themselves to local laws and customs, and at the same time contributed their own Nordic language and culture to the vernacular and the local civilization.

The plight of the cities was serious. Venice, located at the end of the Adriatic and protected by the laguna as a natural fortress, was spared severe attacks by the invaders. It therefore could take the lead when cities began to reemerge economically and politically after the tenth century. Others were less lucky. Duurstede, for example, located south of Utrecht, had intensive trade relations with Norwegian, Danish, and Baltic ports, but was destroyed by the Viking raiders so radically that it never recovered. Its leading function was soon taken over by Bruges, at the mouth of the Zwyn, which profited from the protection of the powerful counts of Flanders and managed to survive the Viking raids.[11]

Yet, these Norsemen changed during the tenth century. By then they had settled in England and Normandy, were masters over the seas surrounding Europe, and maybe simply tired of fighting and pillaging. In any case, they began to switch their activities to trade which began to flourish again in the tenth century. Merchants from Byzantium and Baghdad ventured north, and travelled with their goods through Russia passing Kiev and Novgorod along the way. The Norsemen became their main trading partners. They even established trading posts in Dublin, Hamburg, Schwerin, and on the island of Gotland, and thereby paved the way for the activities of the Hanseatic League.[12] It becomes apparent that the revival of the merchant cities and their international trading networks in northwestern Europe had been facilitated by their worst enemies, the Scandinavians.

### Feudal Competition and Gradual Recentralization

Once again we must revisit the fierce competition between the counts and barons of the post-Carolingian era, since it laid the foundation for a renewed centralization of power, and eventually to the rise of the nation-state. This recentralization had a profound impact on the cities and on urbanity again.

After the partition of the Carolingian empire and the subsequent anarchy of feudal society, attacked and pillaged by the Vikings, the Saracens and the Magyars, the history of Europe becomes extremely complex and hard to grasp. However, if we focus on the rise of the nation-state and thus on the powers that initiated a recentralization of power which eventually forged the map of Europe as we know it since several centuries, there is one fact that stands out and thus can be singled out as a trendsetting and structure-forging phenomenon. That phenomenon involves the fierce competition between the feudal lords in their extended families often possessing extensive territories, called counties and baronial estates. The old French concept *demesne* (domain) is also often used. Naturally, the king, in name, if not in actual fact, the highest feudal lord, had to compete again with the top of these competing lords who often would see possession of the throne as the final success of their competition.

One should bear in mind that this competition was not primarily about goods, services, and money, but about territory, about land. Theoretically, the king as highest lord of the realm, was the sole owner of all the land, but due to the radical decentralization discussed above, that idea was but a fiction. In exchange for loyalty and military service, kings had distributed considerable pieces of land as *fiefs* to their vassals, and since the days of Charlemagne, who could not afford to pay salaries to his *missi dominici*, it had become custom to be paid in natura, often with land—or, of course, to extort such "gifts." Thus, the domains of the counts and barons were their property, and they would do anything to enlarge them in order to enlarge their wealth and power.

Louis VI who reigned in Francia from 1108 till 1137, presents a perfect example of a king who was only lord of his lords in name. His revenues came from his own *demesne* and were rather sparse. Consequently, so was his actual royal power. He was, in fact, just a very large landowner in perpetual competition with his vassals, who constituted a kind of landed gentry. His main policy was to enlarge this domain which he did by warfare with any lord who would cross his path. Feudal lords, the *vassi dominici* of the sovereign, who for the same reasons waged incessant wars among each other, were one after the other divested of their land possessions, either partially or completely. Then instead of returning these portions of territory *in toto* as fiefs to his vassals, he added them to his own *demesne*. In this way, he enlarged his domain and his military power step by step.[13] If his successors would continue this policy of aggressive competition, the royal house would eventually hold the monopoly on a vast territory, and on considerable financial and military means of power. This is precisely what happened.

The dream of Louis VI was realized two centuries later. The House of Capet ruled over France, and actually encountered one formidable competitor to the throne. This competitor descended from the Norsemen, and plagued the Capetian sovereigns as in a nightmare: the House of Plantagenet, successor to the reign of William the Conqueror in England. It was claimed that the Plantagenets should reign in England from the capital, London, and in France from Paris. It led, as we know, to a long and weary war, lasting more than one hundred years, from 1337 till 1453.

In sum, this aggressive competition between feudal lords, and between feudal lords and the royal sovereign, produced reunified king-

doms that between the thirteenth and sixteenth centuries began to take
on the shape and content of true nation-states: administratively unified
territories with clear borders and some sort of national identity. France,
Germany, Spain, Italy, the Netherlands, and the Scandinavian countries were slowly born in this way. Not without strife and conflict, however, as the Netherlands in the sixteenth century and Italy as late as the
nineteenth century have demonstrated. It was far from a smooth evolution. There were, for instance, different degrees and structures of centralization—as the German nation (or nations) at the time demonstrated.
Yet, a distinct pattern emerges from all of this.

As we saw before, the cities reemerged as vital centers of trade,
craftsmanship, and vocational services. They were not afflicted by the
feudal wars of competition. On the contrary, they occupied the profitable position of a third party that can play off of the other two conflicting parties. The cities of Flanders, for instance, were successful in
making deals with the count of the region who marshalled their material and political support in his endless conflicts with lesser feudal lords.
But, at the same, they maintained their bonds with these lords. In exchange, the burghers received and maintained their political and economic liberty within the walls of their cities. Urbanity as a civic and
economic culture could prosper.

Yet, the recentralization discussed above carried a hidden danger
which eventually would pop up in all its brutality in the absolutism of
the *ancien régime*: the growing prominence, politically, economically,
and culturally of the capital, seat of an increasingly interventionist state.
That would, as we shall see next, exert a centrifugal energy on the
various cities in the nation-state, gradually rendering them subservient
politically, economically, and culturally to the interventionist state,
administered in the capital. The capital, as the central seat of the interventionist state, would grow in physical size and political influence.
Most other cities were reduced to provincial towns. Needless to add,
this was potentially detrimental to their urbanity which gradually would
lose much of its original vigor and vitality.

By the sixteenth century, absolutism had taken shape. It would become known as the *ancien régime*, and last until the eighteenth century.
The French Revolution marshalled its symbolic finale, but, as Tocqueville
observed, its decline had already set in long before 1789. We should
briefly look at this centralized, absolutist reign, and take into consider-
ation the peculiar position of cities, in particular vis-à-vis the capital
that, as heart of the nation, began to occupy a crucial position.

## Absolutism and the Tyranny of the Capital

Come the sixteenth century, Western Europe, in particular France and somewhat later England, had concluded the consolidation of central power. Nation-states began to emerge, ruled top-down from the capital by the increasingly absolutist sovereign who commanded over military power and financial resources. As to the latter, the discoveries of the Americas and the opening by force of many Asian countries, yielded prosperous resources. Not just gold, silver, and other precious metals, but also coffee, tea, and scores of spices would be shipped to European markets. At the same time these colonies presented profitable markets for European products. Mercantilist policies insured the royal households of the needed revenues—much needed because, now that the internal struggle with vassals had been concluded successfully, the nation's borders had to be defended and, whenever possible, extended. The seemingly endless rounds of wars between the European nation-states, all of them about territory and commercial interests and lasting deeply into the twentieth century, demanded, of course, large amounts of financial resources.

However, the most interesting part of this centralized absolutism was its social and cultural attraction. Whereas courtly society remained decentralized for a long period of time in countries like Italy and Germany and spread over various urban courts of local princes and bishops, in sixteenth-century Paris (after Francis I) and in seventeenth-century London (after Elizabeth I), the royal court and courtly life developed rapidly into a rather greedy center of societal and cultural energies. Elias analyzed it as a specific institution—*die höfische Gesellschaft*, Courtly Society.[14]

Sombart has argued that the papal courts first in Avignon and then in Rome were the first to develop into courtly societies. They unashamedly exhibited their splendor and wealth and attracted men and women of distinction—military men, intellectual men, artists of sorts. The court of the Roman pope functioned after the fifteenth century as model for the princes and bishops in the Italian city-states, but had a decisive influence beyond Italy on other European courts as well. Here we witness for the first time, Sombart argued, the decline of feudal knighthood, the urbanization of nobility, the formation of the absolutist state, the renaissance of the arts and sciences, the prominence of social talents, the growth of wealth and material prosperity—all of them components of the absolutist courtly society of post-sixteenth-century Europe.[15]

Sombart emphasized in particular the blatant luxury of these courts, consumed by the wealthy who would look down upon any sort of work or labor. They indulged in leisure and conspicuous consumption. He characterized them aptly, and in an ironic mix of languages, as the *"Homo novus der City."*[16] One should add, that the courtiers in this Courtly Society were increasingly exposed to a deep sense of ennui— a penetrating, often rather melancholic sense of boredom, bred by a powerlessness that was imposed on them by the absolutist throne.[17]

The culture of Courtly Society trickled down into the urban bourgeoisie. This was facilitated by the simple fact that nobility and bourgeoisie needed each other direly: in exchange for its high social esteem and political influence the members of the noble estate coveted the often massive wealth of the third, bourgeois estate. In England wealthy merchants or bankers were often ennobled, in France the old *noblesse d'épée* faced the fact that more and more members of the wealthy bourgeoisie were promoted into a new class of nobles, the *noblesse de robe*.

The most usual intermingling of nobility and bourgeoisie, however, happened by means of inter-estate marriage. If a daughter of a wealthy merchant married the son of a respectable noble family, she would be automatically included in the noble estate. But, more importantly, through her the grandchildren of the bourgeois merchant and all their descendants would then be noble by birth. Status was thus exchanged for money. If the finances of her parents demanded it, the marriage of a noble daughter to the son of a wealthy bourgeois family did also occur, but, in that case, of course, the descendants were lost for the noble estate.[18]

Naturally, the opportunities of the wealthy bourgeoisie to ascend to the circles of nobility were limited. This was, however, compensated by a kind of semi-nobility that began to develop within the third estate. In particular, the upper-middle-class merchants and professionals who often occupied influential positions in the government of their city, became known as the urban *patriciat*. In Germany they were called *consules*, urban consuls who commanded not only a considerable amount of influence but also bore great prestige and esteem. In England there was the *gentry* which was not quite noble but more than plainly bourgeois. In the city, a member of the gentry was more than just merchant or banker. He was a Gentleman. This pertained in particular to high-ranking people in the world of banking and high finances. This urban *patriciate*, consisting of a limited number of families, formed the core of the urban power elite.

Often, successful merchants, who had retired from their business and were enjoying much leisure time, would delve into the city archives in search of a glorious heraldic past. Daniel Defoe (1659–1731), the astute sociological observer of his day, made fun of these Gentlemen engaged in the science of heraldry:

> We see the tradesmen of England, as they grow wealthy, coming every day to the herald's office, to search for the coats of arms of their ancestors, in order to paint them upon their coaches, and engrave them upon their plate, embroider them upon their furniture, or carve them upon the pediments of their new houses.... In this search we find them often qualified to raise new families, if they do not descend from old; as was said of a certain tradesman of London, that if he could not find the ancient race of gentlemen, from which he came, he would begin a new race, who should be as good gentlemen as any that want before him.[19]

As to urbanity, this development is, of course, detrimental to the economic and civic culture of absolutist capitals, and of the surrounding towns and cities as well, since they modelled their societal and cultural lives after the Courtly Society in the capital. The luxurious consumption, the boredom of leisure, and the pervasive lack of power and real influence condemned most of these people to an idleness that was at odds with civic participation and economic activities.

## Nationalism, Militarism, and Urbanity

It must be said once more that the process of centralization in Europe differed from country to country in its speed, extensiveness, and intensity. Yet, the process had a basic structure. Reinhard Bendix corroborates this, when he writes: "Western European societies have been transformed from the estate societies of the Middle Ages to the absolutist regimes of the eighteenth century and thence to the class societies of plebiscitarian democracy in the nation-states of the twentieth century."[20] It is, however, as we have seen, in France's history in particular, that one can observe this process of structural change as through a magnifying glass. One ought to bear in mind also that in this chapter we try to analyze the wider political context of the developments in European cities and their urbanity. The modernization of the latter, as discussed in the previous chapter, can, of course, not be isolated from the political developments examined presently.

Tocqueville's structural analyses of the birth of the French Revolution are, despite their age, crucial for an understanding of the centralizing processes which carried fateful consequences for cities and their economic and civic culture.[21] To begin with, the centralization of power in the capital with its centripetal culture that absorbed great amounts of creative energy, was, as Tocqueville observed, detrimental to the cities, large or small, in the country. But Tocqueville simultaneously realized that centralization affected the civil society adversely. It weakened intermediary structures with the result that individualized citizens, anxiously guarding their private interests, were now confronted by abstract, bureaucratic powers which in their turn, through regulations and scores of legal restrictions, guarded the public realm and its interests. This fateful disjunction of the private and the public gave, after the violent demise of *ancien régime* absolutism, rise to a plebiscitarian democracy based primarily on equality, not liberty. It yielded, according to Tocqueville, a democratic tyranny that ruled over individualized citizens with care and softness. We return to this in an instant.

Political representation was, up to the French Revolution, shaped by the feudal estates, and thus collective by nature. After the revolution, representation was no longer collective but individual: individual citizens, not estates, had the right to vote. This equality, as we know, was initially a very restricted one. Scores of individuals were excluded from the political rights. It took women and the lower strata of society, in particular, a long time to gain unlimited franchise. Yet, the principle was clear: not collectivities but individuals were, from now on, the political units of the democratic system. In fact, they were not really citizens, but rather subjects. And they were subjected to a relatively new phenomenon: the nation-state.

It is not easy to construct a clear definition of the nation-state. As we have seen above, nations began to emerge from various tribes and ethnic groups in the Middle Ages, in particular within the Carolingian empire. It took, however, quite some time and many wars and battles, before the present European nations crystallized and established their present borders.

As arbitrary as this may be, I define a nation as a collectivity of human beings who, within a specific territory, share and acknowledge a common past, and who maintain common values, norms, and meanings, expressed in myths, legends, rituals, and artistic expressions. This shared culture gives them a collective identity. Thus, nation as a focus of loyalty, solidarity, and identity, competes with older foci, such as the clan, the estate, or the caste. It also competes strongly with the city and its urbanity. In fact, the nation and nationalism superseded the city and urbanity ever more strongly in the nineteenth and twentieth centuries.

The state can then be defined as the public and legal (constitutional) authority which possesses the monopoly of coercion and extraction, and functions as the dominant administrative institution, differentiated by and independent of organizations such as schools, universities, the army, the unions, voluntary associations, and so on. State-formation, as we have seen, began in the Middle Ages, and came into full swing in the *ancien régime*. After the French Revolution, in particular, nations developed into nation-states with more or less fixed borders and clearly defined rules as to rights and obligations of citizens.[22]

Due to the rise of the nation-state and the centralization of power in the capital, urbanity as an economic and civic culture was succeeded gradually by *nationalism* orchestrated from the capital. In most analyses of nationalism this evolution of solidarity and identification from clan, estate, and caste to urbanity and then to nationalism is not noticed and acknowledged. The peculiar type of urban solidarity which was, as we have seen, rather rational and which combined localism and cosmopolitanism, was now transcended by a type of solidarity which in its inner core was not rational at all. It carried premodern, atavistic notions and was obsessed by the idea that the "sacred" soil and borders of the nation-state had to be defended. This was, of course, acerbated when the notion of "nation" was defined in terms of collective blood-ties, as in the notion of *Volk* and even more fatal in the notion of an allegedly superior *race*.

This is not the place to define and discuss nationalism. It is viewed here as the ideology which puts the nation-state on a pedestal and tries to subordinate all sentiments and actions of loyalty, solidarity, and identity to it. Isaiah Berlin characterized nationalism, based upon Friedrich Schiller's simile, as a bent twig. People who have been subjected collectively to humiliations and degradations develop a sense of national pride and dignity. If systematized and organized into a powerful movement, nationalism may function as the bent twig which may eventually swing back and hit the tormentor. In this sense, Berlin argues, nationalism is indispensable for decolonization and any similar movement of national emancipation.[23]

Naturally, nationalism generally eschews pacifism, especially when the borders of the nation-state and the society within it are threatened, or believed to be under threat. Militarism is in that case the companion of nationalism. The territory of the nation and the borders around it, have to be defended by means of military might. It stands to reason that a less defensive attitude may soon have the upper hand: the extension of the territory—the fateful *Lebensraum* of the Germans, for instance—has been at the forefront of many politicians' minds in the capitals of Europe in the nineteenth and twentieth centuries.[24]

Nationalism and militarism thus functioned as the emotional nutrition and the moral legitimation of a nearly endless string of aggressive international wars—from the post-revolutionary battles of Napoleon to the two world wars of the twentieth century. These wars grew steadily in size and impact, until the limit of total annihilation of the globe was reached during the decennia that followed the Second World War.

All this stands in contrast to cities and their urbanity. One should, as I have emphasized, not romanticize the economic and civic culture of cities. Cities have fought wars in the defense of market interests, or for the enlargement of their market shares. The perpetual strife, and even war, between Lübeck and Denmark are telling examples of this. And cities did support their own nation-state if it would conduct war on powerful competitors, thereby defending or even enlarging their markets. Yet, unlike nation-states, cities have always prospered most in times of peace. Merchants, craftsmen, lawyers, and bankers have at all times been aware of the fact that their private and public interests and welfare were served best by deals, contracts, and compromises, not by wars and battles. That is precisely their functional rationality which we discussed before. Thus, if urbanity was not precisely pacifistic, it was, unlike nationalism, generally averse to belligerence and militarism.

In that respect, the decline of cities and urbanity due to the rise of centralized power whose culture was nationalistic and militaristic, may have contributed much to the fatal wars that have ravaged Europe in the last two centuries. The Second World War in particular witnessed the often total destruction of cities. Dresden, but also many other German cities, Hiroshima and Nagasaki, and recently Bosnia Mosztar and Sarajevo stand out as prime examples of this brand of *urbicide*. Yet, as to centralization, Europe seems to be at the crossroads again. As I shall argue later, the decentralization that began recently in Western Europe may herald the end of a period, which began with the French Revolution and ran up till the 1980s. In the near future Europe may indeed be more a continent of regions and cities (or urban regions) than of nation-states. Yet, as always, Europe is ambiguous in this as well. As developments in Central and Eastern Europe after the revolution of 1989 have demonstrated, decentralization may lead societies into chaos marked by scores of fragmented nationalisms and spurred on by old-fashioned militarism and atavistic feelings of superiority. The events in former Yugoslavia testify to this in a disquieting manner. (Note how, in this unhappy region, genocide has been accompanied by urbicide!) On the other hand, in Western Europe the gradual extension of the European Union may also counteract decentralization and establish a Kafkaesque supersovereignty in Brussels with an all-embracing and suffocating bureaucracy. This too, needless to add, would be detrimental to cities and their urbanity.

Or will Europe manage to rationally combine a certain degree of administrative centralization with various forms of decentralization of power? The role of cities in this process may well be crucial. But then, this role can only be crucial if cities possess a strong and vital urbanity. They can only function economically and politically as powerful units if they exhibit a contemporary type of economic and civic culture. Obviously, a return to the culture of the Hanseatic League is not possible. One never returns to the past successfully. Yet, it should not be forgotten that this urban league did in fact represent a kind of unified European market. Its cities were indeed the nodal points of an early European community that transcended national and regional borders. In that respect, the Hanseatic League may function as an inspiring historical example. Eurocities should occupy a similar strategic economic and political position, if the European Union is to be politically, economically, and socioculturally viable.

But we are way ahead of our argument now. First we will have to remain focused upon a structurally specific form of the nation-state which emerged in the wake of industrialization in the nineteenth century and received its final shape and contents in the twentieth century, particularly in the decades after the Second World War. That is, the nation-state developed into a *welfare state*. Again, there are, of course, many vast national differences, particularly in the extensiveness and intensity of the welfare state. Yet, here too we may discern some basic structural characteristics which, as if viewed through a magnifying glass, are exhibited most clearly by the countries of northwestern Europe, particularly the Scandinavian countries and the Netherlands. However, this is not the place to take these specificities into account. Needless to say, the welfare state is discussed here in view of the changing position of the city and its urbanity.

## Modernity and the Welfare State

We may safely assume that the caring for fellow human beings— infants first and foremost, but also the elderly, the sick, the indigent, and the handicapped—has been a task that people living together have, in most societies, inaugurated themselves albeit in different gradations of intensity and various organizational configurations. In the Western world, we may even find a certain structural development in this care: roughly speaking, from nuclear and extended families to larger associations such as the church, the neighborhood, vocational associations (e.g., guilds), societal voluntary associations (e.g., the British Friendly Societies), and then, in this century, to the welfare state. That is, the gradual centralization towards the nation-state entailed a similar centralization that could be found in the caring activities of organizations. Many voluntary and urban initiatives of charity were, in the end, taken over by the bureaucracies of the welfare state and the related professionals in the world of welfare.

In this centralization and professionalization of welfare a gradual transformation took place from *charity* as a care-as-favor, for which the receiver had to be grateful and from which the provider drew a sense of religious and moral satisfaction, to *welfare-as-right*, that is, as a social right, as a constitutive part of modern citizenship. Such welfare can be demanded by every citizen of the nation-state without any moral obligations attached to it.

T. H. Marshall's by now classic evolutionary theorem of citizenship springs to mind. During the last three centuries, Marshall argued, citizenship has developed along the lines of distinct stages. It began in the eighteenth century with the emergence of *civil rights*, such as freedom of speech, the right to possessions, and the right to draw up contracts: rights necessary for individual freedom. The nineteenth century saw the development of *political rights*, in particular the passive and active franchise, based upon democratic institutions especially the three separate and autonomous powers. These rights enable the citizen to participate fully in democracy. The twentieth century witnessed the emergence of *social rights* which, in Marshall's words, cover "the whole range from the right to a modicum of economic welfare and security to the right to share to the full in the social heritage and to live the life of a civilized being according to the standards prevailing in society."[25]

This rationalization of care is at the same time a professionalization. Care-as-favor is charity produced by well-intentioned, religiously or humanistically inspired amateurs. Care-as-right in the context of a welfare state is performed by persons who have been trained and educated for the job and for which they are remunerated formally. Their caring profession may give them moral satisfaction, but it is not primarily the moral surplus-value these professionals are after, but social influence and political power, in particular. Power and professionalism go hand in hand.[26] A centralized government is crucial to the interests of these professionals, who therefore ought to be viewed as influential proponents of a strong, centralized, extensive and intensive welfare state. This point is important, in view of the main argument that the centralization of political power is quite detrimental to the development of cities and urbanity.

The concept of the welfare state can be used both in the broad sense and in a much narrower, strictly legal and policy-related sense. In the latter, the welfare state refers exclusively to welfare-oriented social legislation and its enactment by specialized welfare agencies. Social security in particular is the essence of the welfare state in this restricted sense. In the broader sense the welfare state is, beyond the formal-legal dimension, a special and specific type of polity, economy, society, and culture. Welfare state in the broad sense is viewed as a comprehensive configuration which typifies a nation-state as a whole.

The concept of welfare state is used here in the broad meaning of the word. The present discussion pertains to the northwestern European welfare state, in particular as it developed intensively and extensively in the Netherlands. Here the welfare state can be seen, as it were, through a magnifying glass. Yet, the basic structural characteristics can also be witnessed in less-developed welfare states, such as the one in the United States.[27] Once more, like Sweden, the Netherlands presents the case of a welfare state with a virtually laboratory-like type of clarity. That is, the basic socioeconomic dimensions and cultural contours of the welfare state as a societal type were uncommonly clear here. This was, I should add hastily, the case up until the 1980s. In that decade a rather radical transformation of the Dutch welfare state set in—a process, incidentally, that has affected Sweden, and all the other welfare states, also.

## The Welfare State and Culture

In terms of polity, the welfare state knows an advanced degree of centralization of power which is concentrated within the state bureaucracies of the capital. The administration and certainly the distribution of welfare to clients are more often than not decentralized to the local communities, yet the final decisions as to the extensiveness and the intensity of welfare provisions are solidly centralized, as are the decisions pertaining to the financing of the system.

Economically, the welfare state presents a mixed economy in that it remains capitalistic and market-oriented, yet imposes rather heavy governmental restrictions on market functions for the sake of the common welfare of the nation. The history of welfare states has demonstrated that it has been very hard to maintain a workable balance between state intervention and freedom of the market. The public sector testified time and again to its inherent tendency to control and even hamper the private sector. Much of this interference, incidentally, was triggered by the desire of the private sector to attract as much state subsidies as possible. This could be observed in education and health care, but also in agriculture, industry, and the service sector.

In terms of society, the welfare state is characterized by an advanced degree of individualization and particularism in which social bonds between citizens present flexible, functional networks rather than strongly institutionalized and traditional roles and relationships. Citizens are bureaucratically labelled as welfare recipients and clients of the welfare system—categorized and thus depersonalized. It is a far-reaching bureaucratization of citizenship in which, paradoxically, Marshall's social rights are circumscribed and officially treated as strictly individual rights.

Moreover, many nonprofit organizations are legally and formally autonomous, yet dependent heavily, in actual fact, on governmental subsidies. As a consequence, governmental, bureaucratic control and regulation increased proportionately. In addition, as we have seen above, the professionals working in these organizations, are state-oriented and view the recipients of welfare primarily as the clients of their rationalized distribution of care and welfare. Society, in other words, is individualized considerably, but its organizations function, even if they are legally independent and autonomous, as extensions of the centralized state. Indeed, Durkheim's warning springs to mind: a society with an overbearing state and strongly individualized citizens is liable to weaken severely the intermediary structures and thereby foster *anomie*. Durkheim called such a society a *monstruosité sociologique!*[28]

In terms of culture, the values, norms, and meanings of the welfare state are usually very modern, and therefore general, vague, and abstract. In fact, the most essential values of the system are rather "thin": efficiency and effectiveness—values believed to be easily quantifiable in statistical terms. Such a predominantly quantitative and functional-rational culture leaves much room for a peculiar type of ethos to be discussed further instantly.

Scores of books and articles have been devoted to the welfare state. The bulk of it is rather one-sided in style and substance, strongly economical, predominantly quantitative-statistical, and policy oriented. Generally, the cultural, historical, and qualitative dimensions remain largely unexposed. They will be over-accentuated on purpose here.[29]

From a cultural-sociological point of view, the remarkable thing about the welfare state is that it lacks a clear and distinctive ideological foundation. As Harold Wilensky argued, the welfare state is essentially a functionally rational technostructure with different degrees of intensity and extensiveness—some societies are far ahead, others lag behind. These differences in pace and scope depend, according to Wilensky, mainly on cultural factors which he terms "ideological roots."[30] The emergence of a welfare state, however, is, according to Wilensky, usually not ideologically motivated. The distributive technostructure which the welfare state essentially is according to Wilensky, will inevitably emerge when a society begins to develop. In the case of a successful development, the demographic composition of a society will begin to change. Due to improved healthcare and other factors a well-developed society will inevitably be subjected to a progressive "greying" of its population. As a result, state interventions as to sufficient welfare arrangements for the elderly become inevitable. And indeed, in most postwar developing nation-states the welfare state began with social security provisions for senior citizens.

Other programs of social welfare and security will usually follow care for the elderly—in particular in the areas of health and education, soon followed by other sectors such as the arts and sports and leisure—depending, that is, on the extensiveness and intensity that one allows the welfare state to attain. When its scope and range of activities have been broadened to such an extent, the welfare state is, of course, much more than a "value-free" and ideologically "neutral" technostructure of distribution. It has indeed become a type of society and culture which is in fact identical to the nation-state. In other words, the nation-state is in essence a welfare state. This happened in most Western European societies and to a much lesser degree in most of the American states.

Here again centralization is at the core of this type of society and polity. In a welfare state, there is an inner drive to accomplish scores of interventions. While it tries to encompass all the dimensions of human life, the welfare state becomes intensive and extensive—and, needless to add, extraordinarily bureaucratic and expensive. Officials in the state bureaucracies and professionals in the various organizations of civil society (schools, universities, hospitals, scores of voluntary organizations, sporting clubs, leisure clubs, etc.) have, of course, a vested interest in this interventionist state, in its maintenance and further expansion. As a result, civil society develops step by step into an extension of the welfare-spending state. Without any absolutist or totalitarian intentions, society and state merge into an undifferentiated mass.

## An Elective Affinity

As Durkheim, among others, argued, a society could not function and survive for long, if a minimal degree of consensus and solidarity were absent. The welfare state could not really perdure, if it were a mere distributive technostructure devoid of any worldview and ethos which contained the basic values, norms, and practical orientations that keep people and their actions together. Without it, a society would eventually plunge into the terror of anomie. Thus, we must address the question as to what precisely the worldview and ethos of a welfare state is, or could be.

Clifford Geertz handsomely defined, as we saw before, the concept of worldview as a set of ideas and theories which express "the assumed structure of reality." A worldview, formerly religious and/or magical, today predominantly scientific and/or technological, contains more or less systematic ideas about an alleged order of nature, society, and history. An ethos is closely tied to a worldview. It indicates how people, within the context of a wordlview, ought to behave morally, how reality is to be experienced emotionally, what kind of aesthetic lifestyle one is supposed to adhere to. In short, an ethos exemplifies "the approved style of life".[31] We might add that an ideology is a worldview-and-ethos in Geertz's sense of the word, but also one that expresses and defends the particular political and material interests of a group. The ideology also legitimizes the actions and ideas of the members of the group in terms of their political and material interests.

Prior to the emergence of the modern welfare state, a historical worldview-and-ethos had been in existence in Europe which unintendedly fit this "value-free" and "neutral" system of welfare arrangements perfectly. It provided the welfare state with its much needed ideological legitimation. In Weberian terms, one could call it an *elective affinity* comparable to the one existing between the Puritan ethic and the spirit of capitalism. This worldview-and-ethos to be discussed in a moment, has helped to ideologically undergird the welfare state which lacks an intrinsic ideology of its own. This has been of great importance to the stability of the welfare state in Western European countries.

I shall sketch next, in broad outlines, this worldview-and-ethos not generated by the welfare state which is, in itself, a value-neutral, technostructure, yet which did demonstrate an unintended elective affinity with it. I shall then compare and contrast it with the worldview-and-ethos of urbanity.

## Worldview of the Welfare State

Policymakers and ideologues of the welfare state—bureaucrats, care professionals, social scientists, politicians, in short, the New Class[32]—have generally testified to an unbridled trust in science and technology. Just as preindustrial people tried to interpret the world and solve the incumbent problems by turning to religion and magic, to priests and magicians, modern people, in particular those at the helm of the welfare state, have turned to science and technology, particularly social science and techniques of social engineering, in a semi-religious fashion. For them, science and technology functioned as a "true" worldview, a kind of secular religion. In fact, scientism and technocracy were the cornerstones of this religion.

*Scientism* and *technocracy* were, for instance, apparent in the trust policymakers generally invested in econometric models of forecasting, and decision making. They were the allegedly solid cornerstones of a truly rational and interventionist policy. Underlying all of this is the conviction that science yields precision, even in policy and politics, and that statistics guarantee the much needed and desired exactness and precision. Both science and statistics render, it is believed, policy and politics efficient, effective, and manipulative. It is needless to add then that they are indispensable to an interventionist state like the welfare state.

Within the New Class the old debate between science and the humanities had been decided in favor of the former (even though it had demonstrable flaws) when it came to an explanation of human actions and interactions, of values, norms, and meanings. Like science, statistics have without doubt advanced our objective knowledge of reality and our capacity to intervene in reality. Yet, we all know that in the real world statistics often serve the hidden agenda of covering up motives and intentions, or legitimating errors of judgment, gaps in knowledge, and inabilities to act or react adequately. In any case, scientism and technocracy served the interventionist purposes of the welfare state well.

Obviously, however, scientism and technocracy have not been generated by the welfare state. On the contrary, they existed long before the emergence of the welfare state. Their theoretical and philosophical origins must be retraced to the eighteenth century. The Enlightenment gave birth to the dream of a steady progress of humanity through scientific precision and technological skill and ingenuity. After the dismissal of religion and magic, Rational Man, the Enlightenment believed, would finally be able to make, to construct, and to further develop reality in all its dimensions—nature, society, culture, and even history (in particular, of course, as in planning, the future). One of the basic Enlightenment doctrines is indeed what the German philosopher and sociologist Hans Freyer has called the "Machbarkeit der Sachen"— that is, the ability to make, to construct reality.[33]

This philosophy stood, of course, in good stead of any interventionist state. It was embraced by absolutist monarchs who from then on were dubbed "enlightened princes," and it served the purposes of the centralized welfare state. Enlightenment rationalism had become somewhat stale at the end of the nineteenth and the beginning of the twentieth century. But it got, so to say, a new lease on life under the regime of the welfare state during the decades after the Second World War. This functionally rational technostructure, this bureaucratic system of distribution of wealth and welfare, that lacked any ideology of its own, adopted, with often visible and audible eagerness, Enlightenment scientism and its concomitant technocracy as its guiding worldview.[34]

Rational planning and bureaucratic organization functioned as the cornerstones of this worldview. It was believed that the allegedly equal distribution of the wealth of the nation and of the various services dispensed by the welfare state, could only be conducted in a just manner, if it were organized in a formalized, unprejudiced, and socioeconomically equal manner. Bureaucratic organization, founded upon scientific principles of public administration, was believed to be the supreme instrument of such a just distribution. Although almost all political parties cooperated in the establishment of the welfare state (it was not the result of an exclusively socialist policy, and capitalism remained a crucial component of its mixed economy), scientism and technocracy were paired to an explicitly egalitarian bent. [35]

The basic tenets of the scientific principles involved were, in general, solidly (neo-)positivistic and behavioristic. The institutional dimensions, like traditional (historically grown) values, norms, and meanings, expressed by customs, folklores, rituals, legends and myths, were usually neglected deliberately—if they were not treated with contempt, as they were allegedly not measurable in a quantitative manner and resisted the almost instinctive urge to build models.

While bureaucratic organization would offer the policymakers and the professionals of the welfare state an instrument through which civil society could be controlled in an interventionist manner, planning developed rapidly into the main instrument by which even the future could be put under rational control—or, so it was believed. Socioeconomic and cultural planning bureaus were set up in order to assist the centralized state in its interventionist task.

It has often been said that the welfare state should be seen and understood as the "progressive," "anti-conservative" prodigy of both liberalism and socialism. This rather facile conclusion, adhered to by both progressive and conservative circles stands in need of revision. In fact, it was Enlightenment positivism with its conservative technocratic and scientistic bent and lesser progressive liberalism and socialism, that was taken up by the New Class protagonists and gatekeepers of the welfare state. One should not be misled here by the anti-positivist and self-proclaimed "left" movement of the 1960s. This was but a short interlude, the ideological contents of which were absorbed and neutralized by the welfare state that expanded rapidly in the 1960s and 1970s.[36] The welfare state managed successfully to incorporate both the socialist emphasis on equality and the liberalist emphasis on individual autonomy and liberty. What remained was an abstract technostructure in which only the numbers game seemed to guarantee efficiency and effectiveness.

It stands to reason that the representatives of the various social sciences, vanguard of the New Class, began to occupy influential positions within this emerging welfare state. The (often self-styled) "left" or progressive, socioscientifically trained rebels of the "babyboomer generation" had been the vanguard of the so-called cultural revolution of 1968. They could have it both ways under the regime of the welfare state: liberal individualism (only very few aspired communist collectivism) and socialist egalitarianism (only very few called for a continuation of class-based inequality). Naturally, they had to come to terms ideologically with the often "right" or conservative positivism inherent to the scientific and technocratic bent of the welfare state. Since the *Positivismusstreit*—the positivism dispute, as it was called in German academia[37]—was full of highly complex philosophical and methodological problems, most members of the New Class decided to stay at the surface of intellectual problems and paid lip service to the basic tenets of the so-called Critical Theory which was hatched in the *Frankfurter Schule*. But having left the university, most of them occupied influential positions in the welfare state. There they were coerced, so to say, to embrace the basic tenets of the (neo)-positivist worldview of the welfare state. Critical Theory—or whatever had trickled down from it—served their progressive conscience, while positivist organizational theory and one-dimensional planning procedures, undergirded by positivist methods and techniques of research, did the rest.[38]

In the 1980s when the waning of the welfare state set in, many members of the New Class had few scruples to abandon the New Left radical stance of their younger days. The hidden technocrats they always had been came to the forefront and applauded processes of privatization and the enlargement of the freedom of the market. They were, in many instances, the first to dismantle the welfare state. To many of them, capitalism was then no longer a morally despicable phenomenon.

## Ethos of the Welfare State

Long before the modern welfare state emerged, the poor, the sick, orphans and widows, the elderly, and the unemployed and unemployable were generally kept on the fringes of society, where they were met with compassion and charity on the part of (usually religiously motivated) individuals and voluntary organizations.[39] As to the latter, since roughly the sixteenth century people began to insure themselves against the unpredictable odds of life, such as illness, disability, and death, through funds that were often related to occupational groups. The British Friendly Societies present a good example. However, it was actually not before the end of the last century that under the pressures of the workers' movement the idea of a *structural* improvement of people's socioeconomic position and the related idea of a structural, state-approved, and assured social security, health care, and education, emerged.

When Mother Teresa received the Nobel Peace Prize for her charitable work in Calcutta, she said in a televised interview that we ought to thank God for the presence of the very poor in this world, because they are the symbol of Christ's humbleness and meaningful targets of our charity and neighborly love. To an inhabitant of a fully modernized welfare state the ethos expressed by these words is incomprehensible. It is as if they descend upon us from a strange world—a world not yet modernized. Apparently, Mother Teresa lives in a world in which welfare and care are still exclusively matters of a religious calling, components of a morally satisfying charity—not components of a social right, not components of citizenship.

After one has become accustomed to welfare and care as a social right, one will not only demand their just and efficient distribution by the state, but also more of it. The services in the areas of social security, health care, education, the arts, etc., offered under the supervision of the state and with main funding by the state, will be consumed not only thoughtlessly, as in a taken-for-granted manner, but also ever more abundantly. Gradually, the fact that somehow all of this has to be financed publicly, is forgotten, while the increasingly heavy burden of progressive taxation is not consciously linked to these public expenses. Due to the complexity of a modern welfare state, it is hard for the average citizen to see a causal connection between the abundant consumption of welfare services on the one hand, and the mounting pressures of state taxation on the other.

The latter is important because it entails a gradual weakening of solidarity, which in origin was the moral cornerstone of the welfare state. The welfare state was based originally on the idea of a proportionate sharing of the public expenses caused by the various welfare programs. Gradually, however, the concrete link between these services on the one hand, and progressive taxation and other financial burdens on the other faded away and was eventually lost from sight. Solidarity—this Durkheimian mortar that keeps society together—became an increasingly hollow concept in the argot of welfare state politicians and policymakers. This was a profound change of ethos.

One should also bear in mind that these social rights were couched in an increasingly more complex network of bureaucratic rules and regulations. Without knowledge and information about all this, many people, in particular the socially and economically most disadvantaged, did not actually receive from the welfare state what they were entitled to. In fact, it was in general the relatively well-to-do middle-classes who knew the ropes of the welfare state, and thus received a bigger share of its benefits. (In the Netherlands there were allegedly people who had specialized in subsidies—where to find them, how to get them, what the legal loopholes were, and so on. They were called facetiously "subsidiologists.")

However, the taken-for-granted and thoughtless consumption of the social securities were not restricted to the services proper of the welfare state. Consumption is, in modernity and certainly within the welfare state, a general attitude and mentality, a kind of ethos. This ethos of consumption stands, of course, in sharp contrast to the work ethic of urbanity and Puritanism.[40] Let us briefly reflect upon it further.

A welfare state can, of course, only be erected in a society that has reached a certain level of material wealth. In affluent countries with state-guaranteed social security, labor is no longer viewed and experienced as the primary and indispensable production of means of existence. Automatization, informatization, and other technological developments have contributed to the situation, in which work is no longer the most crucial factor of life. As demoralizing as unemployment is, it can, due to the welfare state, no longer reduce human life to severe hardship and degrading dependency. This contributed also to a gradual shift of emphasis from production to consumption, from a work ethic to an ethos of consumption.

In this sociocultural and socioeconomic configuration, not only the provisions and services of the welfare state, but also luxury goods, human relations (marriages, friendships), and ideas and theories (religious and/or political ideologies) are consumed and evaluated in terms of personal and individual satisfaction, rather than in terms of public and collective quality and value. If a commodity, a relationship, an idea, ideology, or theory does no longer satisfy emotionally, if one gets bored with it, it is usually disposed of summarily, or exchanged for another commodity, relationship, idea, ideology, or theory.

As a result, there are rapidly changing trends and lifestyles, usually consumed for a while, disposed of and, if the desire arises, exchanged for others. Indeed, this is a throwaway and highly flexible culture. Not just material objects and goods, but also relationships, ideas, ideologies, and theories are subjected to it. Not traditional institutions, such as the family, the church, and the neighborhood enduring the passage of time, surviving many successive generations; but flexible, lowly institutionalized networks are the new patterns, into which this throwaway culture is molded.

The morality aspect of all of this is important. In a society in which labor and productivity still belong to the primary conditions of life, the responsibility of the individual vis-à-vis his fellowmen and vis-à-vis society as a whole still plays a dominant role. This changes rather radically in a comprehensive, bureaucratically organized welfare state. In such a context, responsibility is easily referred to formal and abstract (and thus nonresponsive and nonresponsible) bodies. In fact, responsibility itself has the tendency to generalize and become abstract. It is then no longer the direct and concrete milieu of the family, the neighborhood, or the community, but abstract social and political entities, such as the "environment," or the "Third World," one feels responsible for and committed to. Issues as the sinister fate of political prisoners in far away countries, or that of the bludgeoned baby seals of Nova Scotia appeal to an abstract sense of responsibility and commitment which, incidentally, is not rational and cognitive but, on the contrary, very emotional and intuitive. Arnold Gehlen called it a "hyper-morality." His colleague Helmuth Schelsky spoke of "borrowed misery": affluence and welfare have, to a great extent, done away with misery in Western societies with the result that it has to be "borrowed" from less fortunate, Third World countries. The mass media present this misery directly and semi-concretely in every Western living room.[41]

If the responsibility in this ethos is rather abstract, its concomitant commitment is usually rather thin. One is willing to join a movement by signing a petition but very hesitant when it comes to joining an organization actively and for a longer period of time, let alone a lifetime. One is generally religiously and politically involved, but not prepared to join a church or a political party. Abstract responsibility yields lose commitments.

Naturally, various traditional values lose their validity and legitimacy. Loyalty, trust, and honor, for example, are, in a well-developed welfare state, old-fashioned values. They still do exist but in an abstract, rationalized manner. They have been neutralized, so to say, through legal arrangements. If one's sense of honor has been injured, modern man threatens the offender with a lawsuit, not with a feud or a duel. Organizations insure themselves the loyalty and trust of their employees by means of (often detailed) contracts which stipulate the parameters of rights and responsibilities of both the employer and the employee.

This demise of traditional values like loyalty, trust, and honor is, of course, not just typical of the European welfare state ethos. It is, in actual fact, typically modern and typically Western. Yet, the welfare state, I venture to argue, radicalized the phenomenon.

## Urbanity and the Ethos of the Welfare State

We must now, in conclusion, briefly compare this ethos of the welfare state with urbanity as the early modern culture of the successful trading and manufacturing cities of Europe. It is obvious that the two are, in many respects, each others' opposites. As we have seen in urbanity-as-ethos, a collectively shared notion of common interests and solidarity undergirded an ever active and creative energy and productivity in trade, commerce, manufacturing, and later industry. This was, in fact, a work ethic religiously fortified and reinforced by Puritanism which, in origin and essence, was strongly production oriented.

However, as we have also argued, in the process of modernization urbanity gradually developed into increasingly generalized, abstract, and multiple moralities which gradually superseded the city proper, and attached themselves to larger entities like the region, the nation, and finally the state. Within the context of the welfare state, ethos and morality modernized radically. They generalized and evaporated into bureaucratic and fiscal obligations, and into an abstract type of rather emotional hypermorality. In European early modern cities the rights and responsibilities of the urban ethos were concrete, down to earth, and not at all hypertrophic. In contrast, in a welfare-state context it is often hard to envisage the heavy burden of sharply progressive, direct and indirect taxes as one's share of a collective responsibility and solidarity.

The comprehensive welfare state has erected a bureaucratic technostructure which in actual fact is "value-neutral" and draws its legitimacy from two sources: first from the fact that it allegedly functions as a system of collective services, and second from the fact that it provides its citizens with the needed leeway to indulge in their consumption-oriented lifestyles and activities. It gave rise to a culture whose ethos is radically different from that of early modern urbanity. Responsibility, for example, has now become a bureaucratic issue within a stratified system of duties and obligations: citizens defer responsibility as much as possible to administrations, and within the administrations, another official or counter which bears the brunt of responsibility. In the end it is often the computer that, in cases of failure or error, is held responsible.

Solidarity too is not absent but has lost much of its society-building and anomie-preventing power, since it is not only reduced, as we just saw, to a fiscal and thus very abstract kind of solidarity but also compartmentalized into ad hoc and private interests. Outside this type of fragmented solidarity people want to do their things, if possible in a milieu in which, as is said, "anything goes."

Urbanity, as we saw, combined localism with cosmopolitanism. It was typically bourgeois, although in origin and essence not of the petite bourgeoisie as it produced a rather grand culture of the arts and the sciences. This too, changed drastically in the context of a radical welfare state. As a system of services it is limited to the borders of its own nation, whereas its citizens are morally mesmerized by their privacy and private interests. Even if they travel abroad extensively, they do so mainly as tourists, as customers of the tourist industry, not as conquerors of new worlds and new experiences.

In the arts and sciences the inhabitants of the early modern cities with their vital urbanity transcended the boundaries of their own bourgeois class. Urbanity, I argued, was in a sense a socially free-floating phenomenon. This was at once its strength and weakness. In contrast, arts and sciences in the welfare state are solidly tied to the nation-state often through rather generous state subsidies. Naturally, they are then caught in the webs of administrative bureaucracies and their inherent rules and restrictions. In the arts non-conformity and avant garde are tolerated to a certain extent. They are, however, neutralized through scores of subsidies which compensate for their weak position in the market.

The sciences, in particular the social sciences, are under pressure to produce socially and politically useful results of research and teaching. The carrot of subsidies and the stick of funding cuts are employed to harness them. The upshot is, more often than not, lack of imagination and derring-do. That too is a far cry from bourgeoisie-transcending urbanity.

Urbanity's greatest fruit was probably its liberty vis-à-vis the forces of feudal bondage. It was experienced as (negative) freedom from subjection and, at the very same time, as (positive) freedom to contribute to the common wealth and welfare of the urban community. Freedom was thus intrinsically tied to solidarity and commitment. This, again, is totally different in the ethos of the welfare state, since liberty here is primarily viewed as an existentialist kind of freedom of the autonomous individual mesmerized by his "authenticity."[42] Liberty in the welfare state is part and parcel of an easygoing libertarianism. It lacks an antenna for social and collective solidarity, commitment, and responsibility.

## The Restructuring of the Welfare State

The rapid rise of the intensive and extensive welfare state in most Western European nations after World War II had far reaching effects on the civil society, the polity, and the economy of the nation-states involved. Mostly these effects were not intended or consciously planned.

First and foremost, there was a profound transformation of civil society as the centralized state began to permeate deeply into its institutions and organizations with scores of interventions. In actual fact, the mediating structures of civil society developed gradually into extensions of the centralized state. Society, to put it bluntly, became state, welfare state.

Next, the often massive centralization of power, compressed in the administrative bureaucracies of the capitals, transformed the polity into a functionally rational, uninspiring arena. The professionals and specialists as the main stakeholders in the institutions and organizations of civil society, oriented their aspirations and interests more towards this arena (the central government, the parliament), than to the authorities of their institutions and organizations (the boards, the trustees). In some cases even the clients they served were in their scale of interests subordinated to the central authorities to whom their lobbying activities were directed.

The basic target of the welfare state was, from the start, social security for all citizens, independent of their socioeconomic class or family background. The central government, and thus not the institutions and organizations of civil society, was called upon to function as the main (legal and financial) guarantor of such a safety net. It should enable the redistribution of wealth by means of progressive taxation, and the distribution of welfare services through extensive and intensive subsidies. Once more, such a massive program caused the almost automatic and radical centralization of power. However, the result was not, as has been claimed by conservative critics of the welfare state, a totalitarian or feudal type of society. On the contrary, the centralization of power ran parallel to an ever-growing individualization and liberalization of the citizens of the welfare state who, apart from abstract bureaucratic controls and regulations, enjoyed and maintained a degree of privacy and liberty unrivaled in human history. This was certainly not a return to serfdom.[43]

The welfare state, including its unavoidable centralization of power, was therefore not the exclusive project of left of center political parties. As in the exemplary case of the Netherlands, politically left, center, and right parties have supported the birth and rapid expansion of the welfare state. One should bear in mind that Lord Beveridge, often called the architect of the British welfare state, was not a socialist but a staunch liberal.[44]

A related and very fateful effect was furthermore a rather sharp separation of the public and the private in sociopolitical life, with an ever-growing primacy of the public sphere. This particularly affected the workings of the market. The welfare state rested from the start on a mixed economy. That is, it supported the free-market principle, yet curbed the freedom of the market, whenever deemed necessary. Thus, in the name of the common and public good—welfare and prosperity for all—private initiatives were restrained by means of the very visible hand of the state. This hand was at times a gloved one, full of state subsidies, but often a firm fist, full of regulations, controls, and taxations.

Simultaneously, however, the balance between the primary (agrarian), secondary (industrial), tertiary (for profit service), and quaternary (not-for-profit service) sectors began to change altogether. The shift from the rural and industrial sectors to the profit and nonprofit service sectors is quite a normal feature of a post-industrial society based primarily on knowledge, information, and their related technologies. It received, however, a special dimension in the case of comprehensive welfare states. Here it was not just a shift of influence and power from the productive sector to the service sector, but a landslide shift to the heavily subsidized nonprofit and nonproductive, quaternary sector. This shift exacerbated the separation of the public and the private spheres.

The public sphere had now become predominantly the sphere of state intervention and public spending. The dynamics of the market were neutralized, if not actually paralyzed, by both of them. The quaternary public sector did not move according to the "laws" of competition; rather, it was regulated bureaucratically by state officialdom. It was, moreover, compartmentalized politically into turfs of specialized interests on the part of care and welfare professionals who, even if they worked in and for legally autonomous organizations, were nonetheless heavily dependant economically and politically on the subsidizing state bureaucracies. Gradually the tertiary (for-profit) service sector too was penetrated by these bureaucratic and professional forces in an attempt, on their part, to draw the sector into the sphere of control of the centralized welfare state. This was, for instance, apparent in the areas of health care, education, and public transportation in which the demarcations between public and private, as well as between profit and nonprofit were blurred.

There are, in terms of social justice, many arguments in favor of this predominance and gradual spread of the quaternary sector. However, there is one set of basic, mutually related problems which became ever more apparent in the 1970s and 1980s: (a) not-for-profit service does not create wealth, (b) centralized bureaucracies have the tendency to perpetuate and even multiply autonomously, thus contributing to the gradual ossification and petrification of both civil society and the market, and (c) in conjunction with bureaucrats, professionals tend to promote their own specialized interests, while they rhetorically profess that they serve their clients and the common good.

The moral dimension of this is significant. Where bureaucratic rules and regulations suffocate the energies of individuals and organizations in civil society and hamper the competitive functions of the market, where state subsidies eliminate the working of scarcity and envy, where professionals hold citizens in tutelage as clients—there society begins to develop an (anti-) economic and (anti-) civic culture. In such a situation private initiatives on the part of citizens and organizations begin to wither away. The state is viewed as the main actor in economic, social, and cultural affairs. It does not take much sociological imagination to realize that such a state of affairs is lethal to any viable civil society.

However, before the advanced welfare states of Western Europe could actually slide off on such a downward slope, the economy suddenly turned things around. In the 1970s, when the world economy was rocked by two severe energy crises, and when it also became ever more obvious that national economies were part of and dependent upon global markets and global competitions, the governments of the intensive and extensive welfare states and many representatives of their New Class elites began to realize that the public spending and the inflated economies would sooner or later render their societies and the social security borne by them, to ruin.

By the start of the 1980s it had become obvious that a fundamental restructuring of most welfare states had become adamant. The two most fundamental restructuring processes were decentralization of power and privatization of those parts of the public sector that would materially and qualitatively prosper by it. Private initiatives of citizens and societal organizations were to be fostered by no longer smothering them in webs of bureaucratic rules and regulations. Thus, decentralization and privatization were paired with deregulation.

Provincial, regional, and above all urban authorities, whose power and influence had declined under the reign of the interventionist welfare state, had to be strengthened, if possible by far-reaching transfers of power from centralized authorities. Above all, within the parameters of sustainable growth, in view of an endangered environment, the wealth-producing sectors, in particular the industrial-commercial sector, had to regain vigor and stamina. To start with, in conjunction with sharp cuts in public expenditure, a sizable decrease of state regulations was needed and had to be combined with a national industrial-commercial policy designed in close cooperation with the corporate world. One can, of course, not fail to realize that a very similar decentralization occurred in the United States since the 1980s.

The restructuring of the economies of these welfare states demanded an end to the growing separation and polarization of the public and private spheres. Much of the privatization mentioned before was to be realized by public-private partnerships which had to contribute to a gradual meeting and, at certain points, a merging of the public and the private. There will, of course, always be typically public and typically private tasks and targets. But—and this is novel since it was never an issue during the heyday of the welfare state—it will be necessary to determine unambiguously what their respective core businesses are and should be.

Needless to say, these structural transformations of the welfare state presuppose a concomitant *cultural* transformation. That is, a change in value-orientations, in thought and action, in habits and mentalities. Urbanity could very well be a most important component of this transformation.

## European Unification and Urbanity

As to the European welfare states, there is still another development which, after the 1970s, has contributed to the awareness that a fundamental restructuring of the welfare state through decentralization and privatization were unavoidable. This is the rapid expansion of the common market of the European Union (EU). The welfare state has always been a national phenomenon, since its social security and welfare services could only be enjoyed by the citizens of the nation-state involved. However, national borders begin to lose significance within the EU which seems to develop ever more into a supranational welfare state. Authorities are increasingly transferred and delegated to the EU's epicenter of power, Brussels.

Thus, in addition to the internal and national decentralization of power to "lower" and "lesser" authorities, as discussed in the previous section, national governments also have to transmit power and portions of sovereignty to Brussels. This is definitely a component of the welfare state's restructuring that will affect its appearance and its functioning ever more strongly in the near future. There is, of course, the distinct possibility that Brussels will, in turn, become a bureaucratic Moloch of Kafkaesque dimensions—stifling, or maybe even absorbing at the end of the day, all social, cultural, and economic energies. Some of the regulations pouring out of the EU bureaucracies (which, by the way, are still minute in size) feed this fear.

Yet, there are also signs and signals that such a super-centralization will not take shape. In Brussels, strong forces propagate the principle of *subsidiarity* which means that, if lower authorities can take care of their socioeconomic, cultural, and political businesses, higher authorities should keep their hands off and abstain from political and administrative interference.

It stands to reason that after all that has been said about urbanity, this restructuring of the welfare state will eventually benefit cities and urbanity. Throughout the ages, as Jane Jacobs argued convincingly, cities have functioned as the main wells for the wealth of nations.[45] They are the economic and cultural nodal points in nations as well as regions, and it is precisely their specific economic and civic culture— their urbanity—which is the perfect mental and attitudinal mold for the kind of production nations and regions need. It is therefore not surprising that together with the decentralization and privatization on the one hand and the European unification on the other, a gradual revitalization of cities has occurred ever since the beginning of the 1980s.

An important part of this urban revitalization is the reemergence of urbanity. Just as corporate culture and corporate communication have become crucial issues in the developments of industrial and commercial corporations, so urban culture and urban communication (e.g., the PR activities of cities) have penetrated into the public administrations of cities. Urban economic and civic culture is, in fact, a crucial issue on the agenda of many urban administrations. The concept of "Eurocity" emerged in this decade. It can be expected that Eurocities will play a dominant role in the EU's urban policies of the near future.

This trickles down into the urban community. Inner cities begin to revitalize socioeconomically, culturally, and architecturally. Though in small numbers, people begin to return to the cities, particularly the well-to-do single people, or couples without children. Corporations that have their offices in the city increasingly prefer their employees to live within its boundaries, so as to avoid the loss of time and money in traffic-jammed commuting. In order to reduce the damage done to the environment by this commuting traffic, authorities also try to foster the return of working people from the suburbs and rural areas to the cities. Their main motive, however, is to attract more wealth and affluence to the cities in an attempt to stop progressive socioeconomic decline. Gentrification of inner-city neighborhoods has, in many instances, become an explicit policy.[46]

## Components of Urbanity Still Relevant Today

Naturally, one cannot transfer early modern urbanity to the late modern cities of today. Moreover, as we shall see later, today's cities are in the process of rather far-reaching transformations. That means *a fortiori* that traditional urbanity, as we have discussed in the previous chapters, cannot function *in toto* as a normative model for the culture of the cities of tomorrow. Contemporary post-industrial, late modern cities will, of course, exhibit quite different forms and contents of urbanity.

Yet, we should be hesitant to treat urbanity exclusively as a historical phenomenon, as something of the definitive past. The main question is, of course, given the definition of urbanity discussed before, whether the cities of today and tomorrow are and will be in need of an economic and civic culture. Sociologically, it is hard to fathom how these cities could continue to function as the main engines of our economies and as the main wells of the wealth of nations, while lacking any sort of economic and civic culture. They would, in that case, just exist as fragmented and unstructured bazaars, plagued by scores of centrifugal forces which in the end can only be contained by stiff regulations and very strong formal controls. Needless to say, this is also the ideal milieu for organized crime and scores of civic strife. While their economic and sociocultural vitality would be stifled, these late modern bazaar cities would unavoidably slip off politically into undemocratic, if not anti-democratic circumstances.

Thus it makes sense to investigate if there are certain components of traditional urbanity which still may bear relevance for us today and, perhaps, for tomorrow. Next, we should, of course, search for the contours of a truly contemporary and maybe even future urban culture. The following elements of urbanity as discussed above seem to me to be still relevant today:

1.  Despite its late medieval origins, urbanity, as we have seen before, presents an amazingly modern type of solidarity, namely a functionally rational one which is free from the encapsulating and often stifling bonds of family, territory, religion, and in principle, if not always in actual fact, socioeconomic class and cultural estate.

2. Urbanity is at once local and cosmopolitan which enables us to avoid both moralistic narrow-mindedness, on the one hand, and hyper-moralistic identification with rather abstract world problems, on the other. Urbanity, in other words, may give urban inhabitants a sense of collective identity and maybe even pride, yet such local chauvinism is always tempered by a broader, cosmopolitan vision.

3. Urbanity is an economic ethos and, as such, it is a down-to-earth ethos of work and responsibility. In the well-known typology of Max Weber, urbanity harbors an "ethic of responsibility" (*Verantwortungsethik*) rather than an "ethic of ultimate ends" (*Gesinnungsethik*).[47] As important as leisure and pleasure are for those who live and work in the city, urbanity is first and foremost an ethos of production and civic responsibility rather than of consumption. It is so, however, without religious, traditionalistic, and moralistic motives and overtones. Urbanity, as a rational work ethic, is neither locked in by a traditional *Gemeinschaft*, nor alienated by bureaucratic regulations and professional rules and controls. In a sense, urbanity can be seen as a link between tradition and modernity.

4. Urbanity depends on a fruitful mediation of the public and the private spheres of life. The gradual growing apart of these two domains—centralization of state and individualization of citizens—was, as we saw, endemic to the process of modernization. It reached a peak in the heyday of the welfare state, as is demonstrated by such front-runner welfare states as Sweden and the Netherlands. If, due to the restructuring of these welfare states during the 1980s (decentralization, deregulation, privatization, internationalization), intermediary structures regain their functionality, and if possibly new intermediary structures will emerge, urbanity could again gain prominence and functionality. After all, it is in its nature to foster the mutual dependence of the private and the public. In fact, public-private partnerships can only prosper and function well within the context of a vital and vigorous urbanity.

If one tries to determine which components of urbanity are still relevant and ought to be maintained, pursued, and fostered today, it may be helpful to focus on the conditions that have a distinctly negative impact, as well as on the conditions that bear positively upon a possible revitalization of urbanity. However, I am fully aware of the circularity of such an argument. Therefore, it should not be read as scientific proof of the alleged timeliness of urbanity in today's late modern urban society. With this limitation in mind, I mention only the most obvious of these negative conditions:

1. The polarization of the public and the private spheres of life has been apparent in comprehensive welfare states. This polarization, as we saw, bears strong centrifugal forces which affect the autonomy and vitality of civil society. Obviously, if this centrifugal polarization in society-at-large and in urban habitats in particular, would be perpetuated, there could be,

given the nature of urbanity, very little hope for its revitalization in contemporary or future cities.

2. Narrowly related to this is the antithesis of urbanity and the ethos of the welfare state. As we have seen, the latter is characterized by the primacy of consumption over production, by heavy emphasis on privacy and subjective experiences at the expense of the public commonwealth and the collective history and tradition. All of this is contrary to the work ethic, the emphasis upon civic responsibility, the orientation towards collective interests and enterprises, so typical of urbanity. Here again, if the welfare state is not really and successfully restructured through decentralization, privatization, and internationalization, socioeconomic and cultural conditions will be perpetuated which are square to the economic and civic culture of urbanity.

3. A further negative condition for urbanity and its revitalization into a vital and vigorous economic and civic culture, is the prominent and often powerful position many urbanologists have occupied in urban policy making. Experts of urban design, planning, and housing—often architects, geographers, sociologists, and lately anthropologists (probably in search of new islands and new "natives")[48]—had a considerable impact on the substance and direction of urban policies. However, with the exception of most anthropologists, who have generally managed to maintain their instinct or intuition for urban culture, these urbanologists usually operate from a rather limited methodological frame of reference with little awareness and knowledge of the cultural factor. Urbanity does not exist, because it does not fit the abstract models of the urbanologists. As urban policymakers and their administrative bureaucrats call upon these urbanologists for advice, many contemporary urban development programs are drenched with anti-urbanism.

Positive influences are potentially exerted on urbanity by these conditions:

1. There is, to begin with, the obvious economic and sociocultural need to restructure the welfare state through decentralization, deregulation, and privatization. In Europe, these restructuring processes are reinforced, and perhaps radicalized in the near future, by the rapid unification of the European market and the redistribution of authorities within the European Union. Particularly, the growing emphasis on regions and cities—Euroregions and Eurocities, for instance—as part of a policy of subsidiarity fosters an enlargement of urban autonomy, but also a kind of competition between cities and urban regions across the borders. In this competition, cities need collective identities, they need to profile themselves; in short, they need to engage in city marketing. As in the case of corporations which develop and strengthen their corporate culture for this purpose, cities need to develop their urban cultures, lest they lag behind as faceless bazaars.

2. Within the national welfare states, decentralization, deregulation, and privatization are conducive to the growing autonomy of the cities, in particular the larger cities and metropolises. Only cities that are financially and politically autonomous are in fact city-states, and can function as the fertile soils of vital and vigorous urbanity. As noted above, such a decentralization, deregulation, and privatization is underway in most Western welfare states since the early-1980s. The resurgence of urbanity is also observable in many of its cities, which prior to the 1980s were rather outstanding in their lack of urbanity (e.g., Rotterdam, Manchester, and Glasgow).

3. Despite my comments about the negative impact of urbanologists on urbanity, it should be acknowledged that among them as well changes are visible. Since knowledge is always related to reality, it stands to reason that when urban societies change, knowledge of urbanologists will also eventually alter. To give just one example, the writings of the architectural critic Witold Rybczynski are refreshing, because they keep the main tenets of contemporary urbanological discourse at arm's length and testify to a sound intuitive sensitivity for the cultural dimensions of urban life.[49] Moreover, the establishment of urbanological specialists and their previously rather arcane knowledge and discourse are increasingly invaded by amateur outsiders who look at and talk about the city and city life from a distinctly cultural perspective. Anthropologists (Ulf Hannerz), sociologists (Richard Sennett), economists (Jane Jacobs), and even theologians (Jacques Ellul) and a literary theologian-sociologist (Andrew Greeley) testify to a refreshing wind of intellectual change. In much of their writings there is a distinct awareness of (if not yet a systematic insight into) urbanity. They definitely contribute to a reasonable debate about and scientific research of urbanity as a distinct cultural phenomenon. That may contribute again to a renewed interest in urbanity and the revitalization thereof on the part of urban policymakers.

## Notes

1. Compare Norbert Elias, *Die höfische Gesellschaft* (Darmstadt and Neuwied: Luchterhand, [1969] 1975).
2. See in particular Henri Pirenne, *Medieval Cities: Their Origin and the Revival of Trade*, translated by Frank D. Halsey (Princeton, NJ: Princeton University Press, [1925] 1974), pp. 3–26.
3. Pirenne, ibid., pp. 40–41.
4. See Geoffrey Barraclough, *The Crucible of Europe: The Ninth and Tenth Centuries in European History* (Berkeley and Los Angeles: University of California Press, 1976), pp. 59–60. There were approximately 250 counties, and thus 250 counts each with a staff of ten assistants maximum, covering an area as large as present-day France and Germany and Italy up to Rome. They were not local officials, but almost all noblemen and royal vassals, somehow related to the house of Charlemagne. In fact, as Barraclough writes, "a very small and select group." This, of course, is not by any stretch of the imagination a "civil service."
5. Pirenne, ibid., p. 29.

6. Geoffrey Barraclough, *The Crucible of Europe*, p. 53. Barraclough's verdict is harsh: "The empire put together by Charles the Great was a failure; it had no future; it simply petered out, leaving no direct inheritance.... Frankish conquest fractured the mould of Frankish government; it was like the serpent that died of swallowing more than it could digest." Ibid., p. 54.
7. Barraclough, ibid., p. 69.
8. Barraclough, ibid., pp. 76–78.
9. Cf. Barraclough, ibid., pp. 86–91. See also Marc Bloch, *Feudal Society*, translated by L. A. Manyon (Chicago: University of Chicago Press, [1940] 1970), vol. 1, part 1: "The Growth of Ties of Dependence," in particular ch. 3, pp. 39–59.
10. For this competition see Norbert Elias, *Über den Prozess der Zivilisation*, 1939, volume 2, pp. 143–160: "Über den Monopolismus."
11. Pirenne, *Medieval Cities*, p. 97.
12. See, for this remarkable development, ibid., p. 96.
13. Elias, *Die höfische Geselleschaft*, p. 124.
14. Elias, ibid., passim.
15. Werner Sombart, *Liebe, Luxus und Kapitalismus* (München: Deutscher Taschenbuch Verlag, [1912] 1967), p. 11.
16. Sombart, ibid., p. 21.
17. See in particular the perceptive analysis of Wolf Lepenies, *Melancholie und Gesellschaft* (Frankfurt am Main: Suhrkamp Verlag, 1969).
18. Sombart, *Liebe*, pp. 19–34: "Der neue Adel."
19. The quote is from Defoe's *Complete English Tradesman*, 2d ed. 1727. I found it in Sombart, *Liebe*, pp. 25–26.
20. Reinhard Bendix, *Nation-Building and Citizenship: Studies of our Changing Social Order* (New York: John Wiley & Sons, 1964), p. 2.
21. Compare Alexis de Tocqueville, *L'Ancien Régime et la Révolution* (Paris: Gallimard, [1857] 1980), edited by André Jardin. I subjected this book to a structural-sociological analysis in "Dezelfde wateren aan nieuwe oevers: Alexis de Tocqueville en de Franse Revolutie" (The Same Waters at New Borders: Alexis de Tocqueville and the French Revolution) in *Tijdschrift voor de Studie van de Verlichting en van het Vrije Denken* (*Journal for the Study of the Enlightenment and of Free Thinking*) 17, nos. 3–4 (Brussels, 1989): 289–307. See also Georges Lefebvre, *The Coming of the French Revolution*, translated by R.R. Palmer (Princeton, NJ: Princeton University Press, [1939] 1969).
22. For both definitions I borrowed heavily from Anthony D. Smith, *National Identity*, (Reno, NV: University of Nevada Press, 1991), in particular p. 14.
23. Isiah Berlin, "The Bent Twig," in I. Berlin, *The Crooked Timber of Humanity*, edited by H. Henry, (New York: Vintage Books, [1972] 1992), pp. 238–263.
24. Compare Alfred Vagts, *A History of Militarism—Civilian and Military* (New York: Free Press [1937] 1959).
25. T. H. Marshall, *Class, Citizenship and Social Development* (Chicago: The University of Chicago Press, [1963] 1977), p. 78.
26. Compare, for example, Terence J. Johnson, *Professions and Power* (London: Macmillan, 1972).
27. As always it is hazardous to make general statements about the United States. As to the intensity and extensiveness of welfare efforts, there is a great variety among the different states. Some resemble premodern circumstances, others come close to the Scandinavian and Dutch welfare states. Cf. Harold Wilensky, *The Welfare State and Equality: Structural and Ideological Roots of Public Expenditures*, (Berkeley and Los Angeles: University of California Press, 1975), pp. 32–49.
28. Durkheim, *De la Division du Travail Social*, p. xxxii.

29. Compare for what follows my essay "The Ethos of the Welfare State," *International Sociology* 1, no.4 (1986): 443–457.
30. Harold L. Wilensky, *The Welfare State*, ch. 2: "Economic Level, Ideology, and Social Structure", pp. 15–49.
31. Geertz, *Interpretation of Cultures*, pp. 126–142.
32. See Alvin Gouldner, *The Future of Intellectuals and the Rise of the New Class* (New York: Seabury, 1979) and Barry Bruce-Briggs, ed., *The New Class?* (New Brunswick, NJ: Transaction Publishers, 1979).
33. Hans Freyer, *Theorie des gegenwärtigen Zeitalters* (Stuttgart: Deutsche Verlags-Anstalt, [1955] 1958), pp. 15–31 and passim.
34. Indicative for all of this is the essay by Julien Offray de Lamettrie, *L'homme machine*, published anonymously in Leiden, 1748. For an English translation and critical analysis see Aram Vartanian, *La Mettrie's L'Homme Machine: A Study in the Origins of an Idea*, (Princeton, NJ: Princeton University Press, 1960).
35. Since the papal bull on social justice, *Rerum Novarum* (1891), Roman Catholic Christian Democracy has been influential in the construction of the comprehensive welfare state. See Kees Kersbergen, *Social Capitalism: A Study of Christian Democracy and the Welfare State* (London and New York: Routledge, 1996).
36. Ironically, this was analyzed profoundly and criticized sharply by the guru of the New Left Herbert Marcuse. See his *One-dimensional Man: Studies in the Ideology of Advanced Industrial Society* (Boston: Beacon Press, [1964] 1968).
37. See Theodor Adorno et al., *Der Positivismusstreit in der deutschen Soziologie* (Frankfurt am Main: Luchterhand, [1969] 1972).
38. See Hansfried Kellner and Frank W. Heuberger, eds., *Hidden Technocrats: The New Class and New Capitalism* (New Brunswick, NJ: Transaction Publishers, 1992).
39. Compare Jean-Louis Goglin, *Les misérables dans l'Occident médiéval* (Paris: Editions du Seuil, 1976).
40. Compare P. D. Anthony, *The Ideology of Work* (London: Tavistock, 1977).
41. Arnold Gehlen, *Moral und Hypermoral* (Bonn: Athenäum Verlag, 1969). Helmutyh Schelsky, *Die Arbeit tun die anderen* (Opladen: Westdeutscher Verlag, 1975), pp. 84–85.
42. Compare Theodor Adorno, *The Jargon of Authenticity*, translated by K. Tarnowski and F. Will (London: Routledge & Kegan Paul, [1964] 1973.)
43. See Vic George and Paul Wilding, *Ideology and Social Welfare* (London: Routledge & Kegan Paul, [1976] 1978), in particular, chs. 2–5, pp. 21–105. A more up-to-date account presents their recent book *Welfare and Ideology*, (New York: Harvester Wheatsheaf, 1994).
44. William Beveridge, *Why I Am a Liberal* (London: n.p., 1948).
45. Jane Jacobs, *Cities and the Wealth of Nations*, passim.
46. Compare N. Smith and P. Williams, eds. *Gentrification of the City* (Boston: Allen & Unwin, 1986). Also M. Lang, *Gentrification amid Urban Decline* (Cambridge, MA: Ballinger, 1982).
47. For this typology see Max Weber, "Politics as a Vocation" (1919) in *From Max Weber: Essays in Sociology*, translated by H.H. Gerth and C. Wright Mills (New York: A Galaxy Book. Oxford University Press, [1946] 1962), pp. 120–121.
48. See Ulf Hannerz, *Exploring the City: Inquiries Toward an Urban Anthropology* (New York: Columbia University Press, 1980). A fine specimen of empirical anthropological research is his *Soul Side: Inquiries into Ghetto Culture and Community* (New York: Columbia Press, 1969).
49. Witold Rybczynski, *Looking Around: A Journey Through Architecture* (New York: Penguin Books, 1992).

# 4

# Modernity and the Fragmented City: The Differentiation of Urban Culture

## The City's Disputed Existence

We have seen in the previous chapters of this volume that (a) modernization consists essentially of structural differentiation and cultural generalization, (b) in modernization, cultures too, like the socioeconomic and political structures, tend to differentiate into fragmented and even divisive subcultures, and (c) urbanity as the economic and civic culture of cities had a stimulating effect on modernization, yet was also transformed by it during the course of the past three or four centuries in which modernization progressed rapidly. As to the latter, (late) modern urbanity will, of course, not exhibit the unity and coherence it still had in the days of modernity's debut. The phenomenon of fragmented urbanity, in particular, deserves closer scrutiny.

There are indications that we presently live in a state of late modernity. One powerful socioeconomic and sociopolitical indicator is the fact that these days in America as well as in Europe, we witness the rather rapid demise of the centralized nation state, particularly in the form of the welfare state which we described in the previous chapter as one of the major products of modernization. A second indicator of late modernity is the spectacular developments of advanced technologies, particularly in the fields of space research, transportation, communication, and dissemination of information. Within a relatively short period of time these technologies have rendered the world borderless, if not limitless. In view of all this, we ought to consider and discuss the postmodernist contention that the idea of the city as a delimitable phenomenon has become obsolete. Obviously, if the idea of the city has become meaningless, the idea of urbanity should be abandoned also.

In contemporary urbanological discourse the notion has indeed taken hold that it is no longer sensible to speak of "the city," conceived of as a spatial phenomenon with distinct borders. According to this theory the city as a clearly marked out and demarcated phenomenon has been superseded by the rapid process of urbanization. "Urbanization without Cities" is the telling title of an urbanological treatise.[1] In particular, the large metropolises have spread out into vast urban regions, in which the former distinction between urban and rural space has become senseless. Urbanization has spread out widely from the cities and penetrated deeply into rural areas. A neologism has been coined for this: rurbanization.

Modern technology, in particular the means of rapid transportation of people, goods, services, and above all the communication media and the modern information techniques, have facilitated if not caused the expansion of urban lifestyles far beyond the former borders of the city. Urbanity is, so to say, on the loose; it has left the city as its physical basis and spread to nations and continents. Moreover, the argument continues, people may still work in cities, but many live with their families outside of them, in suburbs. In fact, they constitute, together with the inner cities, huge metropolises in which it is impossible to distinguish clearly between city and non-city.

There are two elements in the non-city argument which ought to be taken into account seriously. To begin with, in many nations there are areas, usually the economically vital ones, in which these metropolitan configurations are located so closely together that it makes sense to speak of one huge, densely urban region with green "spots" within it. Such regions are often called conurbations.

To give an example, the area between Amsterdam, Utrecht, the Hague, and Rotterdam is called in the Netherlands: *Randstad*—that is, "border city"—since it is viewed as one highly urbanized western flank of the country. If one travels by car or by train from, say, Rotterdam to Amsterdam one still sees relatively large portions of rural Holland, yet the whole region is dominated economically and politically by the big cities which still expand annually. The French urbanologist Jean Gottmann coined a name for such an extended urban region: *megalopolis*. He has, for example, designated the northeastern seaboard of the United States, from the south of New Hampshire to the north of Virginia, as one single, densely urbanized area.[2] This area is, according to him, a megalopolis.

But it is questionable whether this makes sense. In view of the wide stretches of rural New England, that in their sometimes vast extension stand in no comparison to the green spots in the Dutch *Randstad*, the megalopolis argument seems to be somewhat far-fetched. This is, of course, a matter of scale, and obviously this scale can be vastly overdrawn. As to the Dutch "border city," it contains urban concentrations with very distinct, and historically very old idiosyncracies: Delft, for instance, or Leiden, let alone Amsterdam, the Hague, and Rotterdam. Despite all the rurbanization in the region, it would be silly to give up calling them "cities," and each one of them has its historically grown, and particular urban culture. The northeastern United States may be called one stretched-out urban region, yet it would be strange, to say the least, to call it a city—a megalopolis—and even stranger to deny the existence of such culturally vastly different cities as Boston and New York.

The second element in the non-city argument carries more weight. It is said repetitively these days that we live, ever since the 1960s and 1970s, in an era in which advanced electronic technologies and the incessant flow of information have solidly transformed our world. In this transformation, scores of traditional borders, limits, and demarcations have begun to evaporate, or—maybe a better phrase—have become porous. Manuel Castells argues that this seminal transformation affected not only the economic modes of production and labor relations but also space, in particular cities and regions. Space, Castells argues, is no longer a space of places but a space of flows, of ever more powerful flows. This has grave consequences for cities as well as for organizations: "the emergence of a *space of flows* which dominates the historically constructed space of places, as the logic of dominant organizations detaches itself from the social constraints of cultural identities and local societies through the powerful medium of information technologies."[3]

This is indeed an important argument. Admittedly, much of our urbanological thinking starts from an idea of the city as a compact space with borders, limits, and demarcations. Informatization and globalization—two closely related processes facilitated by advanced electronic technologies—are in the process of radically changing the spaces we live in, not leastly urban and regional spaces. The octogenarians ruling Communist China reportedly have great problems with the as-of-yet-free flow of information through the Internet. Not only pornography, but even capitalist ideas about free markets and democratic ideas about the free exchange of ideas penetrate deeply into Bejing through the Internet. However, this does not mean that we should abandon the idea of the city altogether. Bejing and Shanghai are still cities, huge cities to which one travels as foreigner and from which one returns after a sojourn. Likewise, Sarajevo which tragically encompasses European history from the beginning of World War I in 1914 to the end of Eastern European Communist rule in the late-1980s, was till recently a lame duck under vicious attacks by Serb guns. It would be strange to deny the "cityness" of Sarajevo.

Yet, late modernity has brought about transformations which compel us to rethink, if not to reinvent the city.[4] The walled-in city has disappeared some centuries ago. Today's late modern city is indeed in many respects a space of flows (Castell), infinitely more flexible than the cities of a few decades ago. The personal computer, the fax, e-mail, and the virtual reality of cyberspace compel us to rethink space, including urban space. But, one would stretch the argument too far, if one would deny the empirical existence of New York and Chicago, Amsterdam and Rotterdam, Toronto and Montreal.

Meanwhile, as we have seen, there has been, and always will be, a rather strong anti-urban animus and the doctrine of the city-past feeds on that animus strongly.[5] The so-called green movement, in association with the philosophical current of postmodernism that generally delights in the evaporation of all borders, distinctions, and dividing lines, takes its ideological toll among urbanologists also. Meanwhile, apart from some elements which deserve attention, the doctrine of anti-urbanism does not stand up to critical analysis.

Often suburbanization is mentioned here as a process which puts the predominance of cities and city life to an end. Yet, it is questionable whether such a sharp opposition between urban and suburban life does actually exist. This may have been the case in the 1950s, but it borders on an outdated cliché today. Actually, nowadays there is a double movement: families with young children prefer to live in the suburbs for obvious reasons (affordable housing, better schools, family-oriented facilities, safety, etc.), young professional couples without children and single managers and professionals often prefer to live in the center of the big city (cultural events, culinary facilities, etc.). Moreover, there are urban governments these days which design policies to attract young families and senior citizens to the inner city again in order to restore the demographic balance.[6]

In many service-oriented occupations in particular, modern electronic technology (telephone, fax, e-mail, etc.) does indeed enable people, as is often argued in the non-city doctrine, to work at home. They actually do not need an office in the city. Yet, the bulk of productive work and their related services, such as banking, insurance, legal assistance, etc. is still located within urban junctions. Here face-to-face contact has not at all been superseded by electronic exchanges. On the contrary, it seems that people need personal contact more than ever. The bulk of routine exchanges of information can be realized through telephones, faxes, and the Internet. This is the functionally rational type of information. It is the non-routine, substantially rational and therefore strategic exchange of information which remains dependent on personal and often also informal encounters. For such encounters one simply has to be present physically. And the social and cultural surroundings of such encounters are and remain, of course, of crucial importance.

Thus, despite cyberspace, virtual realities, and electronic flows, cities, particularly the inner cities, have remained nodal points for trade, industry, allied services, and scores of cultural endeavors. Here one has one's associates and competitors, as it were, within physical reach. Due to the high costs associated with traffic congestion, corporations often prefer their managers and office workers to live in the city. Moreover, and it bears repeating, young professionals and managers, who often maintain flexible, childless partnerships, increasingly prefer to live in the inner city which has infinitely more to offer in terms of leisure and luxury than the communities of suburbia. It fits their lifestyles far better than the suburbs, let alone the rural areas. This, of course, attracts scores of formal and informal service jobs.

Cities compete with each other—to host Olympic games, or to organize cultural festivals, for instance. In this often worldwide competition they present themselves as entities with specific, often unique identities, much like multinational corporations that try to communicate their individual, specific corporate culture and identity. When a city has scored in this competition—hosting the next Olympic Games, for instance—the joy and pride of administrators and city dwellers often knows no bounds. And what about tourists? Do they buy a travel package (roundtrip air fare plus hotel accommodations and city trips) in order to visit Megalopolis, or one of the other limitless and faceless conurbations? Of course not, they go to see and experience Paris, Berlin, Vienna, Amsterdam, Rome, New York, Boston, Chicago, San Francisco, and maybe even Los Angeles! They go there, because these are true cities with vital—that is, inspiring, challenging, and often also exasperating, if not frightening—urban cultures.

The administrations of these cities, in fact, engage in what is called "strategic city-marketing." The most important products to be marketed by cities, it is claimed, are: spaces for offices and industrial plants,

facilities as to housing, schools, the arts and sciences, sports and leisure, shopping, transportation, tourism, and so on.[7] Cities often act
like corporations and try with all PR-means at their disposal, to lure
investors, professionals, businessmen, artists, and tourists to visit them,
and to live and to work within their administratively delineated orbits.
Like corporations emphasizing their corporate identity, cities nowadays
often go to great lengths and spend much money, in order to communicate their urban cultures and identities. They are not faceless non-enti-
ties, as the postmodern non-city doctrine proclaims. On the contrary,
they are social, economic, cultural, and political configurations, often
gifted with a just measure of pride. Often this is symbolized by a slo-
gan: "Amsterdam has it!", which Rotterdammers countered facetiously
with "Yes, but Rotterdam does it!"; or simply, "The Big Apple."

These days, Los Angeles is mentioned as the symbol of the future,
as the late modern metropolis par excellence in which space is being
fragmented socioculturally, economically, and politically, and whose
hard-to-grasp nature consists allegedly of flexible flows. If New York
is the symbol of modernity and modern urbanity, Los Angeles offers a
prime example of the late modern city which in fact is no longer a city.
It allegedly preshadows urban life in the twenty-first century. Let's
take a closer look at this curious phenomenon.

## Tale of a Fragmented City

Los Angeles is, to some, the pinnacle of twentieth-century-urban
misery; to others, the model city of the twenty-first century. If a city
evokes such extreme reactions and emotions, it must somehow possess a special quality. Indeed, whether one likes it or not, L.A. as the
city is usually called, is a statement, it has something to say. In its own
way, it must be a city and it must somehow carry some sort of urbanity.
But the moment one tries to apply the notion of urbanity, as developed
in the previous chapters, one runs into great difficulties, not in the least
because this huge urban sprawl seems to be bereft of any trace of urbanity upon first sight.

L.A. is much in discussion these days. Postmodernists in particular
are prone to celebrate L.A. as the fragmented urban space which offers
countless opportunities for individualization, mobility, and decentralized vitality—a city of postinstitutional networks, preshadowing human life in the twenty-first century. Many Americans, particularly those
from the East coast, and almost all Europeans, usually abhor this urban

sprawl with its notorious traffic congestion, air pollution, and ethnic conflicts. Others, like Mike Davis, who has an intimate knowledge of L.A. and who called this stretched-out piece of urban space a City of Quartz, are more sober in their judgment. Davis focuses on L.A. from a political, "leftist" point of view, and obviously has some axes to grind. Yet his detailed portrait of L.A. is an impressive one.[8]

L.A. is, indeed, a puzzling phenomenon. One ought to try to avoid the extreme pro-and-con positions. When confronted with L.A., one begins to realize how European the notion of urbanity, as the economic and civic culture of cities, really is. Yet, as I tried to demonstrate above, it can still be applied to most American cities—to Boston, New York, Chicago, San Francisco, New Orleans, and Washington, D.C.—not because these cities are European but because they are, like the nation-state, the church, the university, and other institutions, products of Western civilization which have been subjected, like their counterparts in Europe, to the process of modernization. But can the idea of urbanity really be applied to L.A.? Isn't L.A. the best example of a city without urbanity, and a city which verges on economic success and predominance, to boot—gateway to the powerful markets of the Pacific Rim, gateway also to the upsurging markets of Latin America? Isn't L.A. the truly global city, the city of the twenty-first century—in many respects totally different from New York, Boston, and Chicago which belong to the nineteenth and twentieth centuries? They are, in a sense, "Atlantic cities," tied historically, culturally, and economically to Europe and European cities. Urbanity as an originally European phenomenon might be an important issue to them, but can it be applied to L.A.?

L.A. is, like Seattle, Vancouver, Hong Kong, and Singapore, altogether different. These are "Pacific cities" which unlike the "Atlantic cities" are probably going to set the agenda for the global economy of the next century. Isn't the concept of urbanity simply too old-fashioned and European to be applicable to these cities of the future? This argument cannot and should not be dismissed as just another piece of L.A.-city propaganda. Yet, in view of the extreme social, cultural, and political difficulties that L.A. faces—difficulties that to a great extent can be traced back to its vast socioeconomic and cultural diversity and fragmentation and thus have a L.A.-specific nature—one can raise a legitimate question: Shouldn't this city also focus its policies on the development of an up-to-date kind of urbanity?

Pictures of L.A. taken from the air show the conventional American grid structure. This almost grotesquely stretched-out grid is filled mainly by single homes that look remarkably alike: a small front yard and, in many backyards, a small swimming pool. In downtown L.A. there are some high-rise buildings and apartment buildings too, but the main impression remains one of a seemingly endless sea of houses, intersected by streets, avenues, and an extensive freeway system. These public spaces are predominantly filled with cars thereby losing their public-space character.

L.A.—and this cliché is repeated time and again—is the city of mobility, of automobility. However, this mobility is a paradoxical thing. Angelenos move about a lot and they do so almost exclusively by car. As a result, Los Angeles's traffic is incessantly congested which, of course, hampers mobility considerably. Not surprisingly, L.A. is the most polluted urban space in the United States, if not of the world. A Dutch visitor made the astute (and probably typically Dutch) observation that the sidewalks and gutters are so clean in L.A. simply because nobody ever uses them.[9]

In a sense, L.A. does not exist as a city. It certainly is the very opposite of the compact city. Downtown is not the epicenter of economic and cultural vitality. It is not a public space in which people walk, stroll, and saunter. In fact, downtown L.A. is a composite of parking lots, shopping malls, and mostly identical shops and plazas which do not exhibit much urban life. This prompted the "Downtown Strategic Plan" which proposed the construction of four squares surrounded by *avenidas* on which pedestrians can walk and stroll. But is this really what one would call a socioculturally lively and economically vital Downtown?

L.A. lacks a dominant center. It is polycentric. It consists of some thirteen different ethnic groups which are often concentrated in their own neighborhoods. It is a city of immigrants, many of whom are illegal, nonregistered aliens. Its multiculturality has reached such a level that in L.A. there are as many Mexicans as in Guadalajara, the second most-populous city in Mexico. It houses the largest concentration of Filipinos outside Manilla, the largest concentration of Druzes outside Lebanon, and the largest concentration of Koreans outside Seoul. David Rieff aptly dubbed L.A., "the capital of the Third World."[10]

As a result, this city is a display of vast social and economic diversity and inequality, and often exhibits a bewildering cultural pluriformity. It is, in fact, a conglomerate of ethnic communities with enormous differences in social and economic composition. Beverly Hills is the L.A. of the rich and white, whereas the black and poor live in Watts, South Central, and parts of Eastern L.A. Recurrent outbursts of violence remain restricted to these ghettos. Poverty and destitution are geographically confined. The farther away from these ghettos the rich and wealthy live, the more they will entrench themselves in walled-in and guarded neighborhoods. Davis paints a depressing picture of the paranoia this entails: "The social perception of threat becomes a function of the security mobilization, not crime rates." He speaks of the "fortress L.A.".[11]

Spatial segregation is a kind of informal principle in this urban sprawl. It precludes the emergence of citywide disturbances, but also the existence of any sort of vital public space. Angelenos hardly expose themselves to the spaces between the houses and the buildings of their city. They move from their heavily guarded homes to their workplaces in cars in which they spend many, many hours a week due to incessant traffic congestion. Incidentally, 70 percent of these cars transport a single person.

Allegedly, the automobile industry bought the public transportation system in the 1940s, and then helped it to its death. L.A. had to become the city of cars and automobile traffic. This may well be one of the many myths that surround it. The fact is, however, that public transportation does not score high politically in L.A. There is widespread opposition against extension and modernization of the public transportation system, in particular against the proposed construction of an extensive subway system. Allegedly, the affluent and well-to-do fear an all too easy access to their enclaves from the poor neighborhoods. Some homes look like fortresses, and plates with the words ARMED RESPONSE are ubiquitous.

Another observation made by the previously mentioned Dutch visitor—an architectural critic and philosopher—throws light on an aspect of L.A. which may well be very characteristic. Fake, he argues, is hard to distinguish from what is genuine and authentic. Actually, he continues, L.A. is the city of fake, is a fake city, celebrates a cult of fake. He exemplifies this statement by referring to the so-called City Walk. The name is a fraud, he complains, let alone the thing itself. It is a rather artificial kind of strolling area which can only be reached by car. One leaves the car in an underground parking lot, and the parking ticket gains you entrance to a rather small area in which there is not much urban life occurring:

> Here then parades affluent L.A. along shops filled with gimmicks and gadgets, show-windows filled with fancy fair attractions, façades that are each one of them copies of buildings located elsewhere in the city. Here, one could say, the city is most honest, here its "true nature" emerges from the parking lots below. Here the city is what it truly is to many: the image of a city.[12]

Davis is even more outspoken about this Downtown project which, according to him, "is one of the largest postwar urban designs in North America."[13] Despite all the giddy talk about the postmodern scene in Los Angeles, he exclaims, "the new financial district is best conceived as a single, demonically self-referential hyper-structure, a Miesian skyscape raised to dementia."[14]

This Downtown area obviously will not function as the dominant center within a polycentered metropolis which radiates sociocultural, economic, and civic energies to the surrounding satellite centers. L.A. is, in fact, a huge conurbation with a multitude of urbanities, affixed to a multitude of urban regions, communities, neighborhoods, and enclaves. It is then, of course, questionable if such a fragmented, polycentered, mutually unrelated set of urbanities can function as the motor of a vital economic and civic culture.

Thus, the question is raised again, if this metropolis presents an example of the breakdown and failure of urban design and development in the second half of the twentieth century, or should be seen and treated, on the contrary, as the model city of the twenty-first century—the "heteropolis" of the future which foreshadows urban life in the age of cyberspace?[15] Is this urban sprawl which, despite socioeconomic diversity and vast cultural pluriformity, despite sparse architectural experiments—the deconstructionist projects of Frank Gehry, for instance—and consists of architectural uniformities within an extensive grid structure, our immediate urban future? Is this urban agglomeration with its decentralized, yet highly bureaucratized and overregulated public administration, the kind of urban surrounding within which future generations will have to conduct their urban lives? Are we, like today's Angelenos, going to live in the next century in homes like fortresses which systematically and frantically lock out the public spaces of streets, squares, and parks? What indeed is left of urban liberalism in a paranoid social system like L.A.?

Some Dutch experts in architecture, urban development, and urban design believe that the urbanized region between Amsterdam, Rotterdam, the Hague, and Utrecht (the previously discussed *Randstad*) will develop into one metropolitan region, a relatively vast conurbation which will increasingly resemble present-day L.A. They applaud this process because they believe it will produce a "heteropolis" that reflects the age of cyberspace with its decentralization, flexibility, mobility, and rapid and massive electronic transportation of information, much more so than most European cities with their traditional urbanity.

Contrary to this utopian, or maybe rather apocalyptic, vision the obvious fact ought to be emphasized that European cities, even the largest metropolitan areas, are the result of relatively long historical developments which, although in different variations, constitute a history of urbanity. The compact Hanseatic city, with its relatively concrete economic and civic culture is, of course, a thing of the past. However, the modernization of Western cities has not been, as I have argued, a process of annihilation of urbanity. Amsterdam's urban culture is very different from that of Rotterdam, as they again differ decisively from the urbanity of Utrecht and from that of the Hague. It requires a very ahistorical type of argument to maintain that in the Netherlands the cultural idiosyncracies and differences of cities will merge into an L.A.-like urban sprawl and eventually evaporate. Likewise, the urban histories of New York, Hartford, and Boston gave rise to very different urban idiosyncracies which will not vanish and make room for Gottmann's *megalopolis*.

Even if it is a feasible scenario, we ought to resist it with all means possible. The dysfunctions of the L.A. "heteropolis" are obvious. Air pollution here is the worst of all American cities. The mobility of this city, of which postmodernist urbanologists usually speak highly, is clearly a myth. People spend many unproductive hours in their cars, caught up in perpetual traffic jams, while the public transportation system, or what is left of it, is well-nigh premodern. The flexibility, equally applauded by postmodernist ideologues, is, if it is truly a feature of L.A., largely undone by bureaucratic inefficiencies and a multitude of decentralized regulations. And the liberalism that is so dear to most postmodernists is largely destroyed by basic fears that cause an obsessive and, at times, paranoid search for security. Public spaces that are socially dead—streets and avenues filled only with cars, squares and parks where no social intercourse takes place—are indeed eerie places, and in actual fact often dangerous as well.

The main argument against the L.A.-model, however, is that life in this "heteropolis" is subjected, probably more intensively than in any other big city, to a penetrating anomie—a deep sense of meaninglessness and homelessness. People are, in a very fundamental sense of the word, deracinated and have withdrawn from public spaces. They entrench themselves in houses that resemble little fortresses promising uninvited strangers an armed response. Public space is dead and that is devastating to any kind of city.

In short, the argument ought to be turned around. Obviously, L.A. has a lot in its corner, so to speak, since it is an immense reservoir of human capacities and potentialities. Its size and expanse, its socioeconomic pluriformity and multiculturality, its focus on global markets make it a fascinating, chaotic, and often maddening world. Admittedly, this cauldron of impulses constitutes some sort of culture and that is, in a peculiar manner, its idiosyncracy. But if L.A. is going to be a viable, vital, and livable urban environment for its people in the twenty-first century, it will have to work on strengthening its urbanity as its economic and civic culture—a culture that should transcend, not destroy, the present, largely uncontrolled diversity and pluriformity.

## Anomic Cities

There are two sociological a prioris without which a society cannot exist: first, the combination of what Weber, following Toennies, called society-building (*Vergesellschaftung*) and community-building (*Vergemeinschaftung*); and second, the presence of what Weber called a legitimate order (*legitime Ordnung*). These are, of course, rationally constructed "ideal types."

We can be brief about these concepts. Human behavior is, according to Weber, not only subjectively meaningful, symbolic behavior, founded on subjective (conscious or unconscious) motives but also on social behavior, interaction. Weber used the condensed expression "meaningful social action" (*sinnhaftes soziales Handeln*). Today, we would call it "symbolic interaction."

Such an interaction can be based on purely rational considerations and on agreements regarding the promotion of certain interests. It is what Weber called society-building. Transactions on the market come close to this "ideal type." However, social interactions can, ideal-typically, also be founded upon mutual feelings of attraction and emotions of solidarity. This is what Weber called community-building. The family, the circle of close friends, the gathering of fellow-believers are examples of *Vergemeinschaftung*. As both are conceptual constructions, they will rarely occur in pure form in empirical reality. Our daily social actions are usually a mixture of the two; or, in one context we act in terms of society-building, in the next context, our interactions are more of the community-building type. However, with the progress of modernization as rationalization, society-building tends to be more prominent than community-building.

Weber did not address himself explicitly on the important question: how can larger social collectivities, such as multinational corporations, the city, or the state continue to function properly, when it is their exclusive aim to promote their interests, without any community-building component? Moreover, can such social collectivities, predominantly products of society-building, be experienced in the long run by insiders and outsiders as legitimate orders? That is the second a priori.

Human social action never occurs within a sociocultural vacuum, but is always embedded in frames of reference which contain the rules by which behavior is approved or disapproved. The two most important frames are, according to Weber, again ideal-typically, the conventions and the law. They constitute, each in their own way, an order (*Ordnung*).[16] However, conventions and law cannot be juxtaposed. In fact, conventions are in actual fact traditional institutions of which law is a specification. Together they constitute an overarching institutional order—a meaningful *nomos*—which to the people concerned (who act and live within it) ought to be valid, legitimate, and authoritative, lest society disintegrates and falls apart.

This meaningful order, in the long run, no longer functions properly, if it is maintained only in a repressive manner, if it functions as a naked power applying brutish violence to maintain itself. When people do not subject themselves to an order against their will, but comply with it for whatever reason (rational, emotional, traditional, religious, etc.), we may speak of a legitimate, authoritative order. It is an order of basic consensus.

This conceptual exercise, kept brief and thus incomplete, helps to determine the relevance of urbanity to contemporary, fully modernized cities. In these cities, since the public and private spheres have been separated into mutual opposition while the central interventionist state tries to keep them in political and financial tutelage and bondage, the process of community-building is well-nigh impossible. As a result, they have disintegrated steadily into compartmentalized units and relationships of interests. These units of partial interests do no longer constitute a coherent market—they resemble various bazaars. The inhabitants of these cities can hardly identify themselves with their urban environment, or experience any bond of urban solidarity. This negatively affects the civic dimension of urban culture since the political and social participation of urban dwellers declined proportionately.

This entailed a rather severe loss of legitimacy on the part of the cities whose administrations are, as a result, not able to exert an authoritative influence on the urban inhabitants, their organizations and institutions. Thus, the two basic a priori's of societal life fell out, exposing cities not just to socioeconomic crisis, but to political and above all cultural (sociopsychological) crisis as well. Such cities lack a sufficient degree of vigorous urbanity, and slip easily into anomie.

The interesting thing about urbanity was, from the start, that it combined the society-building and the community-building factors of socioeconomic action. Urbanity, as we have seen before, was from the very beginning a functional-rational kind of solidarity. The burghers of the trading cities of the eleventh century banded together in order to defend and promote their economic and political interests against the ruling estates of feudal society. Their main field of operation was the market which soon transcended the surrounding region and could extend far beyond the borders of Western Europe. This was indeed what Weber called society-building. Yet, these merchants, craftsmen, service experts, and urban administrators also experienced an emotional bond. They identified themselves beyond the ties of family, religion, and class with their city, and they often did so with a measure of pride. In a sense, these burghers developed some kind of urban chauvinism. In Weberian terms, their actions were community-building as well. The city was to them not so much a romantic *Gemeinschaft* but above all a meaningful order, a *nomos*, a legitimate and legitimating order.

This is of special importance to us who live either in a city, or outside cities in an advanced urbanized environment. We are all thoroughly urbanized. It is this urbanized environment which constitutes our direct, physical, sociocultural milieu. However, this milieu is, due to a lack of vital urbanity, in danger of losing its legitimacy and authority; it is no longer a *nomos*. This is the cause of social and psychological tensions and conflicts which are infinitely more fundamental and influential than the alleged loneliness of modern, thoroughly urbanized men and women. One could argue, as has been done recurrently, that urban loneliness means freedom and individual autonomy also. As such, it is not necessarily negative. Alienation too is, in all probability, not the correct concept here, because that would include loss of control over one's own life and destiny, loss of personal autonomy and freedom. This is obviously not a dominant trait of modern urban life within a democratic political context. Not loneliness and alienation, then, but a penetrative Durkheimian anomie is the fundamental social and cultural problem of cities without urbanity. It will eventually negatively affect the economic and civic dimensions of urban life.

Anomie is not just normlessness, it is a deep-seated sense of meaninglessness, of illegitimacy, of lack of authority. Modern cities without

urbanity are anomic, because they have developed into incoherent conglomerates of bazaars whose solidarities are, if they do exist at all,
purely functional-rational and oriented to partial interests. Burghers—
if this concept is still applicable—cannot identify themselves with these
often ad hoc structures that lack intrinsic authority and legitimacy. As
a result the civic dimension of urban life, the heart of urban democracy, fades away.

Outside the Western hemisphere and within Europe prior to the eleventh century, there have been cities, sometimes very large ones. But
they were not organized around a coherent market and usually lacked
any trace of civic culture. Yet, anomie was avoided by the existence of
traditional, often sacred bonds of solidarity and authority of a macrostructural nature—the estates of feudal Europe, the extended families
of ancient China, or the castes of Hindu India, for instance. Modern
man has no such bonds at his disposal. Without urbanity the urbanized
and individualized citizen of contemporary industrial society lacks
macrostructural identifications, and lives in an order which is abstractly
bureaucratic and thus rather illegitimate.

Urban society thus presents itself as a meaningless and abstract order which is easily seen as repressive and which, as a result, easily
invites aggressive and criminal behavior. Without urbanity as ground
for legitimacy, city administrators can only counter urban aggression
and criminality by means of an escalating repression; certainly if crime
runs rampant in certain parts of the city and if aggression explodes in
collective acts of public violence. This public repression usually leads
to a spiral of violence which only adds to further decline in legitimacy
and authority.

In other words, the basic question in terms of urban policy is whether
we are able to develop and maintain a contemporary, truly modern
type of urbanity which contributes to a fortification of urban solidarity
among the burghers and to authority on the part of the urban administrators. Traditional intermediary institutions, like the family, the church,
the neighborhood, and voluntary associations seem to have lost much
of their community-building and anomie-preventing power, while the
abstract interventionist authorities remain unable to fill the void of
legitimacy that emerged consequently. Often this void is filled by criminal gangs and organizations.

If modern cities are still able to develop a modern kind of urbanity,
they may well achieve what the welfare state could not: the establishment of a truly modern kind of solidarity and identification in a socio-

economic and political milieu which is open and modern. Such an urban milieu would (a) shield off the forces of anomie, endemic in each radically modernized and thus abstract society, (b) bring together the public and the private spheres of socioeconomic life, and (c) combine the society-building and the community-building actions and interactions of its citizens, albeit, as we shall see, with strong precedence of the former over the latter.

But how should we envisage such a truly modern and contemporary kind of urbanity? Again, we cannot reinstall an early modern type of urbanity in a fully modernized (late modern) society as ours.

### The Contours of Contemporary Urbanity

The cities of today will, to begin with, admittedly lack the community-building force of, for instance, the Hanseatic cities. They are simply too large, too complex, too often subjected to constant socioeconomic changes, too entrenched in the flows and flexibilities brought about by electronic technologies, in order to establish a coherent and emotionally rooted community. Thus, a communitarian definition of contemporary urbanity would not be very adequate. Yet, this is not to say that urbanity as the economic and civic culture of cities would be a thing of the past altogether. It might well be that fully modernized (according to some: postmodern, or better yet, late modern) cities need some measure of urbanity in order to survive economically and politically.

One should constantly bear in mind that Western urbanity has, from the beginning, been a rather rational culture primarily based upon economic and political interests. Emotional identification with the city— urban chauvinism and pride—did not originate from bonds of blood, possession of soil, or religious allegiances, but from common, private, and collective interests—political and material interests. Urbanity is in its origin not primarily a *Gemeinschaft* establishing culture, but first and foremost an economic and civic culture. This was, as we have seen, together with its transnational cosmopolitanism its typically modern dimension and it was this dimension that in fact contributed to the further modernization of the Western world.

In a sense urbanity is comparable to organizational culture in contemporary industrial or commercial corporations. Such a corporate culture is predominantly functionally rational and a very far cry from the kind of community people experience from the family, the church, or the private club. However, a corporate culture does present, if it is sufficiently vital and vigorous, a sense of common identity and common aim, even a sense of collective, corporate pride. As general and rational (i.e., modern) as such an organizational culture may be, it does add to the authority and legitimacy of the corporation. To all involved (management and workers), the corporation with a vital culture constitutes some sort of *nomos*, some sort of legitimate and authoritative order. The same holds true of contemporary urbanity as the "corporate culture" of the modern city.

I have focused on urbanity as a way of life, as a particular form of solidarity, as a worldview and ethos. Admittedly, these are, in Weber's terminology, community-building dimensions. But underlying all of this is the much stronger society-building forces which are exemplified in various urban functions, such as housing, work (trade, industry, public and private services), traffic, leisure and pleasure, arts and sciences. In cities with a vital urbanity these functions are not spatially and functionally separated, as proposed by Le Corbusier in his utopian vision of the Radiant City which we shall discuss later. They are, on the contrary, intertwined and mixed. Through this commingling of functions people are tied together in a functional manner. It is inherent to their private and collective interest to collaborate and to socialize. This is a Durkheimian "organic solidarity" which, as we saw before, has been characteristic of urbanity almost from the beginning. Contemporary urban solidarity will most certainly be strongly organic (i.e., functional). A Dutch architect with a remarkable sensitivity for urbanity formulated this as follows:

> The essence of urbanity is the interweaving of functions, of housing, recreation, playing, learning, working and everything connected therewith, like shopping, greeting, small talk, walking on together, looking at things or participating in doing things—all of this within the codes of social intercourse. It has been a disaster to separate these functions in urban designs.[17]

However, having said this, we should admit that community-building forces also exist in fully modernized, contemporary cities, albeit in a rather vague, general, and "abstract" manner. Moreover, if modernity's functional rationality becomes too dominant, people tend to react rather emotionally, calling for more substantial rationality, and, beyond that, an emotional and allegedly "concrete" experience of community. Not rarely is such an experience neo-romantic, if not posh and *kitschig*. People then claim to yearn for more "we-feelings." With regard to urbanity, we are then usually called upon to embrace romantic notions of an allegedly lost *Gemeinschaft* to be regained by utopian town planning. The Garden City movement was a telling example of this ideology which reemerged recently in what is called *New Urbanism*.[18] One project, presently developed by the Disney Corporation outside Orlando, Florida, is named *Celebration*. It is a compact town for twenty thousand inhabitants reminiscent of a colonial-period village. Only six styles of houses are allowed to be built: classical, Victorian, colonial revival, coastal, Mediterranean, and French. Not amazingly, postmodernist architects who are generally fond of "historical citations," participated in the project. Incidentally, the land was bought by Walt Disney in the 1930s, and the ideas he then had about truly American towns have been taken down from the shelves again by the developers of Celebration.[19] Needless to add that these and similar projects seem appealing because of their rather heavy kitsch value. All of this reminds one of the Jeffersonian vision of the city-on-the-mount. It is Zion vis-à-vis Babylon again, and definitely not a viable model for a vital, contemporary kind of urbanity.

Urbanity ought to remain down-to-earth, predominantly "organic," and functionally rational, if it is to contribute to fruitful contemporary cities and contemporary city life. Community-building sentiments and activities are doomed to remain modern, and therefore rather vague and abstract. Each attempt to render them emotionally warm and "concrete" is rather naive, and probably in the end counterproductive. Society-building interactions and functions in terms of a down-to-earth economic and civic culture founded on political and economic, and private and collective interests have to prevail, if a truly contemporary and modern urbanity will (re)emerge successfully.

This is in line with the original nature of urbanity, as we explored earlier. We also saw, however, that urbanity's modernization led to its gradual decline and demise, causing the emergence of metropolises without a vital urbanity. They are comparable to multinational corporations which lack a vital and invigorating "organizational culture." Such corporations are usually devoid of a strategic sense of direction, while its human resources, generally viewed as their most essential capital, gradually desiccate in bureaucratic formalisms. Just as "corporate culture" has by now become a normal component of modern business administration, it ought to be the primary business of urban administrations these days to develop conscious policies and planning procedures that deal with the development and strengthening of a fully modern and contemporary urbanity. In the recent past policies have often been developed which are lethal to a vital urban culture. For example, the separation of the various urban functions, as Le Corbusier proposed, will contribute sooner or later to the disappearance of urbanity, or, more likely to a very abstract and colorless type of urban culture which hovers above scores of fragmented and conflicting subcultures. Such an urbanity can no longer function as the electrifying and energizing force that cities need in order to be producers of the wealth of nations and hosts of civic democracy.

It must be emphasized that a truly contemporary urbanity will deviate strongly from traditional European urbanity in one specific, very decisive respect: it will not be monocentric but polycentric. Particularly in view of the growing multiculturality of present-day cities, urban habitats will be pluriform socioculturally, politically, and economically. Along these dividing lines various centers with various allegiances and solidarities will emerge and develop. However, having said this much, it should also be emphasized that it will be imperative that contemporary urban policy orchestrate and coordinate these multiple urban centers. That is, contemporary cities should try to maintain one administratively, socioculturally, and economically dominant city center—a geographically determinable Downtown—to which the other centers relate as *satellite-centers*. Los Angeles, for example, may indeed be the prime example of a polycentric, fragmented metropolis, as is claimed in particular by postmodern urbanologists. But, in order to prevent the gradual spread of a pervasive urban anomie, which will also eventually affect the various semi-autonomous centers, this city may have to put prime emphasis upon the sociocultural and economic regeneration and revitalization of its Downtown area.

This argument should also be maintained in view of the so-called *edge cities* which are presently emerging around large urban conglomerates.[20] Unlike suburbs, edge cities integrate homes, jobs, shops, and leisure (in particular sport) facilities. Due to modern communication techniques, service jobs—banks, administrative offices, information and communication businesses, and so forth—can function efficiently outside cities and their Downtown areas. There, land prices are lower and personnel can be housed cheaply and more comfortably. Yet, these edge cities are in fact *satellite cities* which remain dependent on an economically and culturally vital Downtown, where the boutiques, the exclusive restaurants, the museums, the theaters, and the concert halls are. Tourists do not visit edge cities. They stay in Downtown hotels and spend their money in Downtown shops, restaurants, museums, and theaters. Edge cities will soon be ghost towns, if they fail to entertain strong sociocultural and economic lifelines with a Downtown area that functions as the source and center of the region's urbanity. These lifelines are called, in contemporary jargon, networks. Urban networks need a core, a center: an economically, socially, and culturally vital and vibrant Downtown.

## Notes

1.  Murray Bookchin, *Urbanization without Cities: The Rise and Decline of Citizenship* (Montreal and New York: Black Rose Books, 1992). See also Murray Bookchin, *The Limits of the City* (New York: HarperCollins Books, 1974).
2.  Jean Gottmann and Robert A. Harper, *Since Megalopolis: The Urban Writings of Jean Gottmann* (Baltimore, MD: The Johns Hopkins University Press, 1990).
3.  Manuel Castells, *The Informational City* (Oxford: Blackwell Publishers, [1989] 1992), p. 6.
4.  Cf. Peter Hall, *Reinventing the City*, Research Paper 179, (Toronto: Center for Urban and Community Studies, University of Toronto, 1990). I found this reference in a Dutch study on the informational city: Rein B. Jobse and Sako Musterd, *De stad in het informatietijdperk (The City in the Era of Information)*, (Assen: Van Gorcum, 1994), p. 3 and 9.
5.  Cf., e.g., Edward C. Banfield, *The Unheavenly City: The Nature and Future of Our Urban Crisis* (Boston, MA: Little, Brown and Co., [1968] 1970). Morton and Lucia White, *The Intellectual Versus the City: From Thomas Jefferson to Frank Lloyd Wright* (Cambridge, MA: Harvard University Press; The MIT Press, 1962). Peter Hall, *Cities of Tomorrow: An Intellectual History of Urban Planning and Design in the Twentieth Century* (Oxford: Basil Blackwell, 1988). Also Ruth Glass, *Clichés of Urban Doom* (Oxford: Basil Blackwell, 1989).
6.  The following two seemingly opposite views ought to be combined. See Susan Diesenhouse, "As Suburbs Slow, Supermarkets Return to Cities" in the *New York Times* (27 June 1993), p. F5: "Companies see a new frontier in urban markets that many left years ago." See also Witold Rybczynski who views suburbs as integral part of city life, and questions the so-called return to the city: "The so-called back-to-the-city movement of the 1970s fizzled out; high rents, high prices, and high crime have continued to drive young families to the suburbs. Clearly, in one form or another, suburbs are here to stay." W. Rybczynski, "Should Suburbs Be Designed?" in *Looking Around: A Journey Through Architecture* (New York: Penguin Books, 1992), pp. 99–106.
7.  L. van den Berg, L. H. Klaassen, and J. van der Meer, *Strategische City-Marketing* (Schoonhoven: Academic Service, 1990), p. 16.
8.  See Mike Davis, *City of Quartz: Excavating the Future in Los Angeles*, (New York: n.p., 1992).
9.  René Boomkens, "De hoofdstad van de 21ste eeuw" ("The Capital of the Twenty-first Century") in *Expeditie L.A.*, eds. Daan Bakker et al. (Rotterdam: Nederlands Architectuurinstituut, 1995), p. 05/1. This is the report of a study tour to L.A. by Dutch architects, in February 1994.
10.  David Rieff, *Los Angeles: Capital of the Third World* (New York: n.p., 1991).
11.  Davis, *City of Quartz*, p. 224.
12.  René Boomkens, "21ste eeuw," p. 05/2. My translation. Boomkens follows Mike Davis, when he calls L.A. an "image."

13. Davis, *City of Quartz*, p. 228f.
14. Ibid., p. 229.
15. Cf. Charles Jencks, *Heteropolis: Los Angeles—the Riots and the Strange Beauty of Hetero-Architecture* (London: Academy Editions, 1993).
16. For these concepts see Max Weber, "Soziologische Grundbegriffe" (Fundamental Sociological Concepts)" in Max Weber, *Wirtschaft und Gesellschaft*, ch. 1, (Köln and Berlin: Kiepenhauer & Witsch, Studienausgabe, 1964), pp. 22–31.
17. J.F. Berghoef, "Architectuur en stedebouw: spiegel van de samenleving (Architecture and Urban Design: Mirror of Society)" in H. de Haan and I. Haagsma, eds., *Wie is er bang voor nieuwbouw? (Who is Afraid of New Buildings?)* (Amsterdam: Intermediair Bibliotheek, 1981), pp. 49–78. My translation.
18. Peter Katz, ed., *The New Urbanism: Toward an Architecture of Community* (New York: McGraw-Hill, 1994.)
19. I took this information from a perceptive article on New Urbanism by a Dutch journalist under the heading "Utopie van het dorpsplein (Utopia of the Village Square)" by Tracy Metz in *NRC Handelsblad* (6 April 1996), p. 4f.
20. For a vivid, journalistic, and somewhat hyperbolic account see Joel Garreau, *Edge City: Life on the New Frontier* (New York: Anchor Books, Doubleday, 1991).

# 5

# Urbanity and Urban Policy:
# The Cultural Dimensions of Urban Renewal

## Can Urbanity Be Planned?

Planning is endemic to fully modernized societies. Particularly in a welfare state which is so dependent upon rationalization and centralization, planning will function as the indispensable instrument that can harmonize rationally set goals and effective and efficient means. It is not necessary to discuss planning here in detail or to expand upon various planning techniques. Rather, we ought to realize that the heyday of rational planning is over because modern rationalization and centralization, so typical of an extensive and intensive welfare state, are no longer. We now live in a late modern and, according to many, even postmodern, society which is characterized by pervasive nonrational fragmentation and decentralization rather than rational centralization and unification. In such a world, the rational harmonization of ends and means, as in the planning of the welfare-state bureaus, simply does not make sense.

However, there are various ways to define and practice planning. In its most original sense, planning is man's capacity to select goals carefully, and then to design instruments for the realization of these goals. It is, next to the irrational method of trial-and-error, the most fundamental method of human action. As such, planning is an anthropological constant with scores of variations in time and space. One of these variations is a kind of rational planning that emerged in the Western world in the wake of the Enlightenment. It is inseparably connected with the technocratic belief that reality—nature, culture, history, and maybe even life—can be constructed and reconstructed rationally. It is this rationalist variation that, according to many, is currently in decline. However, two reservations are in order here. First, in some areas, in particular in the fields of medicine and biochemistry, rational

147

planning and technocratic engineering are still very prominent. Second, in the socioscientific field as well, the decline of Enlightenment rationalism is not at all universal. Even where it does occur, it does not necessarily entail the end of all planning. The method of trial-and-error may have gained respectability—it is often wrapped in fashionable chaos theories and postmodernist ruminations about flexible flows, borderless networks, and nonrational fragmentations. But at the end of the day normal people will still continue to set goals and design means that are as effective and efficient as possible. This is true *a fortiori* for administrators, politicians, and civil servants who bear responsibility for public goods and public expenditures. They will simply have to engage in planning.

As to cities, urban planning, as we know it today, began at the end of the nineteenth and the beginning of the twentieth century. It was a response to the social miseries of the congested cities which emerged in the wake of industrialization.[1] However, with respect to urban design and planning we ought to address the question of whether urbanity as a historical and, in origin, European economic and civic, culture can be planned—whether it is possible, in other words, to set urbanity as a rational goal of urban policy and to foster it systematically within a comprehensive urban design. In short, can urbanity be planned?

It is often believed that culture, and thus urbanity, resists rational planning. That seems a reasonable conclusion at first sight. Indeed culture is, in essence, a historically grown configuration of values, norms, and meanings, shaped and structured in institutions which are difficult to trace the origins of. Moreover, on the rational drawing board one can design an industrial or bureaucratic organization, pin down its functional differentiation, its command structure, and its proper operational territory. But it is well-nigh impossible to do the same with culture, as one discovers immediately when attempting to grasp such an ephemeral phenomenon like organizational culture.

However, it would be romantic and quite old-fashioned to believe that culture—and thus urbanity—emerges spontaneously, functions autonomously, reaches a summit, and is eventually doomed to decline without the possibility of any rational human interference. In fact, culture would then be viewed, if not as blind fate, as a kind of natural, instead of historical, phenomenon. Of course, culture admittedly has much to do with biological conditions and material needs. The boundaries between nurture and nature are notoriously vague and slippery. However, it also remains a fact that human individuals and human collectivities react differently to these conditions and needs. They somehow construct, maintain, and pass on patterns of behavior (institutions) which are thoroughly historical. With the passage of time, they change their substance and appearance constantly, yet contain very strong seeds of continuity and stability.

Institutions transcend biological conditions and material needs and develop a reality of their own with its own rationality and logic. It is a reality that transcends the individual and individual behavior, the ad hoc, and the here-and-now. This reality indeed acquires, as Durkheim argued, a *sui generis* character. We call it in shorthand, "culture." The culture of the early modern cities in Europe can also be traced back to physical conditions and material needs. It is, however, far more interesting and relevant sociologically that this urban culture soon developed semi-autonomously into a historical and traditional set of urban institutions which embodied a distinct economic and civic culture. It is then a historical and objective phenomenon that can be subjected to rational scrutiny, as is done in this study. It follows that this historical phenomenon can also be subjected to rational policies.

In particular, after one has determined the relevance of urbanity as a historical phenomenon for today's cities and the parameters for a contemporary kind of urbanity, one can try to determine which negative conditions may hamper it and which positive conditions may foster it. This is not a technocratic, old-fashioned, rationalistic kind of cultural engineering; it is a substantially rational planning that fosters, not stifles, freedom and creativity. Karl Mannheim would have called it "planning for freedom."[2]

## Urbanity and Urban Renewal

Sometimes the concept of urbanity and, more often, that of urbanism occurs in discussions and publications about urban policy, urban design, and urban planning. Usually such debates are not clearly defined and rarely do they touch on the issues we discussed previously. If the present analysis is correct in presenting urbanity as an empirical phenomenon with a historically traceable origin and development in the Western world, we must deal with it rationally and scientifically. Urbanity will, in that case, also be relevant to urban policy's various endeavors.

Cultural sociology, as historical and comparative sociology, tries to look behind the façades of society, continuously in search of historical origins, sociocultural developments, and meaningful relationships. This mode of sociologizing digs behind organizational structures searching for latent values and meanings embedded in traditional patterns of thinking, feeling, and acting (i.e., institutions). The cultural sociologist tries to detect and reconstruct solidarity as the cohesive principle underlying the sociological facts of order and disorder. What is generally called "society" or "social structure" in sociology is seen and interpreted by the cultural sociologist as "culture" or "universe of meaning." Underlying social change, the cultural sociologist detects a coherent yet very complex process of modernization; underlying the city, he looks for urbanity. These are not allegedly metaphysical depth-structures but empirical phenomena and processes that can be made "visible" through historical and comparative analysis.

In the preceding chapters we have seen how, in the wake of a spectacular rise since roughly the eleventh century, European cities developed their urbanity, often in contrast to, if not in conflict with, older principles of identity and solidarity. However, under the regime of absolutism and its endemic centralization of power in the capital, cities began to lose their autonomy and power. This process was exacerbated by the interventionist nation-state and particularly by the interventionist welfare state. With this loss of urban power and autonomy came a similar decline in urbanity. Urban culture, we saw, modernized gradually into very general, broad, and abstract collective identities, such as nationalism and patriotism, until, in the end, under the regime of the welfare state, even those sentiments dried up and evaporated. By then, cities had lost their identity and character, their ability to tie people together, to inspire them, and to encourage creative productivity. It meant a decisive ossification of the city's economic culture, much to the detriment of its economic strength and vigor, of course. Civic culture began to lose its stamina at the same time, which resulted in a decline in active democratic participation on the part of the urban dwellers. In consequence, cities became, not just politically but economically, increasingly dependent upon the centralized administrative bureaucracies in the capital.

Meanwhile, central governments may pour great amounts of money into our troubled cities to keep them from submerging to blight, poverty, and destitution—and, we may add, to keep them dependent. Yet it is questionable whether all this money can indeed revitalize the very source of urban renewal: a vital economic and civic culture. Without urbanity these cities will remain disorganized and anomic bazaars, habitats doomed to sociocultural and political lifelessness, if not death. The money poured into these cities by the central government will be all for naught if the plans for urban renewal do not somehow incorporate the cultural factor of urbanity.

Urbanity is a crucial ingredient in the much needed revitalization of our cities. I am, of course, not saying that central governments should stop their financial assistance of cities. Rather, I plead for an incorporation of the cultural factor in all public and private endeavors concerning the revitalization of our cities. As an economic and civic culture, urbanity can fulfil important functions and should therefore be incorporated in all theoretical and practical endeavors of urban design and planning. As Jane Jacobs has forcefully argued, cities are the main sources of the wealth of nations, and if one considers the historical fact that European cities were the cradles of Western democracy, the whole issue takes on a relevance that transcends the parameters of cities.

## Conditions for a Vital Urbanity

A strongly centralized, interventionist state is, as we saw before, incommensurable to the economic and civic vitality of cities. In this respect the tendencies of decentralization, privatization, and internationalization in most Western societies foster the resurgence of cities. If these cities are to function as engines of economy and sources of democratic vitality, they are in dire need of vital economic and civic cultures. Urbanity is, in this respect, necessary for the cities of today and tomorrow.

As to Europe, the gradual shift of power and sovereignty from the nation-states and their capitals to Brussels, the capital of the European Union, will eventually be advantageous to cities and regions, if, that is, the policy of *subsidiarity* is enacted in actual practice: the higher authorities in the European Union concern themselves only with those issues which the lower authorities are unable to deal with adequately—i.e., international relations, international safety, transnational economic developments, and so on. If enacted properly, the subsidiarity principle will eventually provide regions and cities with considerable political clout. It will, in addition, create socioeconomic space to promote and pursue material (economic and political) interests within the context of their own urban and regional cultures. If this actually occurs, the Europe of the regions, Jacques Delors's *l'Europe des régions pas des nations* ("Euroregions"), will in all probability also be a Europe of cities ("Eurocities") and urban regions.[3]

This administrative and political transformation has not concluded yet. Will it continue to alter the power relations between the nation-states, the regions and the cities of Europe, or will there be a political backlash on the part of nation-states that want to maintain their full national sovereignty, and fear the growing power and bureaucratic control of Brussels and the increasing autonomy of cities and regions? The discussions in various European parliaments about the Treaty of Maastricht concentrated predominantly on this question.[4]

There are also questions to be asked about the other transformation in the post-welfare-state society. Will the rifts between the public and the private sectors, between the profit and the non-profit service sectors, between the bureaucratic state and the free market be restored eventually, and brought into a workable balance? Will there be a complex world of super-rational and super-functional organizations in which bureaucratic formalisms run rampant, to which people adjust for the duration of their working hours (which in total amount will decline) while they give themselves to rather informal, and at times irrational activities, thoughts and emotions in their leisure time?[5] That again would contribute to the growing polarization of a public, formal, and purely functionally rational world on the one hand, and a most private, informal, and irrational world on the other. Any social solidarity, let alone urbanity, is hard to conceive of in such a polarized world. Or is this conclusion too fatalistic and rash?

Let us, for the sake of the argument, assume as the most negative scenario that this transformation will indeed continue to affect the economy, the polity, the society, and culture of Western civilization— in some nations and regions more rapidly and radically than in others, of course, but nonetheless. In that case, instead of being a passive victim, urbanity could, on the contrary, function as an instrument of policy by which the transformation is curbed, dampening, as it were, its adverse effects on society. Even if the transformation establishes circumstances that are detrimental to urbanity as an economic and civic culture, policymakers still have the option to strengthen urbanity, to revitalize by all means possible and available, the economic and civic culture of the habitat for which they are responsible. Likewise, citizens and scores of organizations in civil society can, against the tide of these negative conditions, still attempt to promote and strengthen the culture of their city. After all, these conditions are not caused by metaphysical fate but created by men in history.

The first public and private attempts at strengthening urbanity are in themselves proof that urbanity has not been completely erased, that some remnants are still alive. The very awareness that the averse transformation concerns *their* society and *their* city, that it has a negative impact on *their* habitat, is the first step in the direction of urban society-building and urban renewal.

What then, in terms of policy, are the main conditions for a vital, fully contemporary, urbanity which urban authorities, both public and private, ought to heed—conditions that, as a deliberate policy, ought to be fostered and reinforced. The focus of the following discussion is on five basic and general conditions which have been mentioned before but stand in need of further and more coherent discussion: (a) intermediary (or mediating) structures; (b) sociocultural diversity; (c) functional pluriformity; (d) a lively inner city; (e) and prolonged national decentralization plus a combination of centralization and decentralization within cities and urban regions. I shall discuss each now.

## Mediating Structures

A return to the premodern centripetal and concrete community is, as was said repeatedly, neither feasible nor desirable. We live in a thoroughly modernized, predominantly functionally rational, pluralistic society in which the society-building forces are infinitely stronger than the community-building ones. However, the question remains relevant if a certain balance between the public and the private, by means of revitalized intermediary associations, would not be one of the basic necessities or possibilities of present-day society. Such a balance, as we saw before, is crucial to urbanity.

In a manifesto published in the 1970s—almost two decades before the present discussions on civil society—Peter L. Berger and Richard J. Neuhaus argued that modernization gives rise to a radical polarization of the public and the private. Much like Tocqueville and Durkheim, they believe that (a) this very polarization is detrimental to a vital democracy, and (b) this can be ameliorated, if not eradicated, by mediating institutions. They begin their manifesto with three basic propositions: "The first proposition is analytical: Mediating structures are essential for a vital democratic society. The other two are broad programmatic recommendations: Public policy should protect and foster mediating structures, and whenever possible, public policy should utilize mediating structures for the realization of social purposes."[6]

According to both authors, family, neighborhood, the church, and voluntary associations are still the most potentially influential mediating institutions. In them, citizens should regain the power through which they can structure their lives according to their own values and norms. Such vital mediating structures will then function as "able bodies" vis-à-vis *megastructures* that rule and order their lives. Mediating structures help to empower people who have become increasingly powerless under the regime of interventionist nation-states.

Berger and Neuhaus continue, elaborating upon the concept of megastructure: "The most important large institution in the ordering of modern society is the state itself. In addition, there are the large economic conglomerates of capitalist enterprise, big labor, and the growing bureaucracies that administer wide sectors of society, such as in education and the organized professions. All these institutions we call the megastructures."[7]

In a much older study, Robert Nisbet discussed the issue of mediating structures as a quest for community. Likewise, William Kornhauser discussed the political relevance of voluntary associations as the cornerstones of democracy.[8] As these and other theoretical studies demonstrate, mediating structures have drawn the attention of many social philosophers and social theorists. In fact, since Tocqueville, Durkheim, and Weber, the importance of mediating (or intermediary) structures is a perennial theme within the social sciences which led to many critical and, at times, fierce debates. Understandably there was a lull in this debate during the heyday of the welfare state when the polarization of public and private was the normal state of affairs.

Naturally, mediating structures have been the object of debate and action, particularly in the political arena. Anti-democratic radicals, from the Jacobinians of the French Revolution to the Bolsheviks of the Russian Revolution, have systematically attempted to oppress free associations operating outside the total control of the state. It is interesting to read what a French revolutionary, *citoyen* Le Chapelier, had to say about guilds as mediating structures. These words are from his speech in the *Assemblée Constituante* of 1791:

> The bodies in question have the avowed object of procuring relief for workers in the same occupation who fall sick or become unemployed. But let there be no mistake about this: it is for the nation and for the public officials on its behalf to supply work to those who need it for their livelihood and to succor the sick.... It should not be permissible for citizens in certain occupations to meet together in defence of their pretended common interests. There must be no more guilds in the State, but only the individual interest of each citizen and the general interest. No

one shall be allowed to arouse in any citizen any kind of intermediate interest and to separate him from the public weal through the medium of corporate interest.[9]

This is a remarkable quote. First and foremost it is noteworthy because it contains distinct notions of a welfare state in reference to which any kind of self-help on the part of certain interest groups is rejected categorically. Rousseau's theory is applied skillfully: there is, vis-à-vis the general will and the collective interest embodied by the Nation or the State, only the will and the particular interests of the isolated individual citizen. There is no room whatsoever for interest groups located intermediarily between the State and the citizens. That is called pejoratively "corporatism."

Here we find the roots of both socialism (general will, collective interest) and liberalism (particular will, individual interest) which beyond their grave differences joined forces in their opposition against conservatism which was always inclined to champion a strong intermediary field of autonomous associations. Liberals and socialists often call *this* "corporatism." The somewhat strained partnership between these two opposed ideologies would eventually, in the twentieth century, contribute to the birth of the welfare state. When their offspring came of age in the 1970s as a comprehensive welfare state, it appeared to be less fit for life than its parents had hoped for. The centrifugal tendencies of this welfare state gradually tore its fabric to pieces. Its public spending weakened the economy, its bureaucratic centralization rendered it well-nigh ungovernable and unadministrable, and, above all, its perpetual interventions lamed the market as well as civil society. The welfare state's combination of *etatism* and *individualism* weakened the intermediary structures and affected democracy—it delivered citizens to bureaucratic and professional tutelage. Needless to add, this was detrimental to any vital type of urbanity. Devoid of an enticing and electrifying economic and civic culture, the economy and the democracy of cities began to decline.

Incidentally, the almost paranoid fear for and hatred against autonomous associations and organizations which mediate between the state and individual citizens, is essentially alien to the American type of society but has been endemic in most European societies. Prior to 1989, this was very apparent in the communist societies of Eastern Europe, where the animus against mediating structures destroyed civil society first and the economy next. Not surprisingly, the successful revolt against this defunct socioeconomic and political system began in Poland in the remainders of civil society. After all, it was the demand of the workers for an independent workers' union that prompted the fall of the Polish communist regime. However, since 1789, the same animus against autonomous, mediating structures, expressed with admirable clarity in the speech of citizen Le Chapelier, has roamed through most Western European societies like a ghost—sometimes overt and visible, often covert and disguised.[10] In all instances, democracy was in danger of being corrupted.

In this context, the aforementioned subsidiarity principle deserves special interest and relevance. As an administrative principle subsidiarity has been rapidly spreading throughout the European Union. In fact—and this is particularly germane to our subject—there is actually a *chain of subsidiarity*. As we have seen, subsidiarity means that, in matters of public administration, higher echelons should, in their policy and decision making, not interfere in affairs that can be dealt with more adequately (i.e., efficiently and effectively) by lower and lesser authorities. Brussels should not try to do what Westminster can very well handle itself. But—and this is where the chain continues—Westminster ought to leave those affairs to regional and local governments that can be dealt with most efficiently and effectively at the regional and local level. And again, on the local level, subsidiarity means that urban administrations should not interfere in the handling of affairs that can best be dealt with by voluntary associations and citizens' organizations in streets and neighborhoods.

It is not the intention of the chain of subsidiarity to reinstall an old-fashioned corporatism but rather to foster the social, economic, and political participation of citizens, that is, to strengthen the civic culture within a vital civil society. It is the avowed aim of subsidiarity to empower people—people, incidentally, who, thanks to the efforts of the welfare state, received a relatively good education and training and who are generally perfectly capable of utilizing the leeway subsidiarity offers them.

Notably, this chain of subsidiarity gives the idea of mediating structures a different, more complex meaning. For instance if, within the European Union, Brussels eventually would receive the status of a central authority, national governments could well be reduced proportionately to the status of intermediary between this European central authority on the one hand and the provinces and regions, the cities and towns on the other. But again, these lesser authorities may function as mediating structures between the central government of the nation-state on the one hand, and the associations and organizations in which individual citizens enact their active and participatory citizenship on the other.

In other words, analytically (but also in reality) not just traditional institutions like family, the church, neighborhood, and voluntary associations, but also and perhaps even above all, administrative bodies, such as the nation-state, the region and, of course, the city receive a position in the chain of subsidiarity and function there as intermediary structures. This is, of course, important to the main subject of our present discussion. Obviously, a city ought to have its own identity and culture, a vital urbanity that inspires life in an urban civil society. Without such a viable and vital economic and civic culture, cities could not function successfully as mediating links in the transnational chain of subsidiarity. Moreover, they could not keep up with the competition that has emerged internationally between the cities of the world.

The question remains crucial, of course, whether traditional mediating institutions, such as family, the church, neighborhood, and voluntary associations, can still cope with the vagaries of a fully modernized, urban society. The organizational stability and anchorage in a durable institutional tradition has been severely affected in most of these institutions by a deeply penetrating individualism that is fed and fostered by an abstract society.[11] Not only family and the church, but also workers' unions, political parties, sport clubs, and other voluntary associations are, in many instances, in crisis. It is a crisis of group loyalty, collective solidarity, and membership participation.

Sociologically, this is a process of de-institutionalization. It is not as, for instance, Arnold Gehlen believed,[12] the end of institutionalization and thus the end of civilization and the end of history. (Indeed, it was in 1952 that Gehlen wrote about the *post-histoire* of modernity, and in two lectures in 1972 and 1973 he discussed the end of history.)[13] But, how realistic is such an apocalyptic vision? If Gehlen had been right in the 1950s, we certainly should have plunged by now into the abyss of social and cultural anarchy and chaos. That is obviously not the case.

What we have witnessed in the past decades is not the destruction of institutions and a rapid de-institutionalization. Rather, we can observe a late modern type of institutionalization which can perhaps best be coined as "low institutionalization," or "loose institutionalization." For example, in many cases, institutional relations and traditional bonds between human beings have been superseded by *networks* which are not durable and traditional, let alone trans-generational. It is individuals who set up such networks contractually in informal and sometimes also formal manner (marital contracts, for instance). If they have served their purpose, such contracts are ended and new mutual agreements are negotiated and concluded. They are short-term, flexible, facile, mobile—anything but traditional and durable. However, as morally unreliable as they may be (loyalty is in all probability a virtue that does not agree with the nature of modern networks), these mutual agreements do in a way structure human actions, thoughts, beliefs and emotions, and therefore somehow function as institutions.[14] As to mediation, networks mediate first and foremost between individualized parties. As a result, trust, mutual trust, has become a crucial asset in social interactions. It has been defined correctly as the most essential ingredient of social capital.[15]

Naturally, despite this low, or loose, institutionalization, contemporary citizens continue to act collectively in groups, organizations, and associations, However, if they do so, their collective activities must first and foremost serve their particular, and often short-term, interests. This is particularly observable in the political arena. Interest groups engage in all sorts of lobbying and networking by which they try to influence the policy and decision-making offices of the various bureaucratic administrations. Here too, new institutional frameworks have emerged which have mediating functions, albeit in a rather nontraditional fashion.

Finally, as weakened as they may indeed be, there are, after all, still churches, families, unions, schools, universities, clubs, and associations in which citizens act and interact, and through which they voice their particular interests as well as their concerns about the collective interests of the commonwealth. It would be foolish, theoretically as well as practically, to disregard them in the name of some anti-institutional ideology. They remain the cornerstones of a sound civil society and democracy. After all, traditional-institutional settings provide us with a degree of taken-for-grantedness and even with some sort of structural trust with the result that we do not constantly need to explain and negotiate our intentions and interactions. Also, these institutions help us to reduce the complexity of choices to be made in daily life. In a sense, they liberate us from the *Qual der Wahl*, that is, the trouble of choosing. Or, in economic jargon, institutions cut transaction costs. They may very well function as firm parameters for those loosely institutionalized networks in which people act and interact—in some instances promoting private and particular interests, in other instances pursuing goals that represent collective interests. In sum, there is no sociological objection to also calling these networks mediating structures, although one might want to write structures in quotations.

This is of great relevance to urbanity. In fact, from the outset in the early modern era, mediation between public and private has been urbanity's hallmark. Also flexibility of social and economic relations was, from the start the nucleus of this economic and civic culture. Urbanity was one of the carriers of modernization. Therefore, it stands to reason that in our late modern era, as well, this kind of economic and civic culture can still be entrusted to function as the socioeconomic and political stimulant of cities and of urban life, albeit, as we saw before, in an adjusted, thoroughly modernized version. Traditional and highly institutionalized as well as contemporary and lowly institutionalized mediating structures will undergird such a late modern, fully contemporary urbanity. Urban policymakers ought to heed these traditional institutions and late modern networks as the intermediary structures which are the core of democracy and the heart of urbanity.

As to policy and planning, urban administrations can foster traditional institutions and late modern networks through subsidies and the endorsement of professionals working within them, as they once did in the heyday of the welfare state. Yet, the most powerful incentive of these mediating structures, and thus of urbanity, would instead be the conscious decentralization of power in conjunction with deregulation and fiscal accommodation. In the heyday of interventionism scores of initiatives on the part of citizens in intermediary organizations were hampered, if not smothered, by overregulation, bureaucratic control, over-professionalization, and tied fiscal demands. Thus, in conjunction with the subsidiarity principle, urban policy and planning concerning urban mediating structures ought to be conducted as much as is possible and responsible in a non-interventionist spirit.

## Social and Cultural Diversity

Ever since the migration movements of the nineteenth and twentieth centuries, Western cities have become increasingly diverse in terms of the ethnic, cultural, and, in particular, religious composition of their populations. The cities of North America took the lead in this cultural diversification. The cities of Western Europe followed suit ever since the 1960s, when unskilled, manual workers from Turkey, southern Europe, and North Africa were recruited for the lowest, unskilled jobs in the industry and service sectors. Both foreign workers and their employers saw these jobs as temporary ones, but the greater part of these so-called guest workers have, since then, not returned to their home countries. Most of them stayed and brought their families over as well. They are now labelled "migrants" or "immigrants." As has been the case with most "pariah people" (M. Weber) in history, these migrants are concentrated in big cities. European cities were from then on confronted with two related phenomenons that had been previously unknown: ethnicity and cultural diversity. In particular the highly visible presence of Islam was unknown to Western European countries prior to the 1970s.

In terms of policy there are two different strategies that national and urban authorities can apply with regard to such a relatively sudden cultural diversification. One can try to spread the incoming carriers of "alien" cultures spatially in order to neutralize their "alien" values and norms and to secure the predominance of the indigenous culture. As many depend on cheap housing and tend to stick together in the same streets and neighborhoods (generally in the inner cities, where slums offer the desired cheap housing[16]), one would have to use force and/or substantial subsidies to scatter them over the city and the nation. Gentrification, which drives the ethnic poor from their cheap, inner-city dwellings in accordance with the laws of the market, usually does not lead to their spread but to a re-grouping elsewhere.

But even if one could successfully apply a spreading policy, the end result would, in all probability, be a melting pot of cultures that, by definition, lacks the power to entice and stimulate people. It would, above all, perpetuate the culture of poverty, and fail to provide people with a collective identity and pride. It would create a sociocultural climate not at all amenable to a vital urbanity.

The other strategy would be to allow, or even stimulate the physical and spatial specificity of various ethnic cultures within the city, enabling them thus to contribute to the cultural diversity and pluriformity of urban society. China Town and Little Italy are examples of this pluriformity. The mosaic, not the melting pot, is the metaphor to be applied here. However, this should not be interpreted (let alone executed) as a policy of facile and ill-conceived multiculturality. If people would be physically isolated from the rest of society, and enclosed exclusively by their own ethnic culture—their specific life styles, ceremonies, and above all their language—urbanity as an economic and civic culture would be seriously hampered, even damaged. Such facile multiculturality leads easily to centrifugalism and the emergence of separate segments which focus first and foremost on their own segmented material and immaterial interests. This would come close to ethnic ghettoization. Ghettos are by definition closed communities, as Louis Wirth argued in a classic essay on the subject.[17] Cities cut up into ethnic ghettos lose their socioeconomic and cultural coherence, disintegrate into a plurality of bazaars, lack urbanity, and suffer in the end from the paralysis of a pervasive anomie.

However, there are, in the interest of the common good, general rules and laws, to be obeyed by all cultural segments. There are individual and collective human rights and duties to be maintained and executed. There are common and basic customs of civilized behavior to be followed. In Western civilization distinct emancipatory conceptions emerged, in particular those concerning the position and rights of women, which are at odds with the ways in which the sexes relate to each other in many non-Western civilizations. The same holds true with regard to individual human rights which in Western countries supersede collective human rights. In many non-Western cultures it is just the other way around. These basic elements of the Western legal system cannot be set aside for the sake of multiculturality, or out of fear of ethnocentrism.[18] There are also the common curricula and common criteria of educational quality to be maintained in schools. And there is, above all, the national language to be upheld, if alone in order to prepare the next generations of all cultures for society in general and the labor market in particular. As to language, it can be a great asset for people to be bi- or even multilingual, but the dominant language of the nation should be the primary language taught in schools and mastered actively (speaking) and passively (reading) by all citizens irrespective of their ethnic descent.

In view of this common cultural and legal frame of reference it will be adamant to negotiate with (the leaders of) ethnic minorities the terms by which they are able to contribute funds of their cultural specificity to the mosaic of urban society at large. A policy of social and cultural diversity ought to actively stimulate the socioeconomic and cultural cooperation of the various urban subcultures, and to convince each of them that functional solidarity is advantageous, that cooperation strengthens the urban society as a whole and thereby the parts composing it. Of particular importance is the participation of members of ethnic minorities in the political affairs of the city. By also operating in the political arena they partake in dealing with power and contribute to the political emancipation of their people and the civic culture of the city as well.

Only within this context of a shared responsibility can various ethnic and/or religious minorities be invited and stimulated to contribute to the overall urban culture. Such contributions are to the socioeconomic advantage and cultural enrichment of all citizens. As to cultural enrichment, festivals in which cultural minorities present their customs, folklores, and traditions are an example of such a contribution. The city is transformed into a stage, the total body of citizens is the audience, intercultural solidarity and thus the strengthening of urbanity is the result. However, having said as much, we again run into that basic paradox: a lively urbanity can prevent the fragmentation of urban society under the impact of cultural diversity, yet the inherent danger of ghettoization which seems to be inherent in ethnic diversity, presents a sizable threat to a lively and vital urbanity. Somehow urban policy has to break through this fatal circle which, of course, is a task for both the public and the private sectors of society.

We may sum up the argument as follows: as long as cultural diversity is not neutralized by a melting pot strategy or stifled by ghettoization, urbanity is strengthened and intensified by ethnic and/or religious diversity; on the other hand, as long as there is a certain amount of urbanity, that is, a culture of openness, focused upon the mutual promotion of material and immaterial interests—various ethnic minorities will be attracted by the city. It is not at all surprising that since the 1980s a new wave of migration swept over Western nations and entered their cities in particular: political and economic refugees from economically depraved countries, torn apart by civil war and scourged by natural disasters. They raise scores of political, legal, sociocultural, and economic problems. One thing seems certain, nations and cities suffering from a pervasive anomie are unable to cope with these problems adequately. Particularly the big cities in Western Europe and North America will experience a sharp aggravation of their problems, if they lack the structural backbone of a vital urbanity.

In order to realize and maintain an integrated cultural diversity much more is needed than intercultural tolerance, as important as such tolerance naturally is for a peaceful coexistence in a multicultural habitat. Beyond such civil tolerance it will be necessary to institute regular consultations between the community leaders of the subcultural segments and the community leaders of the urban society at large. A shared *modus vivendi* will have to be negotiated, and then instituted in contractual agreements. Thus the various components of urban society can realize and maintain their own culture within the parameters of the law and of internationally accepted codes of human rights. These negotiations can be greatly facilitated, if the parties share a sense of common culture, if urbanity as their shared economic and civic culture is the ultimate spirit of consensus that undergirds the interactions and deliberations of the negotiating parties.

Naturally, there are many obstacles for such a policy of negotiated pluriformity. The most problematic obstacle is, without doubt, the fact that most ethnic minorities possess a distinct, collective, and basic awareness of their cultural identity and background, often called their *heritage* or their *roots*. They differ in this from the indigenous majority of society, most representatives of which have been modernized to such an extent that their collective identity and heritage has, as it were, evaporated. In Western Europe, massive expressions of nationalist pride and patriotic sentiments have actually only occurred during international soccer competitions. As a result, many of them, in particular academic intellectuals and political policy makers, tend to regard ethnicity as a somewhat old-fashioned and obsolete phenomenon. Because they occupy dominant positions in (urban) society, they easily resort to ill-conceived policies of either assimilation or segregation. Both policies are detrimental to urbanity.

The goal of the assimilation policy, often assisted by gentrification, is to force cultural (ethnic) minorities to spread out over an (urban) society which would, if this policy were successful, function indeed as a melting pot. The policy is ill-conceived as it will only exacerbate ethnic sentiments which in the end may evoke various kinds of aggression and violent actions. Urban authorities will then have to restore order, and before you know it, violence spirals out of control. Urban society is then bereft of its legitimacy. What is left, are very anomic cities.

The policy of segregation is often advocated and practiced by minorities themselves albeit equally ill-conceived and detrimental to the urbanity of cities. Often the policy is enacted by means of a benign or sometimes blatantly harmful neglect. It has, together with other semi-autonomous economic developments, already contributed to the emergence of a destitute underclass in the inner cities of many Western societies. Subpar standards in education and training, one of the main causes of unemployment, and a pervasive culture of poverty which robs people of their civic competence, contributing in its turn to unemployment, create anomic neighborhoods that are "no-go areas" for other citizens, and eventually for the police, the fire brigade, and the ambulance service as well. The ghetto is then turned into a jungle, an uncivilized wasteland.

It would, of course, be naive, if not silly, to advocate urbanity as a cure for such grave urban maladies. It goes without saying that urban renewal always costs money. Money is needed for the improvement of education, of housing facilities, and above all for employment schemes within urban areas that are in steadfast decline. It would be even more naive to believe that a mere turnaround in the culture of poverty—a culture of pervasive anomie spreading throughout the neighborhoods of our inner cities—would solve the grave social and economic problems of the big city. Yet, it is also erroneous to focus exclusively on socioeconomic and political factors, as is usually done when the issues of urban unemployment, urban poverty, and the urban underclass are debated. It is the main contention of the present argument that a metropolis lacking urbanity, that is, lacking a vigorous and vital economic and civic culture, is, in fact, robbed of its most essential source of energy and vitality. It is a source whose essence is neither monetary and economic, nor administrative and political, but cultural. This culture consists of values, norms, meanings. Its ultimate goal is legitimacy and averting anomie.

A city without urbanity is devoid of the basic legitimacy which any social body needs in order to act effectively and efficiently. In this sense, urbanity is a necessary precondition for all urban policies, including the war on poverty and destitution. In fact, over the past decades we have, in America and Europe, poured astronomic amounts of money into our cities and their pockets of poverty. It was until now to no avail. These pockets of poverty only grew in number and in size. Time and again this money was like seeds sown on arid wasteland. Is it really naive to believe that this money was wasted, because we have managed to build and maintain cities without urbanity?

## The Urban Functional Mix

In the 1930s architects and experts in urban design and planning held regular conferences, called "Congrès Internationaux d'Architecture Moderne" (CIAM). The main focus of CIAM was the Radiant City of Corbusier. A more adequate and less pretentious name would have been the Functional City. There was the Charter of Athens (1933) in which it was declared that livable housing demanded air, light, and space, and furthermore that urban planning ought to take into account first and foremost the rapid expansion of modern (primarily commercial) traffic. The visionary architect and urban designer Le Corbusier, the aforementioned champion of anti-urbanity, was the motor behind CIAM. He is also celebrated as the inventor of the systematic differentiation of four basic city functions. According to this principle, housing, work, recreation, and traffic ought to be distinguished and planned separately in any truly modern city. Although Le Corbusier hardly received a chance during his lifetime to realize his plans, his architectural and urban-design functionalism, equalled by Ludwig Mies van der Rohe, Frank Lloyd Wright, and Walter Gropius, did exert a considerable influence on the morphology and the culture of modern cities until long after the war.

The undeniable aesthetic quality of most of Le Corbusier's plans was easily lost when his disciples applied his functionalist ideas to the housing projects of the welfare state. Once more, disciples managed to kill the spirit of creativity that still inspired their master and idol, producing dreary casts of originally brilliant designs.[19] Robbed of its aesthetic qualities, Corbusierian functionalism apparently possessed a kind of elective affinity with the bureaucracies of the welfare state, because they embraced it well-nigh thoughtlessly.

This functionalism on the part of architects, urban designers, and urban planners contributed considerably to unaesthetic, if not simply ugly, concrete apartment buildings on the outskirts of the cities (often labelled "instant slums" by the population), to gigantic shopping malls in and outside the city, to unattractive theaters and movie houses in urban centers which were usually deserted in the evenings and the nights, to the rapid development of suburban sleeping cities generally devoid of any trace of urbanity, to a social and economic deterioration of the inner cities, to severe traffic congestions in the early mornings and the late afternoons, to the gradual social decline of streets and neighborhoods—in short, to a general decline of the city as a social and cultural milieu. Needless to say, this separation of urban functions was inimical to any kind of urbanity.

Corbusierian functionalism was, of course, often met with critique but it remained without much effect as long as the official instances of urban planning and design continued to embrace it as allegedly the most effective and efficient "philosophy." Thus, in the 1960s the Functional City was criticized, as functionalism was criticized in the social sciences, in favor of a more critical imagination. Not amazingly, in the 1970s voices within the urban population, but also within the group of urban experts, could be heard which called for the restoration of an anti-functionalist urbanity. When in that decade an old neighborhood of Amsterdam had to be levelled in order to make room for the construction of a subway system, the following piece of graffiti was written on the walls of one of the last houses that still stood erect: "We want a city with neighborhoods in which housing, playing, working, learning, and shopping by young and old happens nearby and criss-cross!"[20] Even a report of the Dutch housing ministry stated, in a rare case of administrative illumination, that urbanity (the concept was not defined or explained) is in fact the intermingling and interweaving of various urban functions. It also acknowledged that the housing functions of the inner cities ought to be upgraded and improved, lest urbanity deteriorate further.[21] We return to this point shortly.

Next to mixing the functions of housing, working, recreation, and traffic, urban policy ought to direct its attention especially to the social and cultural functions of the city. We have seen before that an essential component of urbanity was, from the beginning, the creative vitality of the arts and the sciences within typically urban institutions, such as universities, scientific and architectural academies, academies of the arts, music schools, museums, and so on. With the rise of centralism, certainly within the context of the advanced welfare state, these typically urban institutions began to lose their urban character and quality, as well as their urban focus and orientation.

Universities, for instance, have always been essential to the social and cultural vitality of cities, just as the social and cultural qualities of universities profit from vital urban surroundings. Yet, for purely functionalistic reasons such as more space on cheaper ground, more compact offices, etc., many postwar universities in Europe have been removed from the city and placed at the outskirts, where they are usually located in very functional, very ugly, and very inhumane concrete buildings. It is a loss for the city, it is a loss for the university—a cultural and a social loss. Universities with their slightly eccentric populations of students and teachers can potentially give a special social and cultural flavor to a city and, perhaps boost its economy. In terms of spatial efficiency and costs, it might have been necessary to remove universities from the cities. In terms of social and cultural costs (technically called social capital) which were obviously not taken into account, the damage to both the universities and the cities has been enormous.

The same holds true of oversized shopping malls, located outside the cities in a social no-man's-land. People drive to them, park their van, buy their merchandise, load it in the van, and drive off. It may be very functional but the social and cultural effects are devastating. They are, in fact, rather outdated bazaars, although they generally lack the social functions of bazaars—i.e. the informal meeting of people, the seeing and being seen, the sauntering, the strolling together.

Urban pedestrian malls, successors to nineteenth century arcades, are a different story.[22] They sprang up everywhere within cities during the 1980s, first in America, then also in Europe. They are altogether different from the suburban shopping malls of the previous decades. Rybczynski calls the shopping mall "an influential architectural prototype for our time." He continues to say that its "influence is visible in the wide range of recent public buildings that have adopted the pedestrian mall as an organizing principle—not only museums but also airports, university buildings, and civic centers. Office buildings now incorporate an atrium as a matter of course. So do many hotels."[23] Socially, the mall is, according to Rybczynski, "a democratic, convivial space; it puts the architectural emphasis squarely on the public rather than on the institution." He concludes this little ode to the mall with a reference to urbanity—a concept that he does not define: "City life has always featured unstructured movement in public space, and in that regard the mall building is an unexpected resurgence of urbanity. America may yet become a nation of boulevardiers."[24]

If one takes into account that human beings, as the thoroughly social animals they are, travel the streets, and that, despite their cars, they often do so in the inner cities by walking and strolling, the social dimension becomes exceedingly prominent. They want to see and be seen, saunter and philander, shop and window-shop, eat and drink and gossip. CIAM functionalists and their contemporary successors had and still have no eye for this basic social function which is essential to any vital urbanity. In the heyday of urban functionalism Jane Jacobs's by-now-classic essay on the *Death and Life of Great American Cities* (1961) highlighted the crucial components of urbanity.[25]

Functional diversity, presented here as a vital condition of urbanity, ought to maintain some sort of balance between countless social tensions and conflicts on the one hand, and a guarantee of order and safety for the urban inhabitants on the other. A lively city is always characterized by alternations, varieties, contradictions, and ambiguities—not just in architectural styles, but also first and foremost in styles of living, behavior, and conduct on the part of the urban inhabitants. A city with a lively urbanity is a crazy place. Its inhabitants are not just representatives of a solidly middle class or working class. Bums and hobos, the homeless, drug addicts, derelicts—in short, the social flotsam and jetsam, are an integral part of life in the big city. Throughout their history, cities have been the places of both virtues and vices. Indeed, this may well be the gravest mistake of the functionalist Radiant City: it is a sterile and one-sidedly middle-class, solidly bourgeois conception.

As to the vices of urban life, such as the use and traffic of drugs and related forms of crime, it is questionable whether well-planned and coordinated police actions will be productive, if conducted in terms of middle class norms and values. In view of the (often related) urban afflictions of drug abuse and HIV-contamination, for example, a seemingly lenient policy, as the one enacted in the city of Amsterdam, may be shocking to the proponents of middle-class norms and values. In this policy the emphasis is on prevention rather than on criminalization and police prosecution. Through education and information, through the provision of alternative drugs, like methadone distributed in so-called methadone buses that travel the city, and through the distribution of clean syringes, these typically urban vices and their related criminality are combatted in a non-combative style.[26]

This might seem immoral at first sight, but it is statistically proven to be relatively effective. Part of the policy is to accept the fact that a certain segment of addicts is lost. This relatively small, hard core of drug addicts is treated experimentally as medical cases who, under medical supervision, receive hard drugs. This may well be one moral bridge too far, as one has actually given up all hope and escorts them only to a soft death. As to the many other cases outside the hard core of addiction, one can only hope to alleviate their fate by public and private assistance, and furthermore develop aid programs which hopefully reap some success eventually. It is, however, first and foremost through prevention by means of information and education that one hopes to diminish the size of this group of people among the next generations. Experience has demonstrated that criminalization and tough police actions are generally not very successful.

In a way, the homeless represent the same morally ambiguous problem. Social policy can try to help those who are homeless and jobless for reasons outside their own will within the possibilities and limits of the present welfare state. Yet, large cities do harbor hardcore outsiders, social strangers, radically nonbourgeois vagrants, the unassimilated, and, not to forget, the mentally disturbed. One can only try to alleviate their fate through public and private aid. Job programs, of course, remain the core of preventive measures. But, we should learn to accept the fact that such social ills—ills from the point of view of bourgeois morality—are intrinsic components of urban life, part and parcel of urbanity.

This is even true of public safety. To most of us, it is so-called small criminality, the kind committed by nonviolent burglars, thieves, and pickpockets, that worries and angers us most, when living in a big city. Big crime, such as organized crime, or so-called white-collar crime, is usually something we only read about in the newspapers. Ordinary citizens are rarely the victims of organized crime. Small crime, on the contrary, is what we may encounter each day or night. We therefore fear it, fret over it, and become intensely annoyed by it. Meanwhile, empirical research has demonstrated that in the case of many cities the fear of falling prey to small criminality is greater than the statistical chance of actually suffering for it.

Urban violence has always been with us, and it is not unlikely that the safety in the cities of today is actually greater than in former periods of urban civilization. It is, by comparison, illuminating to read the memoirs of Benvenuto Cellini, an apparently violent man in a very violent environment. This environment was the cities of Renaissance Italy which are generally associated with the fine arts, beauty, and urbane civility. Historical records tell a different story. These towns were not just the cradle of European arts and sciences but also places of violence and aggression. The aforementioned "demonic" aspects of cities were an inherent component of urbanity. It will not be much different today.

Many urban renewal programs of the 1970s and 1980s demonstrate the tendency to (re)shape the urban environment according to middle class values and norms, which are usually heavily infected also with the virus of functional differentiation. Old buildings and houses, worthwhile to renovate, were often radically demolished and replaced by concrete structures, alleged to be "modern" and "functional." In several inner cities older buildings and houses, located on expensive land, were often ruthlessly demolished and then rapidly replaced by uniform, mirror-glassed architectural contraptions, or unattractive parking garages. As a result, the downtown areas of large cities all over the world look alike. They are by definition "faceless."

Gentrification is an important component of this. More than likely people living in old buildings and houses in the center of the city were not asked for their opinions. They were more often than not simply relocated, and lured, or forced into exchanging their allegedly decrepit homes for up-to-date, functional housing projects elsewhere, usually at the outskirts of the city or in suburbia. After the demolition squads have done their jobs, new, modern and functional buildings arise which display an international uniformity, in appearance as well as in use. From a sociocultural perspective there is more involved here than a merely economic calculus. These policies testify to a middle-class mentality which intentionally destroys the ambiguities, the eccentricities, the madness, if you will, of cities. The result is cities without urbanity—faceless cities, dead cities. The appropriate word here is *urbicide.*

## Lively Inner City

Lest its urbanity evaporate, a city needs a point of sociocultural gravity, a field of sociocultural concentration, a space in which the urban functions concentrate, condense, and become, as it were, visible, tangible, concrete. This is why the postwar suburbanization proved fatal to urbanity: while the suburbs functioned as "sleep cities," the housing and socializing functions of the inner city deteriorated. Downtown became the place of irreconcilable opposites: the site of huge office and commercial buildings deserted beyond working hours, and the site of slums and substandard housing for the poor. One can view this fatalistically as the upshot of an unavoidable development, as is often done. One can also view this development as a maldevelopment to be redressed by conscious policies of urban renewal.

This essay takes the latter position, if only because the inner city is crucial to the vitality of urban culture. It is metaphorically speaking, the very heart of urban life from which scores of vital impulses are sent into the surrounding areas, even beyond the city's administrative borders. "The Urban Core," a Dutch sociologist wrote, "is the gist of life in metropolitan society, and a barometer for the shifts and changes which take place."[27] Urban people know this. To them "going to the city" means going to the center, *die Innenstadt, la Cité.* Downtown is the place where "things" are happening.

Much in line with post-modernism it is often argued that (a) cities really no longer exist, and (b) the urban conglomerates of today are radically decentered. The argument of the nonexistence of cities was dealt with in chapter 4. The second, more interesting argument is of special importance to this chapter. It deserves closer scrutiny.

In a perceptive article William Sharpe and Leonard Wallock claimed that "we find ourselves seeking to delineate a 'decentered' city that does not conform to the definitions of the past."[28] There is, they continue, a crisis of semantics here, since the city has become "illegible."[29] The postwar situation of a centered city with surrounding suburbs, intensified by automobile traffic and commuter transport services, has gradually entered a new phase of development in which we now find widely spread urban areas without a center: "American cities are becoming distended and decentered."[30]

In search of proper terminology to describe the decentered city, Sharpe and Wallock leave the urbanological discourse and turn to contemporary literature, where they discern two directions. The first one they call "literary gentrification," expressed by novels that affirm the urban experience of "yuppies." The urban world in these novels is "a largely delocalized city": "Everything is so implicitly urban in the gentrified style that the city as an imaginative or emotional focus, or even just a physical factor, has practically ceased to exist."[31] The second direction in literature is a more conventional one, as it depicts urban life as one of utter decay. The focus is on "urban apocalypse" and on "otherworldly revelations of the dispossessed".[32]

Both authors believe that a "recentralization of the urban field" is unlikely. Yet, at the end of their essay they do discuss countermovements in the reality of urban life: (a) people apparently do not like to live apart from each other, spread out over decentered space; (b) corporate business wants its headquarters to be located in central business districts, where they are surrounded by the best financial services, by their competitors, and by scores of cultural supplies. The thrust of future development, they conclude, may therefore lead toward "a proliferation of new centers rather than toward a homogenous urban field."[33]

It remains unclear what such a "homogenous urban field" actually could be and represent. A brief look at the history of Western cities shows conclusively that cities with urbanity were never homogenous and uniform. There was, certainly in European cities prior to the 1960s, an ethnic homogeneity, but in terms of tastes, styles of life, ideas and emotions Western cities have been places of great social and cultural diversity, certainly if they possessed a vital economic and civic culture. Indeed, pluriformity and pluralism, as we saw, are the main hallmarks of urbanity.

As to urban centers, here too one should not interpret them as fixed spots that remain the same over decades, let alone centuries. On the contrary, urban centers tend to move within the city and the larger a city grows the more complex the center becomes. Within the center too, there have always been shifting nodal points. For some decades, for instance, Greenwich Village was the focus of downtown Manhattan, the place where "things" happened. Later there was a shift to Soho and since then "things" have been moving up or down, but in any case on. Yet, as to Greater New York, the inner city—The City—will for a long time be located somewhere on Manhattan island—never, I dare say, on Staten Island, or in New Jersey, the Bronx or Harlem. Of course, the boroughs can and will develop their own cores as well—satellite centers, as I called them before. Brooklyn Heights is a good example of such a satellite center. It only underlines the vitality of New York City's urbanity.

Incidentally, arguments about the decentered or polycentric nature of contemporary (or postmodern) cities are not always consistent. For example, Jonathan Barnett argues that in the big metropolitan areas of today there are still "vibrant downtowns." These downtowns respond to novel competitive pressures by assuming "new specialized functions," such as

> big office buildings, conventions, tourists, and in a few of the largest cities, the homes of the rich and some young professionals. Certain kinds of business, like banks and corporate headquarters, still need large staffs of clerical workers and benefit from a central location with good public transportation.... The old city's cultural life is also still strong: its museums, theaters and universities.

But then, rather unexpectedly, Barnett embraces the decentered city argument:

> The real centers of urban life have moved to what were once fashionable suburbs. What had been small suburban downtowns are now office centers; the regional shopping malls often have more and better stores than downtown, restaurants and theaters have sprung up along shopping strips that used to offer only filling stations and supermarkets. Corporate offices nestle in old estates or are grouped in office parks.

Barnett concludes that a new urban world has emerged:

> It has no center but is roughly fan-shaped with a highway or main arterial road serving as an extended main street.[34]

The decentered city argument is, in fact, somewhat abstract. Anybody who knows a little about Amsterdam, for example, can tell the visitor from abroad immediately where "things" are happening in this city: concerts, theater performances, peep shows, prostitution centers, drug traffic, "coffee shops" (where soft drugs are sold). It is definitely not in the surrounding suburbs, neither in the outer circle of boroughs, but round and about the ring of canals. This ring—in Dutch the *Grachtengordel*—is in fact a kind of institution and a symbol that stands for all that is ugly and beautiful in this urbanity-loaded capital.

The problem of Rotterdam, on the contrary, is that it lacks a distinct inner city, a socioeconomically and culturally vital Downtown. Rotterdam is indeed a decentered city. This is not due to modern technology, or to some sort of fatal and autonomous development that allegedly afflicts all modern cities. It simply is the result of a very ill-conceived urban planning effort after the Germans had bombed the center to ruins in 1940. The heart was taken out of this city, and a satisfactory replacement has never been found. As a result, unlike Amsterdam whose urbanity is taken for granted by almost everyone, Rotterdam had to make great and enduring efforts to reconstruct its urbanity. This is, without a clear center and core, a very tall order for all urban parties involved.

Another flaw in the decentered city argument is its fatalism. It is as if autonomous developments and "objective" circumstances dictate our passive acceptance of radically fragmented, disheveled, decentered cities. The words of an urbanalogical trio come to mind here: "We have forgotten that it is people—through institutions—who have the central role in building and developing cities, and in bringing about the various transformations embodied in the urbanization process."[35] Urban administrators and politicians, urban businessmen and ordinary urban citizens should take these words to heart. The question is, whether we should condone the progressive fragmentation of urban society and the concomitant decline of urbanity, or fight it by all policy means available.

In a Dutch dissertation on the housing function of the inner city, published in 1971, when the Functional City was still the dominant model of urban planning and design, a tendency was noted to favor and foster living in the city, particularly in its center.[36] There is much dispute about this alleged return-to-the-city. Some claim it has, since then, progressed, albeit at a very slow pace. Others reject the claim and stick to the argument that the inner cities have been abandoned by most middle- and upper-class urbanites, in exchange for a more comfortable life in the suburbs. Rybczynski defends this position: "The so-called back-to-the-city movement of the 1970s fizzled out; high rents, high prices, and high crime have continued to drive young families to the suburbs. Clearly, in one form or another, suburbs are here to stay."[37]

The facts are clear: in 1990, 60 percent of the population of 320 metropolitan areas lived in suburbs, and a majority of jobs was located in suburbs.[38]

Certainly, suburbs will continue to exist and function, but the question is, if in terms of urban policy and design we should not focus our attention again, and this time with more effort, on the inner city as the source of urban energy, as the very foundation of urbanity as an economic and civic culture. Scores of cultural provisions should be concentrated in the downtown area. In a close cooperation of the public and the private sectors there should be a differentiated supply of living spaces—for the old and young, for singles and partners, for one-parent and two-parent families, for the rich and wealthy, as well as for the middle- and lower-income echelons of society. The previously discussed nefarious consequences of gentrification should be placed high on the agenda of urban renewal.[39] Finally, a balance between motorized access and pedestrian areas should be upheld. Public transportation ought to be high on the urban-policy agenda. Above all, there should be lots of public space in which people can stroll, walk and sit, get tired and rest. The urbanity of cities is as much exemplified by their *flaneurs* and *boulevardiers* as by their hard-working businessmen, professionals, and civil servants.

David Rusk, former mayor of Albuquerque (1977–1981), also emphasizes the seminal importance of Downtown, but believes that cities alone cannot bear its multiple financial burdens. In terms of urban public policy he believes strongly in a holistic approach, integrating cities and suburbs from a centralized regional-metropolitan authority. Only then could the progressive decay of inner cities be put to a halt: "In America the 'city' has been redefined since World War II. The real city is now the whole urban area—city and suburb—the metropolitan area. Redeeming inner cities and the urban underclass requires reintegration of city and suburb."[40] It should be noted that Rusk's defense of suburbs contains an equally strong defense of a vital Downtown. As mayor he used to call Albuquerque "a giant suburb in search of a city" and he defended the following urban strategy: "Albuquerque needed to strengthen its urban character. With modest success and much controversy, I promoted downtown Albuquerque as a center of business, government, entertainment, and the arts."[41]

The center—Downtown—should be the essence of the city, its main script, its symbolic representation. The previously mentioned Dutch dissertation formulated the habitus and mentality of Downtown residents succinctly: "They experience the city, in particular its center, in a more integrated manner: they live and work in it, look for their recreation there, and love the volatile and vague contacts in the public domain. In short, they seek and find in the center of the city a surplus of urbanity which is absent elsewhere."[42] And again, there can be, and will increasingly be, a multitude of centers in contemporary metropolises. Yet, urban policies ought to establish and maintain one dominant center—Downtown—to which the other centers, despite their autonomy, relate as satellites.

In sum, the inner city ought to be more than a business center, and a dumping place for the very poor. It ought to be a socioculturally lively place, where one can stroll and philander, eat and drink in sidewalk restaurants, discuss, debate, and gossip, see and be seen, and generally spend one's leisure time until the early hours of the morning—in short, a socially meaningful place. The center should be the very source of urban energies, the very spring of creativity, of artistic avant-garde and cultural renewal, of experiments in the arts and lifestyles.

## Decentralization and Centralization

It is not, in the first place, money that big cities in North America and Western Europe need from the central government, but sovereignty, power, authority, autonomy. A central government can pump great amounts of money into cities, but if they lack a sufficient degree of urbanity, that is, if they are stale and stagnant at their vital core, their economic and civic culture, this money will be to no avail. The same holds true, as was said before, for urban ghettos. One can continue to pour money into them, but this will not reap much fruit if it does not fall on the fertile soil of a solidarity sustaining civic spirit on the part of the ghetto residents. Here too, the people who in the end make up urban society, ought to have (or to regain) the distinctly civic awareness that they have power over their lives and destinies.

In short, there should be, within a chain of subsidiary, a thorough decentralization of power—from the nation-state and its bureaucracies to the cities, and within these from city-hall to the boroughs, districts, neighborhoods, and streets. It is the same in the business corporations which, in the 1970s and 1980s, grew into huge (often global) enterprises because of mergers and takeovers, and which were then forced to decentralize its power toward semi-autonomous business units that could operate flexibly and according to the changes and demands of the market.

Yet, there is, at the same time, need for centralization. In the public world as well as in the private world—the world of public administration and the world of business administration—there is a dire need of a central authority, a top layer of decision making which sets out the overall strategy. This strategy is the context, the set of parameters, within which the semi-autonomous units operate and cooperate. In other words, decentralization is not a pulverization of power, responsibility, and authority. On the contrary, decentralized power, responsibility, and authority are placed within the context of a general and centrally designed strategy to which all segments and units ought to conform and in which they are supposed to partake.

This transformation is comparable to the transformation of a traditional, top-down ruled army to a coordinated set of independent guerilla units which are to a certain extent on their own if it comes to military action, yet stay in touch constantly with a headquarters that designs the overall strategies. The modern, complex, and volatile market demands the decentralization and deconcentration of business corporations into business units. Likewise, today's highly complex and rapidly changing, internationalized societies demand a much more flexible administrative organization than the centralized, bureaucratic and top-down megastructures we grew accustomed to in the heyday of the welfare state. This holds true *a fortiori* for today's urban systems.

All this places rather heavy demands on leadership. The top of such public and private organizations must have the courage to delegate and deregulate, while still bearing the final responsibility for the general course of affairs. It must, in particular, have the imagination and creativity to set the overall goals and strategies of the organization under its command. The Chief Executive Officer of a corporation and the Mayor of a city ought to set the strategic agenda, and forge and radiate the style of their leadership. In this respect, individuals do make a difference. Needless to say, charismatic authority is a decisive component of this corporate and urban leadership.

The combination of decentralization and centralization is particularly visible in the recent developments of European urban regions. In line with the general development of a "Europe of regions," the larger cities of this continent—"Eurocities"—tend to unify surrounding communities into urban regions. Such an urban region consists of several semi-autonomous units with their own administrative authority, yet tied together in an overarching administration which in view of common economic and political interests sets out the overall aims and strategies for the region.

As to the metropolitan regions of America, David Rusk is also an outspoken proponent of such centralized regional authorities. He calls them "metro governments." The present situation with its inherited past of democratic decentralization, is a very fragmented one. Rusk mentions "28,078 special purpose units of local government (transit authorities, water and sewer agencies, and community college districts, for example). Often they are metrowide."[43] He believes in the unification of these fragmented urban authorities according to the traditional, pre-urban county system: "The most direct—and probably most efficient—path to creating metropolitan government in the majority of metro areas is to empower urban county government, have it absorb the functions and responsibilities of all municipal governments within its boundaries, and abolish all municipalities." "This is an action," he adds, "that is fully within the legal powers of most state legislatures even if at present such sweeping urban reorganization is beyond legislators' desires and political powers."[44] Needless to add that such a drastic centralization would run into many problems and obstacles that make the proposal unrealistic. It would, to begin with, unavoidably lead to massive bureaucratization and thus inefficiency. It would also need scores of annexations which would probably destroy local democratic structures that can be of respectable age.

The apparent danger of such metropolitan regions is the gradual loss of their urbanity. Their overarching, centralized urban administrations grow easily into abstract, bureaucratic megastructures with which the urbanites—the people of flesh and blood, living and working within the semi-autonomous units—can impossibly identify. Organized segmented interests too will take advantage of the fragmentation that may take place, when these abstract megastructures unavoidably lose their grip on the semi-autonomous units that can never be wiped out completely, lest one wants to erect a totalitarian society. It therefore stands to reason that large conurbations will develop a pattern in which metropolitan centralization is combined with urban decentralization, comparable to New York City consisting of five independent boroughs. In such an administrative configuration of both coordination and autonomy it is imperative that there is a visible and lively sociocultural heart and center, identified as The City. London, Hamburg, Paris, New York, and Chicago can only avoid the neutralization and evaporation of their remarkable socioeconomic and sociocultural energies, that is to say, they can only avoid the death of their urbanity, if they manage to secure a central space, an inner core in which the urban functions, are concentrated and condensed.

If the planning and policy of the urban regions of Europe do not heed this crucial fact, they may end up in conurbations without urbanity, that is in abstract megastructures that will eventually lose their political power, economic strength, social stamina and cultural pizzazz. It is to be feared next that another megastructure, this time not the nation-state but the overarching European Union with Brussels as its capital, will be eager to fill the void.

## Urban Leadership

Public administration and business administration have much in common these days due to the fact that the public and the private sectors intersect and often merge in ways which would have been unthinkable during the heyday of the comprehensive welfare state. This is, of course, very apparent in those cases in which services that were public formerly, such as transportation, mail, museums, and so forth, have been privatized. These organizations have to transform their office oriented, usually rather bureaucratic culture into a market and client oriented, competitive culture. The general contention is that inspiring leadership is essential for the success of such a cultural turnaround. But also in the private sector some drastic changes have occurred in this respect. Through the wave of takeovers and mergers in the 1980s huge, often global corporations have emerged which demand a kind of strategic steering that is different from the ordinary business administration of former days. Here too a special kind of leadership is required which resembles the statesmanship of the public sector. The strategic entrepreneur, not the super-manager, is needed here. In addition these megastructures will inevitably develop rather substantial bureaucracies which again brings them closer to the public sector.

This remarkable rapprochement between the world of policy and politics on the one hand and that of the market and business on the other is very visible these days in the field of urban administration. Under the regime of the centralized welfare state, European cities in particular were governed in terms of a bureaucratic public administration. City hall was, to all intents and purposes, the locus of the central urban bureaucracy, subsidiary of the nation's welfare state. This has changed drastically and rapidly during the 1980s. Functional decentralization, deregulation, and privatization of various public services compelled urban administrations to approach citizens less as passive receivers of subsidies and state-provided services and more as critical

customers who directly or indirectly (through taxes) pay for the provided services. This meant a rather sweeping change of culture since
urban administrators had to transform their bureaucratic orientation
into a service orientation. They even were confronted now with the
need to engage in competition with other cities. As to the latter, this is
not just the traditional, often jocular competition between neighboring
cities such as the one between Toronto and Montreal, Boston and New
York, or Rotterdam and Amsterdam. The new competition between
cities is serious—worldwide and primarily market-oriented. Rotterdam,
for example, competes fiercely with New York and Kobe to preserve
its status as the largest harbor of the world, while Amsterdam's Schiphol
Airport tries to maintain its status of best transfer airport, competing
primarily with Singapore Airport.[45] Likewise, cities compete worldwide for the hosting of the Olympic Games, the World Exhibition,
various cultural festivals, and in Europe the status of Cultural Capital.
This, of course, compels them to engage in city marketing which not
that long ago would be viewed as an activity unbecoming a public
administration like the government of a city.

In the theory and practice of corporate (or organizational) culture,
leadership has come to occupy a central position. In business administration it is common wisdom these days that an inspiring and even
visionary board at the top of an organization makes a difference. The
chairman of the board, in particular, the Chief Executive Officer (CEO),
is the essential person, the strategically crucial entrepreneur. The CEO
is not a dictatorial super-manager who exerts his infinite power in a
top-down manner. On the contrary, power within the structure of the
modern corporation is delegated to lower echelons and as to these echelons they are usually flattened through scores of decentralizations.
The CEO has power, of course, but it is infinitely more important for
him to have authority, to be trusted and therefore followed because he
is a man with vision and courage. He is the leading strategist who is,
naturally, intelligent and possessed of great business instinct which
also translates into political instinct. He knows the market and its social, cultural, and political surroundings, and he senses trends and transformations in the market and the political arena. In fact, he is a virtuoso
in timing, that is, in deciding when to act, when to wait, when to com-
promise, when to hit. The CEO is an authoritative leader, but not a
führer who wields limitless and dictatorial power. In many respects he
resembles the director of a play or the conductor of an orchestra who
inspires players, explains the meaning of the script or score, and tells

them how to interpret and perform them. The main difference between a CEO and a conductor is the fact that the latter disposes of a finished score written by a composer, whereas the CEO, together with many colleagues, has to compose the score of the corporation while it performs its tasks. That is what is meant by the word corporate strategy. For this strategic task the CEO ought to have a special gift. In the music world this is called musicality. It is a natural talent, a gift that can be triggered and improved through learning and experience. It can, however, not be appropriated from outside. It is a talent one is born with, just as one is born as a gifted musician or a gifted teacher, carpenter, and sportsman.

The urban CEO is, of course, the mayor and these days, maybe more than ever before, he is the figurehead of the urban administration—not just a city manager but an authoritative urban leader. A truly contemporary, forceful, and influential mayor differs from the strong men of former days who, particularly in America, ruled with iron fists over very powerful, top-down organized political machines. These days the mayor is the urban CEO who transcends the perpetual conflicts of socioeconomic and political interests. His is an authoritative, nonpartisan influence which demands a very special skill in the handling of power. Not old-fashioned power games and gimmicks, but the design of long-term strategies and the communication of these strategies to all of the organization's sectors and echelons ought to be his task and prerogative. He is an administrative generalist who has an intimate knowledge of the market, the political arena, the society-at-large, and who is able to put all this in an international perspective.

As in the corporate world, leadership is actually a kind of principle which penetrates into all the sectors and echelons of the urban administration. The mayor and the aldermen foster and inspire leadership even in the least influential sections of the administration. This inspiration stimulates a sense of pride and identification on the part of urban administrators and thus contributes to the vitality of urbanity. Indeed, nothing is more detrimental to the economic and civic culture of a city than an over-bureaucratized administration which lacks vision, self-confidence, and belief in its mission, and which treats citizens in an uninspired way as the passive recipients of public subsidies and services. Urban governments ought to take the lead in the cultural turnaround that transforms cities into lively, exciting places to live, to work, to create and recreate.

What is needed is urban administrations gifted with imagination and the courage to introduce new ideas, new goals and new instruments.

# Notes

1. Compare Peter Hall, *Cities of Tomorrow*, p. 7: "...twentieth-century city planning, as an intellectual and professional movement, essentially represents a reaction to the evils of the nineteenth-century city." Hall underlines the heavy influence of anarchism on the early ideas of urban planning. Cf. also his *Great Planning Disasters* (Berkeley and Los Angeles: University of California Press, 1980).
2. Karl Mannheim, "Planning for Freedom," part 5 of *Man and Society in an Age of Reconstruction*, translated by E. Shils (London: Routledge & Kegan Paul, [1940] 1960), 239–368.
3. In Europe, large cities continue to develop into urban regions which are, comparably to the large cities in the United States, composed of various, fairly autonomous, urban authorities (boroughs). This is not the place to discuss the rather ambiguous concept of region. Its definition and demarcation are generally rather vague. Sometimes economic criteria prevail, as in the case of transnational Euroregions, then again sociocultural dimensions define the region, as in the case of so-called ethnoregions like Wales and Scotland. See, for instance, David McCrone, *Understanding Scotland: The Sociology of a Stateless Nation* (London: Routledge, 1992).
4. For a survey of European politics and European institutions see Stephen George, *Politics and Policy in the European Community* (Oxford: Clarendon Press, [1985] 1990).
5. This was discussed in a witty and insightful manner by Witold Rybczynski, *Waiting for the Weekend* (Middlesex: Penguin Books, 1992).
6. Peter L. Berger and Richard J. Neuhaus, *To Empower People: The Role of Mediating Structures in Public Policy* (Washington, DC: American Enterprise Institute for Public Policy Research, [1977] 1996), pp. 162 f.
7. Ibid., p. 158.
8. William Kornhauser, *The Politics of Mass Society*. Robert Nisbet, *Community and Power* (Oxford: Oxford University Press [1953] 1964). Originally, this book was entitled: *The Quest for Community*. It presents a history of ideas about mediating structures. Naturally, Nisbet's political stance is debatable. Recently, this discussion has flared up again, following John Rawl's influential *A Theory of Justice* (Cambridge, MA: Harvard University Press, 1971) which contains a defense of liberal individualism. Critical reactions emphasized expectedly the need for community. See, for instance, Michael Sandel, *Liberalism and the Limits of Justice*, (Cambridge: Cambridge University Press, 1982). See also more recently Philip Selznick, *The Moral Commonwealth: Social Theory and the Promise of Community* (Berkeley and Los Angeles: The University Of California Press, 1992.) Rawls reformulated his position recently in *Political Liberalism* (New York: Columbia University Press, 1993).
9. Reinhard Bendix, *Nation-Building and Citizenship*, p. 84.
10. The most dangerous and fateful disguise was and still is fascist corporatism. It emphasizes the socioeconomic and political importance of associations but views these as corporations which march according to the dictates of the totalitarian state and its sole political party. Fascist corporatism, therefore, is opposed to the idea of voluntary associations as structures that mediate between the individual citizen and the state. Seen in this light one should be careful with the concept of corporatism which in contemporary debates is employed rather loosely.
11. On the present crisis of voluntary associations in present-day America see Robert Putnam, "Bowling Alone: America's Declining Social Capital," *Journal of Democracy* 6, no.7 (January 1995): 65–79.

12. See in particular Arnold Gehlen, *Urmensch und Spätkultur* (*Original Man and Declining Culture*) (Bonn: Athenäum Verlag, 1956).
13. Compare Arnold Gehlen, "Ende der Geschichte?" in Arnold Gehlen, *Einblicke*, (Frankfurt am Main: Vittorio Klostermann, 1975), 115–135. Francis Fukuyama, *The End of History and the Last Man* (New York: Free Press, 1992).
14. This is not the place to discuss the interesting question of why and how these lowly institutionalized networks which supersede and compete with the traditional institutions, have become so successful in contemporary society. A sound sociological analysis would have to take into account above all, I believe, the rapid development and spread of electronic technology (personal computer, fax, e-mail, portable telephone, etc.), the demise of the interventionist nation-state and in connection therewith the rapid internationalization of society. It is my contention that these developments constitute an advanced stage of industrialization and modernization, and that concepts such as post-industrialism and post-modernism are basically deceptive, if not simply wrong.
15. See Francis Fukuyama, *Trust: The Social Virtues and the Creation of Prosperity* (New York: Free Press, 1995). Also Robert Putnam, *Making Democracy Work: Civic Traditions in Modern Italy* (Princeton: Princeton University Press, 1993) and Robert Putnam, "Bowling Alone: America's Declining Social Capital," *Journal of Democracy* 6, no.7 (January 1995): 65–79.
16. Compare Paul Harrison, *Inside the Inner City: Life under the Cutting Edge* (Harmondsworth and Middlesex: Penguin Books, [1983] 1985). Also Harold Tambs-Lyche, *London Patidars: A Case Study in Urban Ethnicity*, (London: Routledge & Kegan Paul, 1980).
17. Louis Wirth, "The Ghetto," in Louis Wirth, *On Cities and Social Life*, edited by Albert J. Reiss, Jr. (London: Phoenix Press; Chicago: University of Chicago Press, 1964), 84–98. "The ghetto, from the standpoint of biology, was a closely inbreeding, self-perpetuating group to such an extent that it may properly be called a closed community." *On Cities*, p. 90.
18. Proponents of multiculturalism often argue that their opponents are conscious or unconscious ethnocentrists. Ethnocentrism as the worldview and ethos that thinks and speaks in terms of cultural superiority and inferiority is, of course, morally reprehensible. But the anti-ethnocentrism of most multiculturalists is equally reprehensible, since it prevents intercultural dialogues. Such dialogues are, of course, only possible and meaningful, if the dialogue partners come up with arguments and visions based on clear positions. The anti-ethnocentrism of most multiculturalists submerge in the quicksands of relativism which renders true dialogues impossible. See in this respect Richard Rorty's defense of an anti-anti-ethnocentrism in his response to Clifford Geertz: "On Ethnocentrism: A Reply to Clifford Geertz," in Richard Rorty, *Objectivity, Relativism, and Truth: Philosophical Papers*, vol. 1 (Cambridge: Cambridge University Press, 1991), 203–210. See also Charles Taylor, *Multiculturalism and "The Politics of Recognition"* (Princeton, NJ: Princeton University Press, 1992).
19. The legacy of the Bauhaus architects Walter Gropius and Ludwig Mies van der Rohe experienced the same fate. Compare Tom Wolfe, *From Bauhaus to Our House* (New York: Farrar Straus Giroux, 1981).
20. H. de Haan and I. Haagsma, "De veranderde aanblik van Nederland (The Altered Sight of the Netherlands)" in *Wie is er bang voor nieuwbouw?*, edited by H. de Haan and I. Haagsma, p. 19.
21. Centrale Directie van de Volkshuisvesting (Central Directorate of Public Housing), *Verkenningen inzake leefbare stedelijkheid* (*Recoinnoiterings Regarding a Livable Urbanity*) Government Report, the Hague, May 1976.

22. On arcades as crystallizations of modernity see Walter Benjamin, *Das Passagen-Werk* (The Arcades Studies), two volumes, 1930s, (Frankfurt am Main: Suhrkamp Verlag, 1983). Compare also Wolfgang Lauter, *Passages*, (Brussels: Harenberg & Struye, 1992) which gives an illustrated survey of many European arcades.

23. Witold Rybczynski, "At the Mall," in W. Rybczynski, *Waiting for the Weekend*, pp. 144–149. Quote on p. 147.

24. Ibid., p. 148.

24. Jane Jacobs, *Death and Life of Great American Cities*, passim. For a sociological critique that is pertinent but lacks a vision of urbanity, see Herbert J. Gans, "Urban Vitality and the Fallacy of Physical Determinism," in Herbert J. Gans, *People and Plans* (New York: Basic Books, 1968), 25–33.

26. For the opposite approach see Mike Davis, *City of Quartz* (New York: Vintage Books, Random House, [1990] 1992), 266–322: "The Hammer and the Rock."

27. W.F. Heinemeyer, "The Urban Core as Center of Attraction" in *Urban Core and Inner City*, Proceedings of the International Study Week, Amsterdam 11–17 September 1966 (Leiden: E. J. Brill, 1967), 82–99. Quote on p. 83. "The core is in fact functioning as a 'forum publicum': a point of impact, a place of joint meeting for the whole body of citizens." Ibid., p. 85.

28. William Sharpe and Leonard Wallock, "From 'Great Town' to 'Nonplace Urban Realm'", in *Visions of the Modern City: Essays in History, Art and Literature*, edited by William Sharpe and Leonard Wallock (Baltimore, MD: Johns Hopkins University Press, 1987), 1–35. Quote on p. 1.

29. Ibid., p.17f. Compare Kevin Lynch, *The Image of the City* (Cambridge, MA: MIT Press, 1960): "a legible city would be one whose districts, or landmarks, or pathways are easily identifiable and are easily grouped into an overall pattern." Ibid., p. 2ff. Lynch mentions also imageability: "that quality in a physical object which gives it a high probability of evoking a strong image in any observer." Ibid., p. 9. Despite the unattractive jargon, legibility and imageability are indeed useful concepts in reference to urbanity.

30. William Sharpe and Leonard Wallock, *Visions*, p. 11.

31. Ibid., p. 26. The novels they mention are those of Jay McInerney, Paul Rudnick, Tama Janowitz, and Louis Auchincloss. They allegedly testify to "this waning sense of city as a place," "decontextualized social relations," "deracinated inhabitants" and "new forms of urban illegibility." Ibid., p. 26f.

32. Ibid., p. 27f. Novelists mentioned here are Don DeLillo, Madison Smartt Bell, and Paul Auster. The apocalyptic scenario is also vibrant in the social sciences. Compare, for example, *The Inner City in Context: The Final Report of the Social Science Research Council Inner Cities Working Party*, edited by Peter Hall (London: Heinemann, 1981), 130: "All in all, then, major technological changes in the coming decades seem most unlikely to work in favor of the inner city—if anything, the reverse. The most likely scenario by far is one of continued, even accelerated decline and of a greater concentration of deprived people—particularly since the skills demanded to operate the new technologies are likely to be least present among inner city residents." As an antidote to these doomsday scenarios see Ruth Glass, *Clichés of Urban Doom and Other Essays* (Oxford: Basil Blackwell, 1989).

33. Sharpe and Wallock, *Visions*, p. 35. On p. 34 they claim that "the recentering of the urban field may take the form not of a downtown renaissance but of a multinodal development."

34. Jonathan Barnett, *The Elusive City* (New York: Harper & Row Publishers, 1986), 186f.

35. John A. Agnew, John Mercer, and David E. Sopher, eds., *The City in Cultural Context* (Boston, London: Allen & Unwin, 1984), vii.

36. J. den Draak, *De woonfunctie van het stadscentrum* (*The Housing Function of the Inner City*), Ph.D. diss., University of Technology, Delft, 1971.
37. Witold Rybczynski, *Looking Around*, p. 100f.
38. Compare David Rusk, *Cities without Suburbs* (Washington, DC: The Woodrow Wilson Center Press, 1993), 5.
39. Compare N. Smith and P. Williams, eds., *Gentrification of the City* (Boston and London: Allen & Unwin, 1986).
40. Rusk, *Cities*, p. 122.
41. Ibid., p. 127.
42. J. den Draak, *The Housing Function*, p. 223. My translation.
43. Rusk, *Cities*, p. 89.
44. Ibid., p. 92.
45. See Witold Rybczynski, "Airports," in W. Rybczynski, *Looking Around*, p. 139–143.

# *Postscript*
# Urban Destinies

*Libelli habent sua fata*, the Romans allegedly said: booklets have their own destiny. They are texts written by individuals, but these texts acquire autonomy vis-à-vis their creators, even while they are being written. In a sense, the authors are but the mediums for the writing of these texts. When the texts are published as articles, essays, booklets, or even books and volumes, they disengage themselves even more from their "creators." They are (hopefully) read, and the readers transform these texts into their own texts by implanting their personal interpretations. These readings de- and reconstruct the texts, often to such an extent that the original authors cannot recognize them anymore. Everyone who has written texts and managed to get them published, has experienced this feeling when critics comment on them, or when symposiums discuss and debate them. It is an alienating feeling that these are actually not the texts one wrote and intended them to be. Texts have their own destiny and there is not much their authors can do about it. In some cases, certainly in those of sacred texts, like the Koran, the Bible, and the Bhagavad-Gita, books have extremely dense destinies. They laid the foundations of worldwide civilizations. Others, like *Don Quixote*, the plays of Shakespeare, *Ulysses*, or *The Magic Mountain*, set literary standards for decades or even centuries to come.

It is not unusual these days to liken cities to texts. That is an attractive metaphor. In a way, the city is like a palimpsest, that is, a parchment from which texts have been erased partially or totally in order to make room for new texts. A palimpsest is thus a series of textual layers, one on top of the other. In the case of most cities, the earlier texts have rarely been erased *in toto*. The older writings shine through the later ones and contribute in a barely perceptible manner to the present state of affairs. Not amazingly, cities and urbanity have penetrated the world of literature where they ensconced themselves solidly. New York, for example, is actually the main actor in J. R. Dos Passos's novel *Manhattan Transfer* (1925), just as Dublin stands at the center of James

Joyce's *Ulysses* (1922). The urbanity of Vienna is the air which the people in *Der Mann Ohne Eigenschaften* (1930–1943) by Robert Musil breathe. The Belgian poet Paul van Ostaijen puts his Antwerp during the German occupation in World War I at the center of his literary stage in *Bezette Stad* (*Occupied City*) which he wrote in 1920 in Berlin.[1]

But cities have their own destinies, not only in the virtual reality of literature but in real history as well. Some of them, for example, are remembered collectively and legendarily as the sites of tragic events. Dallas will be remembered for decades to come as the place of the fateful presidential assassination on 22 November 1963. Likewise, Sarajevo is solidly entrenched in our collective memory as the location where the assassination of the pretender to the Austrian throne triggered the mass slaughters of World War I, and the collapse of two empires, the Wilhelminian in Germany and the Austro-Hungarian in Central Europe. Tragically, the same city will be remembered as the center of ethnic hatred and inter-ethnic genocidal killings after the collapse of the communist regime. Indeed, in a sense, the twentieth century opened with Sarajevo and closed with it. Equally tragic memories of well-nigh mythological proportions present Hiroshima and Nagasaki, the first victims of our atomic day and age.[2] Needless to say, the name Auschwitz will be forever associated with the hell that human beings can make for their fellow men, particularly when they refuse to see them as fellow men. Indeed, cities can represent hideous destinies.

But cities are also actors in the brighter and happier parts of this century's history. San Francisco hosted the politicians that started the United Nations between April and June 1945. Of course, the UN has been met recurrently with severe criticism. Yet, it is hard to deny that this international organization with its sub-organizations for international justice, education, sciences, culture, and so forth, contributed to a climate of debate and consensus after many decades in which differences were met by violence and open hatred. San Francisco 1945 has contributed a great deal to this postwar turnaround. In 1948, Amsterdam hosted many Christian denominations which founded the World Council of Churches. Religious conflicts and alienations were not solved at once but referred to the conference and seminar rooms. Again, a lot of criticism has been levelled against this international body. Yet, it cannot be denied that it contributed to a fundamental change of the postwar cultural climate—a change which, in the terminology of Norbert Elias, contributed to the process of civilization. Cities have also acquired fame by hosting global events, such as the World Exhibitions in which nations exhibit their main trades and arts. Lasting fame carried, for instance, the World Exhibition of 1867 in Paris, where new products, technological inventions, and artistic innovations from many nations were exhibited. In a sense, the exhibited objects foreshadowed the twentieth century.

As was mentioned before, cities compete fiercely over the hosting of the summer or winter Olympic Games. Sometimes the collective memory is bitter, as in the case of the infamous Olympic Games in Nazi Berlin (1936), or those in Münich (1972) where the murderous attack on the Israeli team by Palestinian terrorists took place. It severely damaged the image of the games as festivals of international brotherhood.[3] Indeed, cities have their own historical destinies and these can be grim and gruesome. In most cases, however, these festivals of international solidarity put host cities in the limelight positively, and if they are organized well, they boost the urban economy and morale.

*Urbes habent sua fata.* That is true, but it is with cities just as with people: in order to be recognized and remembered, they must have a face, a recognizable identity, a personality that engenders trust and loyalty. Urbanity provides cities with just that!

## Notes

1. Jef Bogman, *De Stad als Tekst* (*The City as Text*) (Rotterdam: Van Hezik Fonds 90, n.d.).
2. The Austro-American biochemist Erwin Chargaff begins his memoirs with a description of the crushing blow he sensed, when he heard about the two atomic bombs of Nagasaki and Hiroshima in *Heraclitean Fire: Sketches from a Life before Nature* (New York: The Rockefeller University Press, 1978). Chargaff's comments on the urban cultures of Vienna, where he was a student, and New York, where he lived most of his life, are of particular interest to the present theory of urbanity.
3. The decision to continue the games met with widespread anger and disbelief. The main reason for this decision was, of course, the simple fact that these events represent gigantic economic interests. These material interests apparently superseded the immaterial ideals of solidarity and brotherhood. Sadly enough, political motives will have also led to this insensitive decision to return to business as usual. What would have happened, if the mayor of Munich demonstrated political courage and exerted strong urban leadership by closing the games and ordering a period of mourning? He would certainly have exposed himself to extreme, internal and external political and business pressures. But he would also have saved his city from an indelible blemish and maintained the honor and legitimacy of the Olympic Games. Nonesuch happened, the games continued, and Munich 1972 is forever a dark and murky page in the annals of this international institution.

# Index of Names

# Index of Cities and Towns

# Index of Subjects

absolutism, 33, 44, 64, 83–85, 92–95
administration, business, 176,179; urban, 178–180
affluence, 3, 9, 61f, 110
alienation, 138
ambiguity, urban, 8–14, 40, 65
*am ha"aretz*, 67
*ancien régime*, 38, 76, 83–85, 91f, 95
ancient Asia, 34–36; China, 17, 34, 36, 74; Egypt, 34; India, 17, 34, 36, 74; Judaism, 35; Near East, 34
animus, anti-bourgeois, 39f; anti-capitalist, 39f; anti-urban, 67–72, 120, 128; bucolic, 1
*anomie* (Durkheim), 60, 101, 135–140, 163f
*Anschluss* (Austria), 4f
anthropology, urban, 10, 120f
antiquity, Graeco-Roman, 36, 55f
arcades, 167
artisans, 25f, 30, 42, 63, 67
arts, 40; and crafts, 45
assimilation, policy of, 163
associations, voluntary, 99, 107, 154f, 157
authority, urban, 30, 115f, 138f; "patrimonial" (Weber), 27, 30, 36; "charismatic" (Weber), 176
autonomy, political, 29, 31, 59f, 62f

baby boomer generation, 106
"balkanization", anomic, 66
Baltic ports, 31–32
bankers, 27f, 38, 93, 97
Bay of Biscayne, 31
bazaars, 34, 137, 139, 150
bazaar cities, 17, 34, 39, 72, 75, 118
bias, Western, 17f
blood ties, 24f; blood and soil, 54
bohemia, 39f, 26
"borrowed misery" (Schelsky), 110
boulevardiers, 174

bourgeoisie, 25–31, 38f, 45, 93
bourgeois class, 38; culture, 45; power, 31; style of life, 45
Broadacre City (Wright), 72
brotherhood, universal, 36; Christian, 53
*"bürgerliche Gesellschaft"* (Hegel), 64
burghers, 13, 25, 30, 34, 36, 44, 75f, 139

Calvinism, 24, 55
Capet, House of, 90
Carolingian empire/era, 28f, 85–89, 95
caste, 25, 30, 36, 44
centers, administrative, 26f, 30, 34f, 67, 86
centralization, 175–178
Central Park (New York), 4
charity, 99, 107
chief executive officers, urban, 176–180
Chinatown, 160
Christianity, 9, 35f, 56f
citadels, 26f, 34
Cité, la, 170
cities, American and European, 18f; Atlantic, 131
citizenship, 13, 99–101, 108
city-states, 28f, 41f, 71, 92, 121
civic culture, xii, 11f, 58, passim; competence, 163f; pride, 20; spirit, 175; virtues, 45
*civilitas*, 21
civil society, xii, 58–60, 102f, 112, 115, 152, 158; and urbanity, 60–65; rights, 13, 41, 99f
"civilization, process of" (Elias), 39, 88, 186
class, 36–38, 44f, 66, 118; urban, 25
clanlike bonds, 24f, 36
communities, cultic, 35; urban, 30
communards, 71
Commune of Paris, 71

193